Hamlet

Prince of Denmark

A Tragedy by William Shakespeare

Editor: Anne Deegan

FOLENS

Editor
Hilda O'Sullivan

Design
Karen Hoey

Layout
Oisín Burke

ISBN 978-1-84741-501-1

Contents

Questions and Sample Answers

Preface

This book consists of three parts.

Part 1 begins with background information and includes a brief outline of Shakespeare's life, a note on Elizabethan theatre and Shakespearean English. This section also includes an outline of the principle elements of tragedy so that the student may appreciate *Hamlet* in the wider context of tragedy as a dramatic genre.

Part 2 is a scene by scene study of the text itself. Each scene contains annotations on the difficult vocabulary, expression or lines, plus notes on the dramatic significance of the scene and a commentary on the characters. Questions are suggested as aids to study to reinforce the student's understanding and appreciation of each scene. At the end of each act there is a suggested revision scheme. The strands of the plot are drawn together in a very brief summary. Essential points before proceeding to the next scene are highlighted and there is an assignment which demands a step by step revision of the main points of the plot. This ensures that the student has a clear grasp of one act before going on to the next.

Part 3 is designed for further study after the play has become familiar to the student. It deals with such aspects as Theme, Language, and Characters. Extra questions and essays are given after this section to encourage students to a more in-depth study of the play as a whole.

A glossary of dramatic terms is included so that students may become familiar with the important terms of criticism in the study of drama. For Higher Level students who may be interested in more extensive reading, the suggested reading list is a helpful guide.

Anne Deegan

This book is dedicated to my mother, May Neville,
with thanks for her support and encouragement.

Part 1
INTRODUCTION

Shakespeare's Life

"He was not of an age, but for all time"   (Ben Jonson)

Birth and Parentage

"Sweet Swan of Avon"   (Ben Jonson)

William Shakespeare was born in 1564 in Stratford-upon-Avon. He was the third and eldest surviving child of John Shakespeare and Mary Arden. He had three younger brothers and two sisters. John Shakespeare was a glove-maker by trade and also a successful general agricultural merchant. He rose high in the municipal life of Stratford and was elected a constable, became a chamberlain, an alderman and a bailiff.

There is no record of William Shakespeare's schooling. It is assumed that he attended the grammar school like the sons of other important townsmen in Stratford. However, John Shakespeare fell into debt, his wife's estate was mortgaged and William was taken out of school to work. There is practically no information about William Shakespeare's life during the five years after he left school.

Marriage and Early Career

"For a good poet's made, as well as born"   (Ben Jonson)

In 1582, at the age of eighteen, William Shakespeare married Ann Hathaway who was eight years older than he was. His daughter Susanna was born six months later and twins Judith and Hamnet were born in 1585. The period 1585–1592 is known as the *"lost years"*. Little is known about his departure from Stratford-upon-Avon. There is a popular legend that he had to leave because he had made a powerful enemy of Sir Thomas Lucy of Charlecote for poaching from his land. There are other claims that he became a school master. One way or another the next six years of his life are unrecorded, but in 1592 he already had a reputation as an actor and playwright in London. Robert Greene referred to him in his work *Groatsworth of Witte,* as *"...bought with a Million of Repetance..."* (repetition) as *"...an upstart Crow..."* who *"...supposes he is as well able to bombast out a blanke verse as the best of you: and being an absolute Johannes fac totum, is in his owne conceit the onely Shakes-scene in a countrey"*. It is thought that Shakespeare began his career as a writer by adapting and re-writing plays by other authors.

Player and Playwright

"Soul of the age,/The applause, delight, the wonder of our stage" (Ben Jonson)

Shakespeare wrote several historical plays and comedies between 1588 and 1594. *Romeo and Juliet* in 1594 was his first tragedy. In 1594 he joined the Lord Chamberlain's Company of actors. In 1599 the Lord Chamberlain's Company moved to the Globe Theatre which was owned by the actors and in which Shakespeare had a one-tenth share. By 1598 he was recognised as the greatest English dramatist. In 1603, his company became the King's Majesty Players, known as The King's Men, and came under royal patronage. Between 1601 and 1608 Shakespeare wrote his greatest tragedies as well as several comedies. In a period of just over twenty years he wrote thirty-seven plays as well as many sonnets and poems. One of his patrons was the Earl of Southampton to whom many of his sonnets are addressed.

Death

"We wonder'd, SHAKESPEARE that thou went'st so soon
From the world's stage to the grave's tiring-room"   (I.M.)

The Tempest was the last play Shakespeare wrote in 1611 and sometime after that he retired to Stratford-upon-Avon. He died five years later, at the age of fifty-two, on April 23rd, 1616.

The Folio

"SHAKESPEARE, at length thy pious fellows give
The world thy works"   (L. Digges)

Shakespeare's plays were collected by two of his fellow actors, John Heminge and Henry Condell, and in 1623 the first Folio edition of Shakespeare's work contained plays which had never been printed before. The other nineteen had already appeared separately as quarto volumes. No play in Shakespeare's handwriting is known to exist and it does not appear as if he himself supervised the publication of his plays. Like the quartos, the Folio is full of printers' and other mistakes and for centuries editors have wrangled over the correct interpretation of the quartos and Folio texts. However in the words of Ben Jonson Shakespeare is:

"... alive still, while thy book doth live,
And we have wits to read, and praise to give."

(Quotations from Ben Jonson, I.M. and L. Digges taken from the Prefatory Verses from the First Folio.)

The Elizabethan Theatre

The stage conditions for which a play was written could affect the methods employed in the play. Shakespeare's plays were designed for performance in the Elizabethan theatre. One source of information regarding the structure of Elizabethan theatres is the copy made by De Witt's friend of his drawing in 1596 of the Swan Theatre. A second source is the contract for the Fortune Theatre which gave exact specifications for the theatre which, although square in shape, was to be modelled on the Globe.

The theatres of Shakespeare's day were high, either round, octagonal or square in shape and the stage could be seen from all sides. The interior of the theatre was generally circular and exposed to the open sky. In this open pit audiences had to stand. Three tiers of galleries were around the inside wall with seats for those prepared to pay more and this was roofed. The stage projected out into the pit. Above the stage, against the back wall, the middle gallery served as a kind of balcony overlooking the stage. A canopy stretched forward high above the stage, supported by pillars. These pillars divided the stage into two parts – the front part projecting into the pit. At the back of the second part of the stage was a recess known as the *"rere"* or *"inner"* stage. On either side of this inner stage were dressing rooms. Thus there were four distinct parts to the stage which could be utilised – the front stage, the middle stage where most of the action took place, the rear stage and the upper stage. Curtains were sometimes drawn across the inner stage to separate it but there was no drop curtain.

The construction of the plays was influenced by the stage arrangements. Because the actors were surrounded by the audience this facilitated frequent asides and soliloquies. The actor simply came forward to the front of the stage, out of earshot of the other characters, and revealed what was going on in his mind to the audience. There were few props and no elaborate scenery. This gave the playwright greater freedom in the number of scenes he could introduce, unhampered by any inconvenience of changing scenery. There are seven scenes in the fourth act of *Hamlet*. Scenery was conveyed through language. The atmosphere of darkness is suggested through the words of Hamlet.

> *"'Tis now the very time of night,*
> *When churchyard yawns and hell itself breathes out*
> *Contagion to this world."*   *(Act 3, Scene II)*

This descriptive poetry serves a dramatic purpose.

The chorus in *King Henry V* called the stage *"an unworthy scaffold"* and advised the audience:

"Piece out our imperfections with your thoughts...
Think when we talk of horses that you see them
Printing their proud hoofs i' the receiving earth;
For 'tis your thoughts that now must deck our kings,
Carry them here and there, jumping o'er times,
Turning the accomplishment of many years
Into an hour-glass".

Here Shakespeare directly tells the audience to use their imaginations and dispenses with the dramatic limitations of the stage.

Nevertheless, although there were few props there was plenty of spectacle on stage. In *Hamlet*, the stage directions call for *"drum and colours"*. The plays took place in the afternoon and so the action was presumed to be taking place in daytime unless night was mentioned directly. Reference was made to torches and candles, as in *Hamlet*, to emphasise the darkness.

In Elizabethan drama the emphasis was placed on the delivery of the speeches rather than on staging techniques. Stage management intruded very little on the play.

Elizabethan English

There are many points of difference in grammar, syntax and meaning between Elizabethan English and modern English usage. What may now be considered as bad grammar was the accepted form of the language in Shakespeare's time. It was characteristic of Elizabethan writers to use one part of speech in the place of another. Adjectives could be used as adverbs *"marvellous wisely"* and it was quite common for adjectives to follow the noun, *"an understanding simple and unschool'd"*. Likewise adverbs tended to be placed where they gave most emphasis, *"Rightly to be great/Is not to stir without great argument/But greatly to find quarrel in a straw"*. A noun could be used as an adjective, *"cast thy nighted colour off"* or a verb, *"the cliff/ ... beetles o'er his base into the sea"*. In order to give greater emphasis a double comparative, considered quite incorrect in modern speech, was used in Elizabethan English, *"more nearer"*. Other grammatical discrepancies include the use of *who* for abstract nouns, *"custom, who all sense doth eat"*, the omission of articles, *"the gait of Christian"* and relative pronouns. Usually the omission of a relative pronoun makes very little difference, but sometimes it distorts the meaning *"He smote the sledded Polack (who was) on the ice"*. Students of Shakespeare should not be put off by unfamiliarity of syntax. It is simply a different arrangement of words and usually the meaning is quite clear.

Tragedy

No one tragedy fits perfectly any one definition of it, but the conventions of tragedy require certain tragic elements. A play is not a tragedy simply because it depicts death or suffering. Aristotle considered tragedy to be the fall of princes. Generally, Shakespeare's tragic hero is a man of high degree. Hamlet is a prince. In Greek and Classical tragedy, Fate is usually the cause of the catastrophe and the play portrays the hero's struggle against Fate. Since Fate is preordained, it was a useless struggle ending in the inevitable destruction of the tragic hero. In Classical tragedy the tragic hero is constrained by the gods, by circumstances beyond his control, to act in a certain way. Although Shakespeare introduces a supernatural element into his tragedies, the supernatural is not made responsible for the hero's actions and Hamlet proclaims *"we defy augury"*. In Shakespearian tragedy evil is the cause of the catastrophe. Shakespeare conceived of tragedy as the struggle between good and evil in the world. The tragic hero illustrates the fickleness of fortune, but the hero's own actions and character are responsible for his destruction. There is a feeling of a presiding ultimate power for good and the tragedy always ends on a note of reconciliation.

Generally Shakespeare's heroes possess definite characteristics. The Shakespearian tragic hero is always a man of exceptional nature, a great man with a more powerful consciousness, deeper emotions and a more splendid imagination than ordinary men. He is a sensitive being with a spiritual bias. He has a divided soul, he is torn by an internal struggle. However the tragic hero in Shakespeare's tragedies has some weakness, some flaw which contributes to his downfall. Aristotle called this internal weakness of the hero the *"hamertia"*, the tragic flaw, an essential element in tragedy. Hamlet is painfully conscious that he is neglecting his duty but he cannot will himself to murder his uncle and instead kills Ophelia's father by mistake. The inevitable consequences of this act work themselves out and the result is tragedy.

Aristotle's criterion of good tragedy was that the spectator should experience *"catharsis"*, that is, pity and terror for the tragic hero. According to him catharsis elevated the mind and purified the emotions. The sensitive, tormented Hamlet inspires pity, and the hardened pitiless Hamlet who could *"drink hot blood"* inspires terror.

Tragedy shows man in unsuccessful conflict with circumstances. Although modern tragedy is very different from Classical tragedy or Shakespearian tragedy, the element of conflict is still the essence of tragedy.

Part 2
Text and Scene Analysis

Characters

Claudius	King of Denmark
Hamlet	Son to the late, and Nephew to the present King
Fortinbras	Prince of Norway
Horatio	Friend to Hamlet
Polonius	Lord Chamberlain
Laertes	his Son

Voltimand
Cornelius
Rosencrantz
Guildenstern   Courtiers
Osric
A Gentleman

A Priest
Marcellus
Bernardo   Officers
Francisco   a Soldier
Reynaldo   Servant to Polonius
A Captain

English Ambassadors
Players
Two Clowns   Grave-diggers
Gertrude   Queen of Denmark and Mother to Hamlet
Ophelia   Daughter to Polonius
Lords, Ladies, Officers, Soldiers, Sailors, Messengers, and Attendants
Ghost of Hamlet's Father

Scene: Elsinore in Denmark

Act 1

Scene I

Elsinore.[1] A Platform[2] before the Castle.
Francisco at his post. Enter to him Bernardo.

Bernardo	Who's there?	
Francisco	Nay, answer me. Stand, and unfold[3] yourself.	
Bernardo	Long live the King!	
Francisco	Bernardo?	
Bernardo	He.	
Francisco	You come most carefully upon your hour.	
Bernardo	'Tis now struck twelve; get thee to bed, Francisco.	
Francisco	For this relief much thanks. 'Tis bitter cold,	
	And I am sick at heart.	
Bernardo	Have you had quiet guard?	10
Francisco	Not a mouse stirring.	
Bernardo	Well, good-night.	
	If you do meet Horatio and Marcellus,	
	The rivals of my watch,[4] bid them make haste.	
Francisco	I think I hear them. Stand, ho! Who's there?	

Enter Horatio and Marcellus.

Horatio	Friends to this ground.	
	And liegemen[5] to the Dane.	
Francisco	Give you good-night.	
Marcellus	O! farewell, honest soldier!	
	Who hath relieved you?	
Francisco	Bernardo has my place.	
	Give you good-night.	*[Exit.*
Marcellus	Holla! Bernardo!	
Bernardo	Say,	
	What! is Horatio there?	
Horatio	A piece of him.[6]	
Bernardo	Welcome, Horatio; welcome, good Marcellus.	20
Marcellus	What! has this thing appear'd again to-night?	
Bernardo	I have seen nothing.	
Marcellus	Horatio says 'tis but our fantasy,	
	And will not let belief take hold of him	
	Touching this dreaded sight, twice seen of us:	
	Therefore I have entreated him along	
	With us to watch the minutes of this night;	
	That, if again this apparition come,	
	He may approve our eyes[7] and speak to it.	
Horatio	Tush, tush! 'twill not appear.	30

[1] the residence of the Danish court
[2] where guns and cannon were mounted
[3] reveal
[4] those sharing the duty of the watch
[5] loyal subjects of the king
[6] he is reluctantly present
[7] he may confirm what we have seen

Bernardo	Sit down awhile,
	And let us once again assail your ears,[8]
	That are so fortified against our story,
	What we two nights have seen.
Horatio	Well, sit we down,
	And let us hear Bernardo speak of this.
Bernardo	Last night of all,
	When yond same star that's westward from the pole
	Had made his course to illume that part of heaven
	Where now it burns, Marcellus and myself,
	The bell then beating one, –
Marcellus	Peace! break thee off; look, where it comes again! *40*

Enter Ghost.

Bernardo	In the same figure, like the King that's dead.
Marcellus	Thou art a scholar; speak to it, Horatio.
Bernardo	Looks it not like the King? Mark it, Horatio.
Horatio	Most like. It harrows[9] me with fear and wonder.
Bernardo	It would be spoke to.
Marcellus	Question it, Horatio.
Horatio	What art thou that usurp'st[10] this time of night,
	Together with that fair and war-like form
	In which the majesty of buried Denmark[11]
	Did sometimes march? By heaven I charge thee,
	speak!
Marcellus	It is offended. *50*
Bernardo	See! it stalks away.
Horatio	Stay! speak, speak! I charge thee, speak!

[Exit Ghost.

Marcellus	'Tis gone, and will not answer.
Bernardo	How now, Horatio! You tremble and look pale:
	Is not this something more than fantasy?
	What think you on't?
Horatio	Before my God, I might not this believe
	Without the sensible and true avouch[12]
	Of mine own eyes.
Marcellus	Is it not like the King?
Horatio	As thou art to thyself:
	Such was the very armour he had on *60*
	When he the ambitious Norway combated;
	So frown'd he once, when, in an angry parle,[13]
	He smote the sledded Polack[14] on the ice.
	'Tis strange.
Marcellus	Thus twice before, and jump[15] at this dead hour,
	With martial stalk[16] hath he gone by our watch.

Margin notes:

[8] you will have to listen again

[9] torments

[10] to usurp is to take possession of something unlawfully; the ghost is an usurper for disturbing the peace of the night and for assuming the likeness of the king

[11] the dead king of Denmark

[12] the palpable and true assurance

[13] parley; dispute

[14] struck the king of Poland who was on a sledge

[15] exactly

[16] in a military manner

Horatio In what particular thought to work I know not;
       But, in the gross and scope[17] of my opinion,
       This bodes[18] some strange eruption[19] to our state.

Marcellus Good now, sit down, and tell me, he that knows, *70*
       Why this same strict and most observant watch
       So nightly toils the subject of the land;[20]
       And why such daily cast of brazen cannon,[21]
       And foreign mart[22] for implements of war;
       Why such impress of shipwrights,[23] whose sore task
       Does not divide the Sunday from the week;[24]
       What might be toward,[25] that this sweaty haste
       Doth make the night joint-labourer with the day:
       Who is't that can inform me?

Horatio   That can I;
       At least, the whisper goes so. Our last King, *80*
       Whose image even but now appear'd to us,
       Was, as you know, by Fortinbras of Norway,
       Thereto prick'd on[26] by a most emulate[27] pride,
       Dar'd to the combat: in which our valiant Hamlet – [28]
       For so this side of our known world esteem'd him –
       Did slay this Fortinbras; who, by a seal'd compact,
       Well ratified by law and heraldry,
       Did forfeit, with his life, all those his lands
       Which he stood seiz'd of, to the conqueror;
       Against the which, a moiety competent[29] *90*
       Was gaged by our King; which had return'd
       To the inheritance of Fortinbras,
       Had he been vanquisher; as, by the same covenant,
       And carriage of the article design'd,[30]
       His fell to Hamlet. Now, sir, young Fortinbras,
       Of unimproved mettle hot and full,[31]
       Hath in the skirts of Norway[32] here and there
       Shark'd up[33] a list of lawless resolutes,
       For food and diet,[34] to some enterprise
       That hath a stomach in't,[35] which is no other – *100*
       As it doth well appear unto our state –
       But to recover of us, by strong hand
       And terms compulsatory, those foresaid lands
       So by his father lost. And this, I take it,
       Is the main motive of our preparations,
       The source of this our watch, and the chief head[36]
       Of this post-haste and romage[37] in the land.

Bernardo I think it be no other but e'en so;[38]
       Well may it sort, that this portentous[39] figure
       Comes armed through our watch, so like the King *110*
       That was and is the question of these wars.

[17]in general terms
[18]foretells
[19]disaster
[20]makes the subjects toil
[21]why are cannons cast in bronze made every day?
[22]market
[23]why are shipbuilders being forced into service?
[24]they even work on Sundays
[25]imminent
[26]spurred on
[27]envious
[28]King Hamlet
[29]an equivalent part
[30]according to the terms of the article drawn up
[31]inexperienced and impetuous
[32]on the borders of Norway
[33]snapped up (like a shark)
[34]they enlisted for their keep
[35]that requires courage
[36]origin
[37]commotion
[38]just that
[39]ominous

Horatio

A mote⁴⁰ it is to trouble the mind's eye.
In the most high and palmy⁴¹ state of Rome,
A little ere the mightiest Julius fell,⁴²
The graves stood tenantless⁴³ and the sheeted dead
Did squeak and gibber in the Roman streets;
As stars with trains of fire⁴⁴ and dews of blood,
Disasters in the sun; and the moist star⁴⁵
Upon whose influence Neptune's⁴⁶ empire stands
Was sick almost to doomsday with eclipse;⁴⁷   120
And even the like precurse⁴⁸ of fierce events,
As harbingers⁴⁹ preceding still the fates
And prologue to the omen coming on,
Have heaven and earth together demonstrated
Unto our climatures and countrymen.
But, soft! behold! Lo! where it comes again.

Re-enter Ghost.

I'll cross it,⁵⁰ though it blast me. Stay, illusion!
                    [Ghost spreads its arms.
If thou hast any sound, or use of voice,
Speak to me:
If there be any good thing to be done,   130
That may to thee do ease and grace to me,
Speak to me:
If thou art privy⁵¹ to thy country's fate,
Which happily foreknowing may avoid,
O! speak!
Or if thou hast uphoarded in thy life
Extorted treasure in the womb of earth,
For which, they say, you spirits oft walk in death,
                    [Cock crows.
Speak of it: stay, and speak! Stop it, Marcellus.

Marcellus   Shall I strike at it with my partisan?⁵²   140
Horatio   Do, if it will not stand.
Bernardo   'Tis here!
Horatio   'Tis here!
                    [Exit Ghost.

Marcellus   'Tis gone!
We do it wrong, being so majestical,
To offer it the show of violence;
For it is, as the air, invulnerable,
And our vain blows malicious mockery.
Bernardo   It was about to speak when the cock crew.
Horatio   And then it started like a guilty thing
Upon a fearful summons. I have heard,
The cock, that is the trumpet to the morn,   150

                    Doth with his lofty and shrill-sounding throat
                    Awake the god of day; and at his warning,
                    Whether in sea or fire, in earth or air,
                    The extravagant and erring spirit[53] hies   [53]wandering beyond limits
                    To his confine; and of the truth herein
                    This present object made probation.[54]   [54]proof
Marcellus   It faded on the crowing of the cock.
                    Some say that ever 'gainst[55] that season comes   [55]just before
                    Wherein our Saviour's birth is celebrated,
                    The bird of dawning[56] singeth all night long; 160   [56]the cock
                    And then, they say, no spirit can walk abroad;
                    The nights are wholesome; then no planets strike,
                    No fairy takes,[57] nor witch hath power to charm, [57]charms
                    So hallow'd[58] and so gracious is the time.   [58]sanctified
Horatio   So have I heard and do in part believe it.
                    But, look, the morn, in russet[59] mantle clad,   [59]a coarse greyish cloth
                    Walks o'er the dew of yon high eastern hill;
                    Break we our watch up; and by my advice
                    Let us impart what we have seen to-night
                    Unto young Hamlet; for, upon my life,   170
                    This spirit, dumb to us, will speak to him.
                    Do you consent we shall acquaint him with it,
                    As needful in our loves, fitting our duty?
Marcellus   Let's do't, I pray; and I this morning know
                    Where we shall find him most conveniently.
                                                              [Exeunt.

Scene Analysis

The scene takes place on a platform before the castle in Elsinore, Denmark. A sense of dramatic tension is carefully built up. It is midnight and bitterly cold. Bernardo is clearly nervous since he challenges the guard and he does not want to be left alone for any length of time. He tells Francisco:

> "If you do meet Horatio and Marcellus,
> The rivals of my watch, bid them make haste."

Marcellus' question:

> "What! has this thing appear'd again to-night?"

indicates that the soldiers fear a *"dreaded sight"*. The fact that it has already been seen twice prepares the audience for the appearance of the ghost. Marcellus has asked Horatio to watch with them, but from the beginning Horatio is sceptical. He says it is a *"fantasy"*.

We do it wrong, being so majestical,
To offer it the show of violence   *(Marcellus, Act 1, Scene I)*

His ears are *"fortified"* against their story. But even the sceptical Horatio is inspired with fear at the appearance of the ghost in the likeness of the dead king.

> *"It harrows me with fear and wonder."*

Horatio is an important witness. He would not have believed:

> *"Without the sensible and true avouch*
> *Of mine own eyes."*

Horatio describes the ghost, giving details which authenticate the ghost's appearance in:

> *"...that fair and war-like form*
> *In which the majesty of buried Denmark*
> *Did sometimes march".*

Horatio connects the appearance of the ghost with:

> *"some strange eruption to our state".*

From the conversation of the friends we pick up the background information necessary for the development of the plot. Horatio tells of the likelihood of an attack by Fortinbras to regain lands forfeited by his dead father in battle with the late king of Denmark. When the ghost reappears Horatio is determined to confront it so as to establish:

> *"If there be any good thing to be done",*

but with the coming of dawn:

> *"...it started like a guilty thing*
> *Upon a fearful summons"*

and disappeared.

The fact that the ghost appears twice emphasises its probable importance in the play. The scene ends with the decision to inform the young Hamlet of the apparition. This points to the reappearance of the ghost as Horatio says:

> *"...for, upon my life,*
> *This spirit, dumb to us, will speak to him."*

Scene II

A Room of State in the Castle. Flourish.
Enter the King, Queen, Hamlet, Polonius, Laertes, Voltimand,
Cornelius, Lords and Attendants.

King	Though yet of Hamlet our dear brother's death
	The memory be green,[1] and that it us befitted
	To bear our hearts in grief, and our whole kingdom
	To be contracted in one brow of woe,[2]
	Yet so far hath discretion fought with nature
	That we with wisest sorrow[3] think on him,
	Together with remembrance of ourselves.
	Therefore our sometime sister,[4] now our queen,
	The imperial jointress[5] of this war-like state,
	Have we, as 'twere with a defeated joy,
	With one auspicious and one dropping eye,[6]
	With mirth in funeral, and with dirge[7] in marriage,
	In equal scale weighing delight and dole,[8]
	Taken to wife: nor have we herein barr'd[9]
	Your better wisdoms, which have freely gone
	With this affair along. For all, our thanks.
	Now follows, that you know: young Fortinbras,
	Holding a weak supposal[10] of our worth,
	Or thinking by our late dear brother's death
	Our state to be disjoint and out of frame,[11]
	Colleagued with the dream of his advantage,[12]

Line markers: 10, 20

[1] fresh

[2] united in mourning; the kingdom is described as a face contracted in grief

[3] moderated grief

[4] our former sister-in-law

[5] joint owner of the kingdom

[6] one eye happy and one eye sad

[7] grief

[8] sorrow

[9] ignored

[10] poor opinion

[11] disorganised and disordered

[12] together with his hope of gaining advantage

He hath not fail'd to pester us with message,
Importing the surrender of those lands
Lost by his father, with all bands of law,
To our most valiant brother. So much for him.
Now for ourself, and for this time of meeting.
Thus much the business is: we have here writ
To Norway, uncle of young Fortinbras,
Who, impotent and bed-rid, scarcely hears
Of this his nephew's purpose, to suppress   30
His further gait[13] herein; in that the levies,[14]
The lists, and full proportions,[15] are all made
Out of his subject;[16] and we here dispatch
You, good Cornelius, and you, Voltimand,
For bearers of this greeting to old Norway,
Giving to you no further personal power
To business with the King more than the scope
Of these delated articles allow.[17]
Farewell and let your haste commend[18] your duty.

Cornelius
Voltimand }   In that and all things will we show our duty.   40
King   We doubt it nothing: heartily farewell.
                                    [Exeunt Voltimand and Cornelius.
And now, Laertes, what's the news with you?
You told us of some suit;[19] what is't, Laertes?
You cannot speak of reason to the Dane,
And lose your voice.[20] What wouldst thou beg, Laertes,
That shall not be my offer, not thy asking?
The head is not more native to the heart,
The hand more instrumental to the mouth,
Than is the throne of Denmark to thy father.
What wouldst thou have, Laertes?   50

Laertes   Dread[21] my lord,
Your leave and favour to return to France;
From whence though willingly I came to Denmark,
To show my duty in your coronation,
Yet now, I must confess, that duty done,
My thoughts and wishes bend again toward France
And bow them to your gracious leave and pardon.

King   Have you your father's leave? What says Polonius?
Polonius   He hath, my lord, wrung from me my slow leave
By laboursome petition, and at last
Upon his will I seal'd my hard consent: 60
I do beseech you, give him leave to go.

King   Take thy fair hour,[22] Laertes; time be thine,
And thy best graces spend it at thy will.
But now, my cousin[23] Hamlet, and my son, –

[13]progress
[14]troops raised for active service
[15]the roster of soldiers and military supplies
[16]the Norwegian people

[17]i.e. they are restricted to the terms set out in the document
[18]express

[19]request

[20]waste your breath

[21]revered

[22]take the opportunity
[23]the word cousin was used to denote any close relative

Hamlet	[*Aside*] A little more than kin, and less than kind.[24]
King	How is it that the clouds still hang on you?
Hamlet	Not so, my lord; I am too much i' the sun.[25]
Queen	Good Hamlet, cast thy nighted colour[26] off,

And let thine eye look like a friend on Denmark.
Do not for ever with thy vailed lids[27]   70
Seek for thy noble father in the dust:
Thou know'st 'tis common; all that live must die,
Passing through nature to eternity.

Hamlet	Ay, madam, it is common.
Queen	If it be,

Why seems it so particular with thee?

Hamlet	Seems, madam! Nay, it is; I know not 'seems'.

'Tis not alone my inky cloak, good mother,
Nor customary suits of solemn black,
Nor windy suspiration of forc'd breath,[28]
No, nor the fruitful river in the eye,[29]   80
Nor the dejected haviour of the visage,[30]
Together with all forms, modes, shows of grief,
That can denote me truly. These indeed seem,
For they are actions that a man might play:
But I have that within which passes show;
These but the trappings[31] and the suits of woe.

King	'Tis sweet and commendable in your nature, Hamlet,

To give these mourning duties to your father:
But, you must know, your father lost a father;
That father lost, lost his; and the survivor bound   90
In filial obligation for some term
To do obsequious[32] sorrow. But to persever
In obstinate condolement is a course
Of impious[33] stubbornness; 'tis unmanly grief:
It shows a will most incorrect to heaven,
A heart unfortified, a mind impatient,
An understanding simple and unschool'd:
For what we know must be, and is as common
As any the most vulgar thing to sense,
Why should we in our peevish opposition   100
Take it to heart? Fie! 'tis a fault to heaven,
A fault against the dead, a fault to nature,
To reason most absurd, whose common theme
Is death of fathers, and who still hath cried,
From the first corse[34] till he that died to-day,
'This must be so.' We pray you, throw to earth
This unprevailing[35] woe, and think of us
As of a father; for let the world take note,

[24]Hamlet is both his nephew and his son by marriage but he does not feel kindly towards his uncle

[25]i.e. in the sunshine of the marriage festivities; also a proverbial saying meaning to be put out of house and home; there could also be a pun on 'son'

[26]black

[27]downcast eyes

[28]sighs

[29]tears

[30]dejected expression of the face

[31]superficial dress

[32]appropriate to funeral rites

[33]irreverent

[34]corpse

[35]ineffective

You are the most immediate to our throne;
And with no less nobility of love   *110*
Than that which dearest father bears his son
Do I impart toward you. For your intent
In going back to school in Wittenberg,[36]
It is most retrograde[37] to our desire;
And we beseech you, bend you to remain
Here, in the cheer and comfort of our eye,
Our chiefest courtier, cousin, and our son.

Queen Let not thy mother lose her prayers, Hamlet:
I pray thee, stay with us; go not to Wittenberg.

Hamlet I shall in all my best obey you, madam.   *120*

King Why, 'tis a loving and a fair reply:
Be as ourself in Denmark. Madam, come;
This gentle and unforc'd accord of Hamlet
Sits smiling to my heart; in grace whereof,
No jocund[38] health that Denmark drinks to-day,
But the great cannon to the clouds shall tell,
And the King's rouse[39] the heavens shall bruit[40]
        again,
Re-speaking earthly thunder. Come away.
        [Flourish. Exeunt all except Hamlet.

Hamlet O! that this too too solid flesh would melt,
Thaw and resolve itself into a dew!   *130*
Or that the Everlasting had not fix'd
His canon[41] 'gainst self-slaughter! O God! O God!
How weary, stale, flat, and unprofitable
Seem to me all the uses of this world!
Fie on 't! O fie! 'tis an unweeded garden,
That grows to seed; things rank and gross[42] in
        nature
Possess it merely. That it should come to this!
But two months dead! Nay, not so much, not two:
So excellent a king; that was, to this,
Hyperion[43] to a satyr,[44] so loving to my mother   *140*
That he might not beteem[45] the winds of heaven
Visit her face too roughly. Heaven and earth!
Must I remember? Why, she would hang on him,
As if increase of appetite had grown
By what it fed on; and yet, within a month,
Let me not think on't: Frailty, thy name is woman!
A little month; or ere those shoes were old
With which she follow'd my poor father's body,
Like Niobe,[46] all tears; why she, even she, –
O God! a beast, that wants discourse of reason,   *150*
Would have mourn'd longer, – married with mine
        uncle,

---

[36]university in Germany founded in 1502, a famous establishment of study

[37]contrary

[38]cheerful

[39]toast
[40]sound

[41]divine law

[42]corrupt and coarse

[43]Greek sun god, splendidly handsome
[44]a mythological creature, part man, part goat, which exemplified lechery
[45]allow

[46]Niobe wept so bitterly when her twelve children were slain by Leto, that Zeus turned her into a fountain of stone which flowed with her tears

My father's brother; but no more like my father
Than I to Hercules.[47] Within a month,
Ere yet the salt of most unrighteous[48] tears
Had left the flushing in her galled[49] eyes,
She married. O! most wicked speed, to post
With such dexterity[50] to incestuous[51] sheets!
It is not, nor it cannot come to good;
But break, my heart, for I must hold my tongue!

Enter Horatio, Marcellus, and Bernardo.

Horatio	Hail to your lordship!	160
Hamlet	I am glad to see you well:	
	Horatio, or I do forget myself.	
Horatio	The same, my lord, and your poor servant ever.	
Hamlet	Sir, my good friend. I'll change[52] that name with you.	
	And what make you from Wittenberg, Horatio?	
	Marcellus?	
Marcellus	My good lord!	
Hamlet	I am very glad to see you. *[To Bernardo]* Good	
	even, sir.	
	But what, in faith, make you from Wittenberg?	
Horatio	A truant disposition, good my lord.	
Hamlet	I would not hear your enemy say so,	170
	Nor shall you do mine ear that violence,	
	To make it truster of your own report	
	Against yourself. I know you are no truant.	
	But what is your affair in Elsinore?	
	We'll teach you to drink deep ere you depart.	
Horatio	My lord, I came to see your father's funeral.	
Hamlet	I prithee, do not mock me, fellow-student;	
	I think it was to see my mother's wedding.	
Horatio	Indeed, my lord, it follow'd hard upon.	
Hamlet	Thrift, thrift, Horatio! The funeral bak'd meats	180
	Did coldly furnish forth the marriage tables.	
	Would I had met my dearest[53] foe in heaven	
	Ere I had ever seen that day, Horatio!	
	My father, methinks I see my father.	
Horatio	O! Where, my lord?	
Hamlet	In my mind's eye, Horatio.	
Horatio	I saw him once; he was a goodly king.	
Hamlet	He was a man, take him for all in all,	
	I shall not look upon his like again.	
Horatio	My lord, I think I saw him yesternight.	
Hamlet	Saw who?	190
Horatio	My lord, the King your father.	
Hamlet	The King, my father!	

[47]son of Jupiter, famous for his physical strength and courage
[48]false
[49]irritated
[50]speed
[51]canon law considered marriage with a deceased brother's widow to be incest

[52]Hamlet will exchange the word friend instead of servant

[53]direst, i.e. most hated

[54] control your amazement

[55] attentive

[56] from head to toe

[57] staff of command

Horatio Season your admiration[54] for a while
With an attent[55] ear, till I may deliver,
Upon the witness of these gentlemen,
This marvel to you.

Hamlet For God's love, let me hear.

Horatio Two nights together had these gentlemen,
Marcellus and Bernardo, on their watch,
In the dead vast and middle of the night,
Been thus encounter'd. A figure like your father,
Armed at points exactly, cap-a-pe,[56]   200
Appears before them, and with solemn march
Goes slow and stately by them: thrice he walk'd
By their oppress'd and fear-surprised eyes,
Within his truncheon's[57] length; whilst they, distill'd
Almost to jelly with the act of fear,
Stand dumb and speak not to him. This to me
In dreadful secrecy impart they did,
And I with them the third night kept the watch;
Where, as they had deliver'd, both in time,
Form of the thing, each word made true and good, 210
The apparition comes. I knew your father;
These hands are not more like.

Hamlet But where was this?

Marcellus My lord, upon the platform where we watch.

Hamlet Did you not speak to it?

Horatio My lord, I did;
But answer made it none; yet once methought
It lifted up its head and did address
Itself to motion, like as it would speak;
But even then the morning cock crew loud,
And at the sound it shrunk in haste away
And vanish'd from our sight.   220

Hamlet 'Tis very strange.

Horatio As I do live, my honour'd lord, 'tis true;
And we did think it writ down in our duty
To let you know of it.

Hamlet Indeed, indeed, sirs, but this troubles me.
Hold you the watch to-night?

Marcellus / Bernardo We do, my lord.

Hamlet Arm'd, say you?

Marcellus / Bernardo Arm'd, my lord.

Hamlet From top to toe?

Marcellus / Bernardo My lord, from head to foot.

Hamlet Then saw you not his face?

Horatio	O yes! my lord; he wore his beaver[58] up.		[58]lower front part of the
Hamlet	What! look'd he frowningly?	*230*	helmet which could be raised
Horatio	A countenance more in sorrow than in anger.		
Hamlet	Pale or red?		
Horatio	Nay, very pale.		
Hamlet	And fix'd his eyes upon you?		
Horatio	Most constantly.		
Hamlet	I would I had been there.		
Horatio	It would have much amaz'd you.		
Hamlet	Very like, very like. Stay'd it long?		
Horatio	While one with moderate haste might tell a hundred.		
Marcellus Bernardo	Longer, longer.		
Horatio	Not when I saw it.	*240*	
Hamlet	His beard was grizzled, no?		
Horatio	It was, as I have seen it in his life, A sable[59] silver'd.		[59]black
Hamlet	I will watch to-night; Perchance 'twill walk again.		
Horatio	I warrant it will.		
Hamlet	If it assume my noble father's person,		

I'll speak to it, though hell itself should gape
And bid me hold my peace. I pray you all,
If you have hitherto conceal'd this sight,
Let it be tenable[60] in your silence still;   [60]kept
And whatsoever else shall hap to-night,
Give it an understanding, but no tongue: *250*
I will requite[61] your loves. So, fare you well.   [61]repay
Upon the platform, 'twixt eleven and twelve,
I'll visit you.

All	Our duty to your honour.		
Hamlet	Your loves, as mine to you. Farewell.		

[Exeunt Horatio, Marcellus, and Bernardo.

My father's spirit in arms! All is not well;
I doubt[62] some foul play: would the night were come!   [62]suspect
Till then sit still, my soul. Foul deeds will rise,
Though all the earth o'erwhelm them, to men's eyes.

[Exit.

Scene Analysis

The court scene contrasts with the previous cold night scene with its ghostly apparition. Claudius addresses his counsellors, thanking them for their co-operation and tries to justify his hasty marriage so soon after the death of the king. His speech is somewhat forced as he uses antithesis to give the impression that it is normal to have:

> *"...one auspicious and one dropping eye,*
> *With mirth in funeral, and with dirge in marriage."*

A little more than kin, and less than kind.   (Hamlet, Act 1, Scene II)

His *"weighing delight and dole"* sounds contrived. Claiming that he mourns his brother *"with wisest sorrow"*, Claudius passes on to matters of state. He is fully aware of the threat of Fortinbras to the state of Denmark but he is in control of the situation and sends Voltimand and Cornelius to old Norway with a diplomatic request to restrain his nephew.

Next Claudius gives Laertes his attention and we get an idea of the important position of his father, Polonius, in the court. The king is prepared to give Laertes anything he wants:

> *"... What wouldst thou beg, Laertes,*
> *That shall not be my offer, not thy asking?"*

Claudius willingly gives permission to Laertes to return to France. Yet he withholds his consent to Hamlet's return to Wittenberg. When the king finally turns his attention to

Hamlet, who is noticeably in the background, it is obvious that all is not well between them. The king's attempt to treat Hamlet as his own son is coldly rebuffed:

> "But now, my cousin Hamlet, and my son," –
> Hamlet (Aside) "A little more than kin, and less than kind."

Hamlet's sharp aside is a bitter comment on the fact that the marriage of his mother to his uncle makes Claudius more than a cousin, but he cannot call him his father, since he is his uncle. There is the double sense of kind which means friendly and also refers to descent. The king shows a degree of insensitivity in asking Hamlet the cause of his gloom. His question points to the fact that Hamlet is not a happy man:

> "How is it that the clouds still hang on you?"

Hamlet's reply is sharp and cryptic:

> "Not so, my lord; I am too much i' the sun."

suggesting that in fact he is surrounded by too much festivity. There is a pun on sun and son, a reminder that Hamlet has no wish to be the son of Claudius and there is a possible underlying reference to the fact that Hamlet has been disinherited by his uncle. It is evident from the queen's words that Hamlet, by his very dress and manner, is a stark contrast to the court. She pleads with him:

> "Good Hamlet, cast thy nighted colour off,
> And let thine eye look like a friend on Denmark."

She, at least, realises that he is mourning his father:

> "Do not forever with thy vailed lids
> Seek for thy noble father in the dust:"

but she does not share her son's grief. For her, death is *"common"*. She does not understand her son's grief:

> "Why seems it so particular with thee?"

Hamlet's answer:

> "Seems, madam! Nay, it is; I know not seems."

is an angry protest against sham and hypocrisy, a firm rejection of hypocritical mourning *"the trappings and the suits of woe"*. Hamlet's grief is seen as *"Obstinate condolement"* by the king and he accuses Hamlet of *"impious stubbornness"* and *"unmanly grief"*. But Claudius is shrewd. He seeks Hamlet's friendship for practical reasons:

> "You are the most immediate to our throne".

O! that this too too solid flesh would melt,
Thaw and resolve itself into a dew!

(Hamlet, Act 1, Scene II)

Both the king and queen ask him not to return to Wittenberg, but Hamlet's reply is pointedly addressed solely to his mother:

"I shall in all my best obey you, madam."

In fact Hamlet ignores the king's speech. Nevertheless Claudius is relieved at:

"This gentle and unforc'd accord of Hamlet".

In the light of Hamlet's grief, the king's call that:

"... the King's rouse the heavens shall bruit again"

seems out of place.

When Hamlet is left alone we see that his state of mind is almost suicidal. He wishes to die but is imbued with a religious awareness that suicide is wrong.

"O! that this too too solid flesh would melt,
Thaw and resolve itself into a dew!
Or that the Everlasting had not fix'd
His canon 'gainst self-slaughter!"

In his soliloquy he reveals the cause of such deep depression. His father is not even dead two months and within a month his mother has married his uncle. Hamlet's feelings are mixed: grief at the death of his father *"So excellent a king"*, shocked disbelief at his mother's unfeeling attitude *"a beast... would have mourn'd longer"*, anger at her *"most wicked speed"* and disgust that she could go *"With such dexterity to incestuous sheets"*. Hamlet's heart is breaking, yet he must hold his tongue as his uncle is now the recognised king of Denmark to whom Hamlet is now subject.

The arrival of his friends interrupts Hamlet's melancholic thoughts and he seems genuinely pleased to see them. When Horatio explains that he came to the funeral, Hamlet's reply is bitter:

"I prithee, do not mock me, fellow-student;
I think it was to see my mother's wedding."

There is a special bond of friendship between Horatio and Hamlet as Hamlet confides to Horatio his feelings about his mother's remarriage:

"Would I had met my dearest foe in heaven
Ere I had ever seen that day, Horatio!"

Horatio is momentarily startled when Hamlet says:

"My father, methinks I see my father."

and this gives him the opportunity to tell Hamlet of the ghost. Hamlet listens carefully to Horatio's report. His questions are practical and to the point. He does not doubt his friend but he is careful to check details:

"Then saw you not his face?"

Hamlet determines to keep watch himself that night. He knows exactly what he must do:

"I'll speak to it, though hell itself should gape
And bid me hold my peace."

This prepares us for Hamlet's encounter with the ghost in *Scene IV*.

Scene III

A Room in Polonius' House.
Enter Laertes and Ophelia.

Laertes	My necessaries are embark'd. Farewell:
	And, sister, as the winds give benefit[1]
	And convoy is assistant,[2] do not sleep,
	But let me hear from you.
Ophelia	Do you doubt that?
Laertes	For Hamlet, and the trifling[3] of his favour,
	Hold it a fashion[4] and a toy in blood,[5]
	A violet in the youth of primy nature,[6]
	Forward, not permanent, sweet, not lasting,
	The perfume and suppliance of a minute;
	No more.
Ophelia	No more but so?
Laertes	Think it no more:
	For nature, crescent,[7] does not grow alone
	In thews[8] and bulk; but, as this temple waxes,[9]
	The inward service of the mind and soul
	Grows wide withal.[10] Perhaps he loves you now,
	And now no soil nor cautel[11] doth besmirch
	The virtue of his will; but you must fear,
	His greatness weigh'd, his will is not his own,
	For he himself is subject to his birth;
	He may not, as unvalu'd persons do,
	Carve for himself; for on his choice depends
	The safety and health of this whole state;
	And therefore must his choice be circumscrib'd[12]
	Unto the voice and yielding of that body[13]
	Whereof he is the head. Then if he says he loves you,

10

20

[1] are favourable
[2] transport is available
[3] not serious
[4] i.e. not lasting
[5] the sport of youth
[6] springtime
[7] growing
[8] physical strength
[9] as the body grows
[10] Laertes is suggesting that Hamlet's mind will outgrow Ophelia
[11] deceit
[12] limited
[13] the consent of the state

It fits your wisdom so far to believe it
As he in his particular act and place
May give his saying deed; which is no further
Than the main voice of Denmark goes withal.
Then weigh what loss your honour may sustain,
If with too credent[14] ear you list his songs,   30   [14]believing
Or lose your heart, or your chaste treasure[15] open   [15]honour
To his unmaster'd importunity.[16]   [16]persistent requests
Fear it, Ophelia, fear it, my dear sister;
And keep you in the rear of your affection,
Out of the shot and danger of desire.
The chariest[17] maid is prodigal[18] enough   [17]most careful
If she unmask her beauty to the moon;   [18]very free
Virtue herself 'scapes not calumnious strokes;[19]   [19]injurious reports
The canker[20] galls the infants of the spring   [20]worm that preys upon
Too oft before their buttons be disclos'd, [21]   40   blossoms
And in the morn and liquid dew of youth   [21]before the buds are open
Contagious blastments are most imminent.
Be wary then; best safety lies in fear:
Youth to itself rebels, though none else near.

Ophelia   I shall th' effect of this good lesson keep,
As watchman to my heart. But, good my brother,
Do not, as some ungracious pastors do,
Show me the steep and thorny way to heaven,
Whiles, like a puff'd and reckless libertine,[22]   [22]playboy
Himself the primrose path[23] of dalliance[24] treads, 50   [23]the way of worldly
And recks not his own rede.[25]   pleasure
                                                              [24]flirtation
Laertes   O! fear me not.   [25]heeds not his own advice
I stay too long; but here my father comes.

                    Enter Polonius.

A double blessing is a double grace;
Occasion smiles upon a second leave.
Polonius   Yet here, Laertes! Aboard, aboard, for shame!
The wind sits in the shoulder of your sail,
And you are stay'd for. There, my blessing with thee!
And these few precepts[26] in thy memory   [26]principles
Look thou character.[27] Give thy thoughts no tongue,   [27]inscribe
Nor any unproportion'd[28] thought his act.   60   [28]immoderate
Be thou familiar, but by no means vulgar;
Those friends thou hast, and their adoption tried,[29]   [29]tested their friendship
Grapple[30] them to thy soul with hoops of steel;   [30]grip hard
But do not dull thy palm with entertainment[31]   [31]don't wear out your hand
Of each new-hatch'd, unfledg'd comrade. Beware   in greeting
Of entrance to a quarrel, but, being in,
Bear't that th' opposed may beware of thee.
Give every man thine ear, but few thy voice;

³²judgment

Take each man's censure,³² but reserve thy
> judgment.
Costly thy habit as thy purse can buy,   70
But not express'd in fancy; rich, not gaudy;
For the apparel oft proclaims the man,
And they in France of the best rank and station
Are of a most select and generous, chief in that.
Neither a borrower, nor a lender be;
For loan oft loses both itself and friend,

³³economising

And borrowing dulls the edge of husbandry.³³
This above all: to thine own self be true,
And it must follow, as the night the day,
Thou canst not then be false to any man.   80
Farewell; my blessing season this in thee!

Laertes   Most humbly do I take my leave, my lord.
Polonius The time invites you; go, your servants tend.
Laertes   Farewell, Ophelia; and remember well
What I have said to you.
Ophelia   'Tis in my memory lock'd,
And you yourself shall keep the key of it.
Laertes   Farewell.

> [Exit.

Polonius What is't, Ophelia, he hath said to you?
Ophelia   So please you, something touching the Lord
Hamlet.

³⁴by Mary

Polonius Marry,³⁴ well bethought: 90
'Tis told me, he hath very oft of late
Given private time to you; and you yourself
Have of your audience been most free and bounteous.
If it be so, – as so 'tis put on me,
And that in way of caution, – I must tell you,
You do not understand yourself so clearly

³⁵befits

As it behoves³⁵ my daughter and your honour.
What is between you? Give me up the truth.
Ophelia   He hath, my lord, of late made many tenders
Of his affection to me.   100
Polonius Affection! pooh! you speak like a green girl,

³⁶inexperienced
³⁷offers of payment

Unsifted³⁶ in such perilous circumstance.
Do you believe his tenders,³⁷ as you call them?
Ophelia   I do not know, my lord, what I should think.
Polonius Marry, I'll teach you: think yourself a baby,
That you have ta'en these tenders for true pay,

³⁸set a higher price on yourself; take care of yourself
³⁹not to drive the point too hard
⁴⁰pressed

Which are not sterling. Tender yourself more dearly; ³⁸
Or, – not to crack the wind of the poor phrase,³⁹
Running it thus, – you'll tender me a fool.
Ophelia   My lord, he hath importun'd⁴⁰ me with love   110
In honourable fashion.

Polonius	Ay, fashion you may call it: go to, go to.	
Ophelia	And hath given countenance to his speech, my lord,	
	With almost all the holy vows of heaven.	
Polonius	Ay, springes to catch woodcocks.[41] I do know,	[41]considered easy game as they were easy to entrap
	When the blood burns, how prodigal[42] the soul	[42]freely
	Lends the tongue vows. These blazes, daughter,	
	Giving more light than heat, extinct in both,	
	Even in their promise, as it is a-making,	
	You must not take for fire. From this time 120	
	Be somewhat scanter of your maiden presence;	
	Set your entreatments at a higher rate	
	Than a command to parley. For Lord Hamlet,	
	Believe so much in him, that he is young,	
	And with a larger tether[43] may he walk	[43]rope which allows freedom of movement
	Than may be given you. In few, Ophelia,	
	Do not believe his vows, for they are brokers,[44]	[44]go-betweens
	Not of that dye which their investments[45] show,	[45]financial transactions; also means clothes
	But mere implorators[46] of unholy suits,	[46]people who urge
	Breathing like sanctified and pious bawds,[47] 130	[47]panderers
	The better to beguile.[48] This is for all:	[48]deceive
	I would not, in plain terms, from this time forth,	
	Have you so slander any moment's leisure,	
	As to give words or talk with the Lord Hamlet.	
	Look to't, I charge you. Come your ways.	
Ophelia	I shall obey, my lord.	

[Exeunt.

Scene Analysis

In contrast to the public court scene, *Scene III* is a private family scene. Laertes, about to depart for France, bids farewell to his sister Ophelia, warning her against believing that Hamlet's love could be everlasting. Laertes's advice is based on his understanding that Hamlet *"is subject to his birth"* and would not marry a girl of Ophelia's class. He lectures Ophelia about virtue and honour, pompously asserting:

> *"The chariest maid is prodigal enough*
> *If she unmask her beauty to the moon;"*

Ophelia agrees to keep *"the effect of this good lesson"* but she shows some spirit in reprimanding her brother:

> *"Do not, as some ungracious pastors do,*
> *Show me the steep and thorny way to heaven,*
> *Whiles, like a puff'd and reckless libertine,*
> *Himself the primrose path of dalliance treads,*
> *And recks not his own rede."*

Polonius tells Laertes to hurry and then proceeds to delay him with a long speech. It is a long sermon full of platitudes:

> *"Be thou familiar, but by no means vulgar;"*

> *"Take each man's censure, but reserve thy judgment."*

His advice shows a wariness of people and a degree of self-interest:

> *"Those friends thou hast, and their adoption tried,*
> *Grapple them to thy soul with hoops of steel;*
> *But do not dull thy palm with entertainment*
> *Of each new-hatch'd, unfledg'd comrade."*

Polonius' advice to his son could have been summarised in the final idea *"to thine own self be true"* and even this has an undertone of looking after oneself first. Polonius' maxims roll off the tongue and sound very high-minded but he takes little heed of his own advice:

> *"Give thy thoughts no tongue"*

> *"Give every man thine ear; but few thy voice"*

Polonius wants to know what Laertes said to Ophelia and he too disapproves of the relationship between Hamlet and Ophelia. He chastises her:

> *"...I must tell you,*
> *You do not understand yourself so clearly*
> *As it behoves my daughter and your honour"*

The dramatic importance of this scene is that it draws attention to a developing relationship between Hamlet and Ophelia. From Ophelia's account to her father, we learn that Hamlet has:

> *"...of late made many tenders*
> *Of his affection to me".*

Ophelia seems to believe in Hamlet's sincerity, claiming:

> *"...he hath importun'd me with love*
> *In honourable fashion."*

Polonius mocks her naivety *"you speak like a green girl"* and in the harsh language of the business world he diminishes Hamlet's vows:

> "...they are brokers,
> Not of that dye which their investments show,
> But mere implorators of unholy suits,
> Breathing like sanctified and pious bawds,
> The better to beguile."

Ophelia is confused by her father's and brother's attitude:

> "I do not know, my lord, what I should think."

Polonius tells her:

> "I would not, in plain terms, from this time forth,
> Have you so slander any moment's leisure,
> As to give words or talk with the Lord Hamlet."

Ophelia obeys without argument.

Scene IV

The Platform.
Enter Hamlet, Horatio and Marcellus.

Hamlet	The air bites shrewdly;[1] it is very cold.	[1] bitterly
Horatio	It is a nipping and an eager[2] air.	[2] sharp
Hamlet	What hour now?	
Horatio	I think it lacks of twelve.	
Marcellus	No, it is struck.	
Horatio	Indeed? I heard it not. It then draws near the season	
	Wherein the spirit held his wont[3] to walk.	[3] custom
	[A flourish of trumpets, and ordnance shot off, within.	
	What does this mean, my lord?	
Hamlet	The King doth wake to-night and takes his rouse,[4]	[4] carouses
	Keeps wassail,[5] and the swaggering up-spring reels;[6]	[5] holds a drinking party
		[6] a wild German dance
	And, as he drains his draughts of Rhenish down,[7] *10*	[7] Rhine wine
	The kettle-drum and trumpet thus bray out	
	The triumph of his pledge.[8]	[8] toast
Horatio	Is it a custom?	
Hamlet	Ay, marry, is't:	
	But to my mind, though I am native here	
	And to the manner born,[9] it is a custom	[9] brought up to it
	More honour'd in the breach than the observance.[10]	[10] more honourable to break than to keep
	This heavy-headed revel east and west	
	Makes us traduc'd and tax'd[11] of other nations;	[11] disgraced and blamed
	They clepe[12] us drunkards, and with swinish phrase	[12] call
	Soil our addition;[13] and indeed it takes *20*	[13] blacken our reputation
	From our achievements, though perform'd at height,	

¹⁴the best part of our merit

¹⁵natural tendency
¹⁶enclosurers; the reason
is described as being
defended by fence and
forts
¹⁷corrupts
¹⁸pleasing
¹⁹one's innate temperament
²⁰determined by the stars;
chance

²¹the small amount of evil

²²burial clothes

²³buried

²⁴communication

The pith and marrow of our attribute.[14]
So, oft it chances in particular men,
That for some vicious mole of nature in them,
As, in their birth, wherein they are not guilty,
Since nature cannot choose his origin, –
By the o'ergrowth of some complexion,[15]
Oft breaking down the pales[16] and forts of reason,
Or by some habit that too much o'er-leavens[17]
The form of plausive[18] manners; that these men,   30
Carrying, I say, the stamp of one defect,
Being nature's livery,[19] or fortune's star,[20]
Their virtues else, be they as pure as grace,
As infinite as man may undergo,
Shall in the general censure take corruption
From that particular fault. The dram of eale[21]
Doth all the noble substance of a doubt,
To his own scandal.

                                 Enter Ghost.

Horatio	Look, my lord, it comes.
Hamlet	Angels and ministers of grace defend us!

Be thou a spirit of health or goblin damn'd,   40
Bring with thee airs from heaven or blasts from hell,
Be thy intents wicked or charitable,
Thou com'st in such a questionable shape
That I will speak to thee. I'll call thee Hamlet,
King, father; royal Dane, O! answer me!
Let me not burst in ignorance; but tell
Why thy canoniz'd bones, hearsed in death,
Have burst their cerements;[22] why the sepulchre,
Wherein we saw thee quietly inurn'd,[23]
Hath op'd his ponderous and marble jaws,   50
To cast thee up again. What may this mean,
That thou, dead corse, again in complete steel
Revisit'st thus the glimpses of the moon,
Making night hideous; and we fools of nature
So horridly to shake our disposition
With thoughts beyond the reaches of our souls?
Say, why is this? wherefore? What should we do?
                                 [The Ghost beckons Hamlet.

Horatio	It beckons you to go away with it,
	As if it some impartment[24] did desire
	To you alone. 60
Marcellus	Look, with what courteous action
	It waves you to a more removed ground:
	But do not go with it.
Horatio	No, by no means.

Hamlet	It will not speak; then, I will follow it.
Horatio	Do not, my lord.
Hamlet	Why, what should be the fear?
	I do not set my life at a pin's fee;
	And for my soul, what can it do to that,
	Being a thing immortal as itself?
	It waves me forth again; I'll follow it.
Horatio	What if it tempt you toward the flood, my lord,
	Or to the dreadful summit of the cliff 70
	That beetles o'er his base[25] into the sea,
	And there assume some other horrible form,
	Which might deprive your sovereignty of reason
	And draw you into madness? Think of it;
	The very place puts toys[26] of desperation,
	Without more motive, into every brain
	That looks so many fathoms to the sea
	And hears it roar beneath.
Hamlet	It waves me still. Go on, I'll follow thee.
Marcellus	You shall not go, my lord. 80
Hamlet	Hold off your hands!
Horatio	Be rul'd; you shall not go.
Hamlet	My fate cries out,
	And makes each petty artery in this body
	As hardy as the Nemean[27] lion's nerve.
	[Ghost beckons.
	Still am I call'd. Unhand me, gentlemen,
	[Breaking from them.
	By heaven! I'll make a ghost of him that lets[28] me
	I say, away! Go on, I'll follow thee.
	[Exeunt Ghost and Hamlet.
Horatio	He waxes[29] desperate with imagination.
Marcellus	Let's follow; 'tis not fit thus to obey him.
Horatio	Have after. To what issue will this come?
Marcellus	Something is rotten in the state of Denmark. 90
Horatio	Heaven will direct it.
Marcellus	Nay, let's follow him.
	[Exeunt.

[25]that juts out

[26]fancies

[27]mythical monster slain by Hercules

[28]hinders

[29]grows

Scene Analysis

Scene IV takes us back to the opening scene. The two intervening scenes heighten the anticipation of the ghost's reappearance. This time the suspense is heightened by the presence of Hamlet for whom the ghost's appearance is so significant. Again, the cold, lonely atmosphere of the opening scene on the platform is evoked. As they watch they hear the sounds of revelry coming from the castle – a contrast to their cold and lonely vigil.

The scene begins with rather aimless conversation about the cold and Hamlet talks about the Danish custom of wassailing. Hamlet's shocked exclamation at the appearance of the ghost leaves us in little doubt that he recognises him as his father, although he wonders at his *"questionable shape"*. Although the others beg Hamlet not to, he follows it. He shows no fear:

> *"Be thou a spirit of health or goblin damn'd,*
> *Bring with thee airs from heaven or blasts from hell*
> *Be thy intents wicked or charitable,*
> *Thou com'st in such a questionable shape*
> *That I will speak to thee:"*

Hamlet understands: *"My fate cries out"* and shows unusual roughness towards his friends in his determination to act:

> *"...Unhand me gentlemen,*
> *By heaven! I'll make a ghost of him that lets me."*

Scene V

Another part of the Platform.
Enter Ghost and Hamlet.

Hamlet	Whither wilt thou lead me? Speak; I'll go no further.
Ghost	Mark me.
Hamlet	I will.
Ghost	My hour is almost come,
	When I to sulphurous¹ and tormenting flames
	Must render up myself.
Hamlet	Alas! poor ghost.
Ghost	Pity me not, but lend thy serious hearing
	To what I shall unfold.
Hamlet	Speak; I am bound to hear.
Ghost	So art thou to revenge, when thou shalt hear.
Hamlet	What?
Ghost	I am thy father's spirit;
	Doom'd for a certain term to walk the night, 10

¹fiery

28

	And for the day confin'd to fast in fires,	
	Till the foul crimes done in my days of nature	
	Are burnt and purg'd away. But that I am forbid	
	To tell the secrets of my prison-house,	
	I could a tale unfold whose lightest word	
	Would harrow up[2] thy soul, freeze thy young blood,	[2]lacerate
	Make thy two eyes, like stars, start from their spheres,	
	Thy knotted and combined locks to part,	
	And each particular hair to stand an end,	
	Like quills upon the fretful porpentine: 20	
	But this eternal blazon[3] must not be	[3]proclaiming the secrets of eternity
	To ears of flesh and blood. List, list, O list!	
	If thou didst ever thy dear father love –	

Hamlet   O God!

Ghost   Revenge his foul and most unnatural murder.

Hamlet   Murder!

Ghost   Murder most foul, as in the best it is;
But this most foul, strange, and unnatural.

Hamlet   Haste me to know't, that I, with wings as swift
As meditation or the thoughts of love,   30
May sweep to my revenge.

Ghost   I find thee apt;[4]

[4]quick to understand

And duller shouldst thou be than the fat weed
That roots itself in ease on Lethe wharf,[5]

[5]the underworld river of forgetfulness

Wouldst thou not stir in this. Now, Hamlet, hear:
'Tis given out that, sleeping in mine orchard,
A serpent stung me; so the whole ear of Denmark
Is by a forged process[6] of my death

[6]false account

Rankly abus'd;[7] but know, thou noble youth,

[7]corruptly deceived

The serpent that did sting thy father's life
Now wears his crown.   40

Hamlet   O my prophetic soul!
My uncle!

Ghost   Ay, that incestuous, that adulterate beast,
With witchcraft of his wit, with traitorous gifts, –
O wicked wit and gifts, that have the power
So to seduce! – won to his shameful lust
The will of my most seeming-virtuous queen.
O Hamlet! what a falling-off was there;
From me, whose love was of that dignity
That it went hand in hand even with the vow
I made to her in marriage; and to decline   50
Upon a wretch whose natural gifts were poor
To those of mine!
But virtue, as it never will be mov'd,
Though lewdness[8] court it in a shape of heaven,[9]

[8]lust
[9]in the form of an angel

[10] glut itself

[11] unsuspecting
[12] a poisonous plant

[13] mercury

[14] curdle
[15] sour

[16] a scab
[17] encrusted
[18] leper-like

[19] without receiving the Eucharist, unprepared and unannointed
[20] examination of conscience; confession

[21] anything

[22] morning
[23] ineffective

[24] add

[25] head
[26] foolish
[27] wise sayings, proverbs
[28] impressions

So lust, though to a radiant angel link'd,
Will sate[10] itself in a celestial bed,
And prey on garbage.
But, soft! methinks I scent the morning air;
Brief let me be. Sleeping within mine orchard,
My custom always in the afternoon,   60
Upon my secure[11] hour thy uncle stole,
With juice of cursed hebona[12] in a vial,
And in the porches of mine ears did pour
The leperous distilment; whose effect
Holds such an enmity with blood of man
That swift as quicksilver[13] it courses through
The natural gates and alleys of the body,
And with a sudden vigour it doth posset[14]
And curd, like eager[15] droppings into milk,
The thin and wholesome blood. So did it mine;   70
And a most instant tetter[16] bark'd about,[17]
Most lazar-like,[18] with vile and loathsome crust,
All my smooth body.
Thus was I, sleeping, by a brother's hand,
Of life, of crown, of queen, at once dispatch'd;
Cut oft even in the blossoms of my sin,
Unhousel'd, disappointed, unanel'd,[19]
No reckoning[20] made, but sent to my account
With all my imperfections on my head:
O, horrible! O, horrible! most horrible!   80
If thou hast nature in thee, bear it not;
Let not the royal bed of Denmark be
A couch for luxury and damned incest.
But, howsoever thou pursu'st this act.
Taint not thy mind, nor let thy soul contrive
Against thy mother aught;[21] leave her to heaven,
And to those thorns that in her bosom lodge,
To prick and sting her. Fare thee well at once!
The glow-worm shows the matin[22] to be near,
And 'gins to pale his uneffectual[23] fire;   90
Adieu, adieu! Hamlet, remember me.
                                              [Exit.

Hamlet   O all you host of heaven! O earth! What else?
And shall I couple[24] hell? O fie! Hold, hold, my heart!
And you, my sinews, grow not instant old,
But bear me stiffly up! Remember thee!
Ay, thou poor ghost, while memory holds a seat
In this distracted globe.[25] Remember thee!
Yea, from the table of my memory
I'll wipe away all trivial fond[26] records,
All saws[27] of books, all forms, all pressures[28] past   100

	That youth and observation copied there;
	And thy commandment all alone shall live
	Within the book and volume of my brain,
	Unmix'd with baser matter.[29] Yes, by heaven!
	O most pernicious woman!
	O villain, villain, smiling, damned villain!
	My tables,[30] – meet it is I set it down,
	That one may smile, and smile, and be a villain;
	At least I'm sure it may be so in Denmark: [Writing.
	So, uncle, there you are. Now to my word; 110
	It is, 'Adieu, adieu! Remember me.'
	I have sworn't.

[29]unimportant things

[30]notebook

Horatio	[Within] My lord! my lord!
Marcellus	[Within] Lord Hamlet!
Horatio	[Within] Heaven secure him!
Marcellus	[Within] So be it!
Horatio	[Within] Hillo, ho, ho, my lord!
Hamlet	Hillo, ho, ho, boy! Come, bird,[31] come.

[31]they have been using the call of falconers

Enter Horatio and Marcellus.

Marcellus	How is't, my noble lord?
Horatio	What news, my lord?
Hamlet	O! wonderful.
Horatio	Good my lord, tell it.
Hamlet	No; you will reveal it.
Horatio	Not I, my lord, by heaven!
Marcellus	Nor I, my lord.
Hamlet	How say you, then; would heart of man once think
	it? 120
	But you'll be secret.

Horatio }	Ay, by heaven, my lord.
Marcellus }	
Hamlet	There's ne'er a villain dwelling in all Denmark,
	But he's an arrant[32] knave.
Horatio	There needs no ghost, my lord, come from the grave,
	To tell us this.
Hamlet	Why, right; you are i' the right;
	And so, without more circumstance at all,
	I hold it fit that we shake hands and part;
	You, as your business and desire shall point you, –
	For every man hath business and desire,
	Such as it is, and, for mine own poor part, 130
	Look you, I'll go pray.
Horatio	These are but wild and whirling words, my lord.
Hamlet	I am sorry they offend you, heartily;
	Yes, faith, heartily.

[32]downright

Horatio	There's no offence, my lord.
Hamlet	Yes, by Saint Patrick,³³ but there is, Horatio,

And much offence, too. Touching this vision here,
It is an honest ghost, that let me tell you;
For your desire to know what is between us,
O'ermaster't as you may. And now, good friends,
As you are friends, scholars, and soldiers,   140
Give me one poor request.

Horatio What is't, my lord? we will.

Hamlet Never make known what you have seen to-night.

Horatio
Marcellus } My lord, we will not.

Hamlet Nay, but swear't.

Horatio   In faith,
My lord, not I.

Marcellus   Nor I, my lord, in faith.

Hamlet Upon my sword.³⁴

Marcellus   We have sworn, my lord, already.

Hamlet Indeed, upon my sword, indeed.

Ghost *[Beneath]* Swear.

Hamlet Ah, ha, boy! sayst thou so? Art thou there, truepenny?³⁵
Come on. You hear this fellow in the cellarage,³⁶   150
Consent to swear.

Horatio   Propose the oath, my lord.

Hamlet Never to speak of this that you have seen,
Swear by my sword.

Ghost *[Beneath]* Swear.

Hamlet Hic et ubique?³⁷ Then we'll shift our ground.
Come hither, gentlemen,
And lay your hands again upon my sword:
Never to speak of this that you have heard,
Swear by my sword.

Ghost *[Beneath]* Swear.   160

Hamlet Well said, old mole! Canst work i' the earth so fast?
A worthy pioner!³⁸ Once more remove, good friends.

Horatio O day and night, but this is wondrous strange!

Hamlet And therefore as a stranger give it welcome.
There are more things in heaven and earth, Horatio,
Than are dreamt of in your philosophy.
But come;
Here, as before, never, so help you mercy,
How strange or odd soe'er I bear myself,
As I perchance hereafter shall think meet   170
To put an antic disposition³⁹ on,
That you, at such times, seeing me, never shall,
With arms encumber'd⁴⁰ thus, or this head-shake,

³⁴swearing on a sword
was considered binding
because its hilt is in the
form of a cross

³⁵honest fellow (a minting
term)
³⁶the cellar; down below

³⁷here and everywhere

³⁸ a mine digger

³⁹ crazy behaviour

⁴⁰ folded

Or by pronouncing of some doubtful phrase,
As, 'Well, well, we know,' or, 'We could, an if we
  would;'
Or, 'If we list to speak,' or, 'There be, an if they might;'
Or such ambiguous giving out, to note
That you know aught of me: this not to do,
So grace and mercy at your most need help you,
Swear.   *180*

Ghost   [Beneath] Swear.
Hamlet   Rest, rest, perturbed spirit! So, gentlemen,
With all my love I do commend me to you:
And what so poor a man as Hamlet is
May do, to express his love and friending to you,
God willing, shall not lack. Let us go in together;
And still your fingers on your lips, I pray.
The time is out of joint;[41] O cursed spite,   [41] in disorder
That ever I was born to set it right!
Nay, come let's go together.   *190*

                        [Exeunt.

Scene Analysis

The high dramatic point of *Act I* is when Hamlet comes face to face with his father's ghost. The ghost hints at *"the secrets of my prison-house"*. He is doomed to *"sulphurous and tormenting flames"*. The tormented ghost cries out *"List, list, O list!"* and calls for the revenge of his *"foul and most unnatural murder"*. Hamlet is shocked but he has only one thought:

> *"Haste me to know 't, that I, with wings as swift*
> *As meditation or the thoughts of love,*
> *May sweep to my revenge."*

It was claimed that King Hamlet was stung by a serpent, but the ghost reveals:

> *"The serpent that did sting thy father's life*
> *Now wears his crown."*

Hamlet's exclamation *"O my prophetic soul!"* suggests that he had suspected something of the sort. The ghost laments the *"falling-off"* of his *"most seeming-virtuous queen"* before he relates exactly how he was murdered by Claudius. The distraught Hamlet is tortured by the ghost's words:

> *"O all you host of heaven! O earth! What else?*
> *And shall I couple hell? O fie! Hold, hold, my heart!"*

He is particularly moved by the father's parting words *"remember me"*. He vows never to forget:

> *"...Now to my word;*
> *It is, 'Adieu, Adieu! Remember me.'*
> *I have sworn't".*

His friends are concerned at his *"wild and whirling words"*. He makes them swear not to reveal what they have seen, not to hint or give knowing looks about his behaviour even if he should *"put an antic disposition on"*. It would seem as if he has formed a plan of action already, yet he baulks at what he must do:

> *"...O cursed spite,*
> *That ever I was born to set it right!"*

This contradicts his initial impulse to sweep to his revenge and marks the beginning in Hamlet's mind of the central conflict in the play.

REVISION

> *"Something is rotten in the state of Denmark."*   (Marcellus, Act 1, Scene IV)

The ghost of the late king of Denmark appears to the guards and is witnessed by Hamlet's friend Horatio. They inform Hamlet and he arranges to watch with them. Claudius, brother of the dead king, now rules Denmark and has married Gertrude, his brother's widow. He sends ambassadors to Norway to ask the king there to prevent the planned invasion of Denmark by Fortinbras, his nephew. Claudius grants permission to Laertes, son of Polonius, to return to France but asks Hamlet to stay in court. Both the king and queen beg Hamlet to cease mourning his father's death. Alone, Hamlet expresses his contempt for the king and his disgust at his mother's hasty remarriage. Laertes warns his sister Ophelia against Hamlet's attentions and her father forbids her to see Hamlet. The ghost appears while Hamlet is on watch with his friends and informs Hamlet that he was poisoned by Claudius, who had seduced Queen Gertrude. He demands revenge and Hamlet swears to obey but he curses the fate that imposes this duty on him.

Points to Note

1. The soldiers are convinced that the ghost they have seen is real; they are expecting it to appear again and so the audience is prepared to accept the appearance of the ghost.

2. There is a state of unrest in Denmark. There are war-like preparations, *"post-haste and romage in the land"*.

3. Denmark was an elective monarchy so the son did not necessarily have to succeed the father.

4. Hamlet suspects foul play even before he meets the ghost.

5. We learn indirectly of Hamlet's courtship of Ophelia. According to Polonius, Ophelia has been *"most free and bounteous"* with her time and, according to Ophelia, Hamlet has *"made many tenders"* of his affection.

6. By the end of *Act 1*, Hamlet is already struggling between his impulse to avenge his father's death and his reluctance *"to set it right"*.

Revision Assignment

Give your impression of Hamlet's character up to the end of *Act 1*, assessing his relationship with (a) his dead father; (b) his mother; (c) Claudius; (d) his friends.

Revenge his foul and most unnatural murder.   (Ghost, Act 1, Scene V)

Act 2

Scene I

A Room in Polonius' House.
Enter Polonius and Reynaldo.

Polonius   Give him this money and these notes, Reynaldo.
Reynaldo   I will, my lord.
Polonius   You shall do marvellous wisely, good Reynaldo,
Before you visit him, to make inquiry
Of his behaviour.
Reynaldo   My lord, I did intend it.
Polonius   Marry, well said, very well said. Look you, sir,
Inquire me first what Danskers[1] are in Paris;
And how, and who, what means, and where they keep,[2]
What company, at what expense; and finding
By this encompassment[3] and drift of question   *10*
That they do know my son, come you more nearer
Than your particular demands[4] will touch it:
Take you, as 'twere, some distant knowledge of him;
As thus, 'I know his father, and his friends,
And, in part, him.' Do you mark this, Reynaldo?
Reynaldo   Ay, very well, my lord.
Polonius   'And, in part, him; but,' you may say, 'not well:
But if't be he I mean, he's very wild,
Addicted so and so'; and there put on him
What forgeries[5] you please; marry, none so rank   *20*
As may dishonour him; take heed of that;
But, sir, such wanton, wild, and usual slips
As are companions noted and most known
To youth and liberty.
Reynaldo   As gaming, my lord?
Polonius   Ay, or drinking, fencing, swearing, quarrelling,
Drabbing:[6] you may go so far.
Reynaldo   My lord, that would dishonour him.
Polonius   Faith, no; as you may season[7] it in the charge.
You must not put another scandal on him,
That he is open to incontinency;[8]   *30*
That's not my meaning; but breathe his faults so
    quaintly[9]
That they may seem the taints of liberty,
The flash and outbreak of a fiery mind,
A savageness in unreclaimed blood,[10]
Of general assault.[11]

[1] Danes
[2] lodge
[3] circling around
[4] direct questions
[5] false reports
[6] associating with drabs (prostitutes)
[7] qualify
[8] promiscuity
[9] delicately
[10] untamed passion
[11] affecting everyone

Reynaldo	But, my good lord, –
Polonius	Wherefore should you do this?
Reynaldo	Ay, my lord,
	I would know that.
Polonius	Marry, sir, here's my drift;
	And, I believe, it is a fetch of warrant:[12]
	You laying these slight sullies on my son,
	As 'twere a thing a little soil'd i' the working,
	Mark you,
	Your party in converse, him you would sound,
	Having ever seen in the prenominate[13] crimes
	The youth you breathe of guilty, be assur'd,
	He closes with you in this consequence;[14]
	'Good sir,' or so; or 'friend' or 'gentleman,'
	According to the phrase or the addition[15]
	Of man and country.
Reynaldo	Very good, my lord.
Polonius	And then, sir, does he this, – he does, – What
	was I about to say? By the mass I was about to say
	something: where did I leave?
Reynaldo	At 'closes in the consequence'. At 'friend or so,' and
	'gentleman.'
Polonius	At 'closes in the consequence', ay, marry;
	He closes with you thus: 'I know the gentleman;
	I saw him yesterday, or t'other day,
	Or then, or then; with such, or such; and, as you say,
	There was 'a gaming; there o'ertook in's rouse;[16]
	There falling out at tennis;' or perchance,
	'I saw him enter such a house of sale,'
	Videlicet,[17] a brothel, or so forth. See you now;
	Your bait of falsehood takes this carp[18] of truth;
	And thus do we of wisdom and of reach,
	With windlasses,[19] and with assays of bias,[20]
	By indirections find directions out:
	So, by my former lecture and advice
	Shall you my son. You have me, have you not?
Reynaldo	My lord, I have.
Polonius	God be wi' you; fare you well.
Reynaldo	Good my lord!
Polonius	Observe his inclination in yourself.[21]
Reynaldo	I shall, my lord.
Polonius	And let him play his music.[22]
Reynaldo	Well, my lord.
Polonius	Farewell!

40

50

60

70

[Exit Reynaldo.

[12] a trick which is justified

[13] above named

[14] he confides in you with this result

[15] title

[16] overcome by drunkenness

[17] that is to say

[18] fish

[19] to proceed by an indirect method (a hunting metaphor; windlass = a circuit made to trap game)

[20] indirect attempts (a bowling metaphor; a bowl has a weight on one side so that it has to be bowled in a curved course to hit the mark)

[21] judge him yourself

[22] play his tune

Enter Ophelia

           How now, Ophelia! what's the matter?

Ophelia	Alas! my lord, I have been so affrighted.
Polonius	With what, in the name of God?

23private sitting room

Ophelia	My lord, as I was sewing in my closet,[23]

24short tight jacket, laced to the trousers or hose, which was always kept fastened

Lord Hamlet, with his doublet[24] all unbrac'd;[25]

25unfastened

No hat[26] upon his head; his stockings foul'd,

26hats were worn indoors in company

Ungarter'd, and down-gyved to his ankle;[27]

27fallen down around his ankles like gyves (fetters)

Pale as his shirt; his knees knocking each other;   *80*

28meaning

And with a look so piteous in purport[28]

As if he had been loosed out of hell

To speak of horrors, he comes before me.

Polonius	Mad for thy love?
Ophelia	My lord, I do not know;

But truly I do fear it.

Polonius	What said he?
Ophelia	He took me by the wrist, and held me hard,

Then goes he to the length of all his arm,

And, with his other hand thus o'er his brow,

He falls to such perusal of my face

As he would draw it. Long stay'd he so;   *90*

At last, a little shaking of mine arm;

And thrice his head thus waving up and down,

He rais'd a sigh so piteous and profound

That it did seem to shatter all his bulk

And end his being. That done, he lets me go,

And, with his head over his shoulder turn'd,

He seem'd to find his way without his eyes;

For out o' doors he went without their help,

And to the last bended their light on me.

Polonius	Come, go with me; I will go seek the King. *100*

This is the very ecstasy of love,

29quality

Whose violent property[29] fordoes itself[30]

30destroys

And leads the will to desperate undertakings

As oft as any passion under heaven

That does afflict our natures. I am sorry –

What! have you given him any hard words of late?

Ophelia	No, my good lord; but, as you did command,

I did repel his letters and denied

His access to me.

Polonius	That hath made him mad.

I am sorry that with better heed and judgment   *110*

31observed

I had not quoted him;[31] I fear'd he did but trifle,

32ruin

And meant to wreck[32] thee; but, beshrew my

33damn my suspicion

   jealousy![33]

34natural to old men

By heaven, it is as proper to our age[34]

> To cast beyond ourselves[35] in our opinions
> As it is common for the younger sort
> To lack discretion. Come, go we to the King:
> This must be known; which, being kept close,[36]
>   might move
> More grief to hide than hate to utter love.[37]
> Come.
>
> [Exeunt.

[35] to over-reach ourselves; to be over-calculating

[36] hidden

[37] this love if hidden might cause more grief than the hatred it would cause by being publicised.

Scene Analysis

Time has passed since the end of *Act 1*. Laertes has reached France and *Scene I* begins with Polonius instructing Reynaldo to investigate, deviously, Laertes's behaviour. Polonius' *"lecture and advice"* to Reynaldo is characterised by deceit and underhandedness. Polonius will not allow *"particular demands"* but insists on *"encompassment and drift of question"*. He tells Reynaldo that he can put on him *"What forgeries you please"*. Despite all his preaching to his son his standards of moral behaviour are not very high. He permits Reynaldo to hint at such vices as gaming, drinking, fencing, swearing, quarrelling and *"drabbing"* as he considers such behaviour as merely *"the taints of liberty"*. Reynaldo is surprised:

> *"But, my good lord, –"*

but Polonius is prepared to justify maligning his son:

> *"Your bait of falsehood takes this carp of truth."*

Polonius goes through so many unnecessary details that he loses the thread of his argument:

> *"And then, sir does he this, – he does, – What was I about to say?*
> *By the mass I was about to say something: where did I leave?"*

Ophelia enters, obviously upset, and tells of her encounter with Hamlet. His strange conduct denotes his love for her. He perused her face *"As he would draw it"*. His love for Ophelia will never be the same as he no longer believes in the fidelity of women. But Hamlet does not relinquish his love for Ophelia without a struggle. Ophelia wonders at his sigh:

> *"...so piteous and profound*
> *That it did seem to shatter all his bulk*
> *And end his being."*

Polonius thinks *"This is the very ecstasy of love."* He thinks that Ophelia's rejection of him has made Hamlet mad. He admits that he has been wrong about Hamlet's feelings for Ophelia. He is shocked by Ophelia's account of her meeting with Hamlet and hurries off to report to the king.

Scene II

A room in the Castle. Flourish.
Enter King, Queen, Rosencrantz, Guildenstern and Attendants.

King	Welcome, dear Rosencrantz and Guildenstern!

King   Welcome, dear Rosencrantz and Guildenstern!
Moreover[1] that we much did long to see you,
The need we have to use you did provoke
Our hasty sending. Something have you heard
Of Hamlet's transformation; so I call it,
Since nor the exterior nor the inward man
Resembles that it was. What it should be,
More than his father's death, that thus hath put him
So much from the understanding of himself,
I cannot dream of: I entreat you both,   *10*
That, being of so young days brought up with him,
And since so neighbour'd to his youth and humour,
That you vouchsafe your rest[2] here in our court
Some little time; so by your companies
To draw him on to pleasures, and to gather,
So much as from occasion you may glean,
Whether aught to us unknown afflicts him thus,
That, open'd,[3] lies within our remedy.

Queen   Good gentlemen, he hath much talk'd of you;
And sure I am two men there are not living   *20*
To whom he more adheres.[4] If it will please you
To show us so much gentry[5] and good will
As to expend your time with us awhile,
For the supply and profit of our hope,
Your visitation shall receive such thanks
As fits a king's remembrance.

Rosencrantz   Both your Majesties
Might, by the sovereign power you have of us,
Put your dread pleasures more into command
Than to entreaty.

Guildenstern   But we both obey,
And here give up ourselves, in the full bent,[6]   *30*
To lay our service freely at your feet,
To be commanded.

King   Thanks, Rosencrantz and gentle Guildenstern.

Queen   Thanks, Guildenstern and gentle Rosencrantz;
And I beseech you instantly to visit
My too much changed son. Go, some of you,
And bring these gentlemen where Hamlet is.

Guildenstern   Heavens make our presence, and our practices,
Pleasant and helpful to him!

Queen   Ay, amen!

---

[1] besides

[2] consent to stay

[3] revealed

[4] is close to
[5] courtesy

[6] intention

40

[Exeunt Rosencrantz, Guildenstern and some Attendants

Enter Polonius.

Polonius	The ambassadors from Norway, my good lord,	*40*
	Are joyfully return'd.	
King	Thou still hast been the father of good news.	
Polonius	Have I, my lord? Assure you, my good liege,	
	I hold my duty, as I hold my soul,	
	Both to my God and to my gracious king;	
	And I do think – or else this brain of mine	
	Hunts not the trail of policy[7] so sure	
	As it hath us'd to do – that I have found	
	The very cause of Hamlet's lunacy.	
King	O! speak of that; that do I long to hear.	*50*
Polonius	Give first admittance to the ambassadors;	
	My news shall be the fruit to that great feast.	
King	Thyself do grace to them, and bring them in.	

[Exit Polonius.

He tells me, my sweet queen, that he hath found
The head and source of all your son's distemper.[8]

Queen	I doubt it is no other but the main;	
	His father's death, and our o'erhasty marriage.	
King	Well, we shall sift[9] him.	

Re-enter Polonius, with Voltimand and Cornelius

Welcome, my good friends!
Say, Voltimand, what from our brother Norway?

Voltimand	Most fair return of greetings, and desires.	*60*
	Upon our first, he sent out to suppress	
	His nephew's levies, which to him appear'd	
	To be a preparation 'gainst the Polack;	
	But, better look'd into, he truly found	
	It was against your Highness: whereat griev'd,	
	That so his sickness, age, and impotence	
	Was falsely borne in hand,[10] sends out arrests	
	On Fortinbras; which he, in brief, obeys,	
	Receives rebuke from Norway, and, in fine,	
	Makes vow before his uncle never more	*70*
	To give the assay of arms[11] against your Majesty.	
	Whereon old Norway, overcome with joy,	
	Gives him three thousand crowns in annual fee,	
	And his commission to employ those soldiers,	
	So levied as before, against the Polack;	
	With an entreaty, herein further shown,	

[Giving a paper.

That it might please you to give quiet pass
Through your dominions for this enterprise,

[7] does not follow the scent of political affairs

[8] disorder

[9] examine

[10] used

[11] to take up arms

On such regards of safety and allowance
As therein are set down.   80

King   It likes us well;[12]
And at our more consider'd time we'll read,
Answer, and think upon this business:
Meantime we thank you for your well-took labour.
Go to your rest; at night we'll feast together:
Most welcome home.
                                    [Exeunt Voltimand and Cornelius.
Polonius   This business is well ended.
My liege, and madam, to expostulate[13]
What majesty should be, what duty is,
Why day is day, night night, and time is time,
Were nothing but to waste night, day, and time.
Therefore, since brevity is the soul of wit,[14]   90
And tediousness the limbs and outward flourishes,[15]
I will be brief. Your noble son is mad:
Mad call I it; for, to define true madness,
What is't but to be nothing else but mad?
But let that go.
Queen   More matter, with less art.
Polonius   Madam, I swear I use no art at all.
That he is mad, 'tis true; 'tis true 'tis pity;
And pity 'tis 'tis true: a foolish figure;[16]
But farewell it, for I will use no art.
Mad let us grant him, then; and now remains   100
That we find out the cause of this effect,[17]
Or rather say, the cause of this defect,[18]
For this effect defective comes by cause;[19]
Thus it remains, and the remainder thus.
Perpend.
I have a daughter, have while she is mine;
 Who, in her duty and obedience, mark,
 Hath given me this: now, gather, and surmise. *[Reads.*
 To the celestial, and my soul's idol, the most
 beautified Ophelia. –   110
That's an ill phrase, a vile phrase; 'beautified' is a
vile phrase; but you shall hear. Thus:
In her excellent white bosom, these, &c.–
Queen   Came this from Hamlet to her?
Polonius   Good madam, stay awhile; I will be faithful.
           Doubt thou the stars are fire;
           Doubt that the sun doth move;
           Doubt truth to be a liar;
           But never doubt I love.
O dear Ophelia! I am ill at these numbers:[20]   120
I have not art to reckon my groans; but that I

Margin notes (left column):

[12]it pleases us

[13]debate

[14]good sense; to be brief is the essence of good sense
[15]appearance and dress; embellishments

[16]figure of speech

[17]result
[18]imperfection
[19]this effect, which should be called a defect, must have some cause

[20]metrical feet, verses

love thee best, O most best! believe it. Adieu.
*   Thine evermore, most dear lady, whilst*
this machine[21] *is to him,*
                              HAMLET   [21]body
This in obedience, hath my daughter shown me;
And more above, hath his solicitings,
As they fell out by time, by means, and place,
All given to mine ear.

King   But how hath she
Received his love?
Polonius   What do you think of me?
King   As of a man faithful and honourable.
Polonius   I would fain[22] prove so. But what might you think, *130*   [22]gladly
When I had seen this hot love on the wing,
As I perceived it, I must tell you that,
Before my daughter told me, what might you,
Or my dear Majesty, your queen here, think,
If I had play'd the desk or table-book,[23]   [23]notebook, i.e. if he had
Or given my heart a winking, mute and dumb,   kept it a secret
Or look'd upon this love with idle sight;
What might you think? No, I went round to work,
And my young mistress thus I did bespeak;
'Lord Hamlet is a prince, out of thy star;   *140*
This must not be:' and then I precepts gave her,
That she should lock herself from his resort,[24]   [24]reach
Admit no messengers, receive no tokens.
Which done, she took the fruits of my advice;
And he, repulsed, – a short tale to make, –
Fell into a sadness, then into a fast,
Thence to a watch,[25] thence into a weakness,   [25]sleeplessness
Thence to a lightness; and by this declension
Into the madness wherein now he raves,
And all we wail for.   *150*

King   Do you think 'tis this?
Queen   It may be, very likely.
Polonius   Hath there been such a time, – I'd fain know that, –
That I have positively said, ''Tis so,'
When it prov'd otherwise?
King   Not that I know.
Polonius   Take this from this, if this be otherwise:
                    [*Pointing to his head and shoulder.*
If circumstances lead me, I will find
Where truth is hid, though it were hid indeed
Within the centre.
King   How may we try it further?
Polonius   You know sometimes he walks for hours together
Here in the lobby.   *160*

²⁶tapestry (called after Arras in France where many famous tapestries were woven)

²⁷drivers of carts

²⁸perhaps it is Hamlet's opinion that Polonius fishes for secrets; fishmonger was an Elizabethan slang word for a pimp

²⁹flesh

³⁰understanding; there is a double meaning of becoming pregnant

³¹subject matter; Hamlet takes the word in the sense of trouble

Queen	So he does indeed.
Polonius	At such a time I'll loose my daughter to him;
	Be you and I behind an arras[26] then;
	Mark the encounter; if he love her not,
	And be not from his reason fallen thereon,
	Let me be no assistant for a state,
	But keep a farm, and carters.[27]
King	We will try it.

Enter Hamlet, reading.

Queen	But look, where sadly the poor wretch comes reading.
Polonius	Away! I do beseech you, both away.
	I'll board him presently.

      [Exeunt King, Queen, and attendants.
        O! give me leave.

	How does my good Lord Hamlet?	170
Hamlet	Well, God a-mercy.	
Polonius	Do you know me, my lord?	
Hamlet	Excellent well; you are a fishmonger.[28]	
Polonius	Not I, my lord.	
Hamlet	Then I would you were so honest a man.	
Polonius	Honest, my lord!	
Hamlet	Ay, sir; to be honest, as this world goes, is to be one man picked out of ten thousand.	
Polonius	That's very true. my lord.	
Hamlet	For if the sun breed maggots in a dead dog, being a good kissing carrion,[29] – Have you a daughter?	180
Polonius	I have, my lord.	
Hamlet	Let her not walk i' the sun. Conception[30] is a blessing; but not as your daughter may conceive. Friend, look to't.	
Polonius	How say you by that? *[Aside]* Still harping on my daughter: yet he knew me not at first; he said I was a fishmonger: he is far gone, far gone: and truly in my youth I suffered much extremity for love; very near this. I'll speak to him again. What do you read, my lord?	190
Hamlet	Words, words, words.	
Polonius	What is the matter, my lord?	
Hamlet	Between who?	
Polonius	I mean, the matter[31] that you read, my lord.	
Hamlet	Slanders, sir: for the satirical rogue says here that old men have grey beards, that their faces are wrinkled, their eyes purging thick amber and plum-tree gum, and that they have a plentiful lack of wit, together with most weak hams: all which, sir,	200

	though I most powerfully and potently believe, yet I hold it not honesty to have it thus set down; for you yourself, sir, should be old as I am, if, like a crab, you could go backward.	
Polonius	[Aside] Though this be madness, yet there is method[32] in't. Will you walk out of the air, my lord?	[32]logic
Hamlet	Into my grave?	
Polonius	Indeed, that is out o' the air. [Aside.] How pregnant[33] sometimes his replies are! A happiness that often madness hits on, which reason and 210 sanity could not so prosperously be delivered of.[34] I will leave him, and suddenly contrive the means of meeting between him and my daughter. My honour-able lord, I will most humbly take my leave of you.	[33]full of meaning [34]bring forth
Hamlet	You cannot, sir, take from me any thing that I will more willingly part withal; except my life, except my life, except my life.	
Polonius	Fare you well, my lord. [Going.	
Hamlet	These tedious old fools!	

Enter Rosencrantz and Guildenstern.

Polonius	You go to seek the Lord Hamlet; there he is. 220	
Rosencrantz	[To Polonius] God save you, sir! [Exit Polonius.	
Guildenstern	Mine honour'd lord!	
Rosencrantz	My most dear lord!	
Hamlet	My excellent good friends! How dost thou, Guildenstern? Ah, Rosencrantz! Good lads, how do ye both?	
Rosencrantz	As the indifferent children of the earth.	
Guildenstern	Happy in that we are not over-happy; On Fortune's cap we are not the very button.[35]	[35]the highest point
Hamlet	Nor the soles of her shoe? 230	
Rosencrantz	Neither, my lord.	
Hamlet	Then you live about her waist, or in the middle of her favours?	
Guildenstern	Faith, her privates[36] we.	[36]ordinary men; pun on private parts
Hamlet	In the secret parts of Fortune? O! most true; she is a strumpet.[37] What news?	[37]fortune is considered a whore as she gives her favours to all men and is inconstant
Rosencrantz	None, my lord, but that the world's grown honest.	
Hamlet	Then is doomsday near; but your news is not true. Let me question more in particular: what have you, my good friends, deserved at the hands of Fortune, 240 that she sends you to prison hither?	
Guildenstern	Prison, my lord!	
Hamlet	Denmark's a prison.	
Rosencrantz	Then is the world one.	

Hamlet	A goodly one; in which there are many confines, wards, and dungeons, Denmark being one o' the worst.
Rosencrantz	We think not so, my lord.
Hamlet	Why, then, 'tis none to you; for there is nothing either good or bad, but thinking makes it so: to me *250* it is a prison.
Rosencrantz	Why, then your ambition makes it one; 'tis too narrow for your mind.
Hamlet	O God! I could be bounded in a nutshell, and count myself a king of infinite space, were it not that I have bad dreams.
Guildenstern	Which dreams indeed, are ambition, for the very substance of the ambitious is merely the shadow of a dream.
Hamlet	A dream itself is but a shadow. *260*
Rosencrantz	Truly, and I hold ambition of so airy and light a quality that it is but a shadow's shadow.
Hamlet	Then are our beggars bodies, and our monarchs and outstretched heroes the beggars' shadows.[38] Shall we to the court? for, by my fay,[39] I cannot reason.

Rosencrantz ⎫
Guildenstern ⎭ We'll wait upon you.

Hamlet	No such matter; I will not sort you with the rest of my servants, for, to speak to you like an honest man, I am most dreadfully attended. But, in the *270* beaten way of friendship, what make you at Elsinore?
Rosencrantz	To visit you, my lord; no other occasion.
Hamlet	Beggar that I am, I am even poor in thanks; but I thank you: and sure, dear friends, my thanks are too dear a halfpenny. Were you not sent for? Is it your own inclining? Is it a free visitation? Come, come, deal justly with me: come, come; nay, speak.
Guildenstern	What should we say, my lord?
Hamlet	Why anything, but to the purpose. You were sent *280* for; and there is a kind of confession in your looks which your modesties have not craft enough to colour: I know the good King and Queen have sent for you.
Rosencrantz	To what end, my lord?
Hamlet	That you must teach me. But let me conjure you, by the rights of our fellowship, by the consonancy[40] of our youth, by the obligation of our ever-preserved love, and by what more dear a better proposer

[38]beggars are real people with bodies (because they are not ambitious) and kings and heroes are the beggars' shadows because their dreams are unreal

[39]faith

[40]friendship

	could charge you withal, be even and direct with me,	290
	whether you were sent for or no!	
Rosencrantz	[Aside to Guildenstern] What say you?	
Hamlet	[Aside] Nay, then, I have an eye of you. If you love me, hold not off.	
Guildenstern	My lord, we were sent for.	
Hamlet	I will tell you why; so shall my anticipation prevent your discovery, and your secrecy to the King and Queen moult no feather.[41] I have of late, – but wherefore I know not, – lost all my mirth, forgone all custom of exercises; and indeed it goes so heav-ily with my disposition that this goodly frame, the earth, seems to me a sterile promontory;[42] this most excellent canopy, the air, look you, this brave o'er-hanging firmament, this majestical roof fretted[43] with golden fire, why, it appears no other thing to me but a foul and pestilent congregation of vapours. What a piece of work is a man! How noble in reason! how infinite in faculty! in form, in moving, how express and admirable! in action, how like an angel! in appre-hension,[44] how like a god! the beauty of the world! the paragon[45] of animals! And yet, to me, what is this quintessence[46] of dust? Man delights not me; no, nor woman neither, though, by your smiling you seem to say so.	300

310 |
Rosencrantz	My lord, there was no such stuff in my thoughts.	
Hamlet	Why did you laugh then, when I said, 'Man delights not me?'	
Rosencrantz	To think, my lord, if you delight not in man, what lenten[47] entertainment the players shall receive from you. We coted[48] them on the way; and hither are they coming, to offer you service.	320
Hamlet	He that plays the king shall be welcome; his Majesty shall have tribute of me; the adventurous knight shall use his foil and target;[49] the lover shall not sigh gratis; the humorous man[50] shall end his part in peace; the clown shall make those laugh whose lungs are tickle o' the sere;[51] and the lady shall say her mind freely, or the blank verse shall halt for't. What players are they?	
Rosencrantz	Even those you were wont to take delight in, the tragedians of the city.	330
Hamlet	How chances it they travel? Their residence, both in reputation and profit, was better both ways.	
Rosencrantz	I think their inhibition[52] comes by the means of the late innovation.[53]	

[41] lose nothing

[42] high piece of land surrounded by water

[43] adorned

[44] understanding; perception
[45] model of perfection
[46] the most essential substance (the fifth substance, the others being earth, air, fire and water)

[47] poor, since lent is a period of fast and penance
[48] passed
[49] small shield
[50] a man dominated by an eccentric trait; a stock character
[51] easily moved to laughter; a sere is the catch on the lock of a gun which can be easily released
[52] refusal of permission
[53] change; an allusion to the order forbidding a dramatic performance in London. Shakespeare's own company was not allowed to perform in the Christmas festivities of 1601 due to their performance of *Richard II*, which it was felt contributed to the conspiracy of Essex and Southampton

Hamlet	Do they hold the same estimation they did when I was in the city? Are they so followed?
Rosencrantz	No, indeed they are not.
Hamlet	How comes it? Do they grow rusty?
Rosencrantz	Nay, their endeavour keeps in the wonted pace: but *340* there is, sir, an eyrie of children,[54] little eyases,[55] that cry out on the top of question, and are most tyrannically clapped for't: these are now the fashion, and so berattle[56] the common stages,[57] – so they call them, – that many wearing rapiers are afraid of goose-quills,[58] and dare scarce come thither.
Hamlet	What! are they children? Who maintains 'em? How are they escoted?[59] Will they pursue the quality[60] no longer than they can sing?[61] Will they not say afterwards, if they should grow themselves to com- *350* mon players, – as it is most like, if their means are no better, – their writers do them wrong to make them exclaim against their own succession?
Rosencrantz	Faith, there has been much to-do on both sides: and the nation holds it no sin to tarre[62] them to controversy. There was, for a while, no money bid for argument,[63] unless the poet and the player went to cuffs in the question.
Hamlet	Is it possible?
Guildenstern	O! there has been much throwing about of brains. *360*
Hamlet	Do the boys carry it away?
Rosencrantz	Ay, that they do, my lord; Hercules and his load too.[64]
Hamlet	It is not very strange; for my uncle is King of Denmark, and those that would make mows[65] at him while my father lived, give twenty, forty, fifty, a hundred ducats a-piece for his picture in little.[66] 'Sblood, there is something in this more than natural, if philosophy could find it out.
	[Flourish of trumpets within.
Guildenstern	There are the players. *370*
Hamlet	Gentlemen, you are welcome to Elsinore. Your hands, come then; the appurtenance[67] of welcome is fashion and ceremony. Let me comply with you in this garb, lest my extent[68] to the players – which, I tell you, must show fairly outward – should more appear like entertainment than yours. You are welcome; but my uncle-father and aunt-mother are deceived.
Guildenstern	In what, my dear lord?

[54]nest; a topical reference to the growing popularity in Elizabethan England of children's companies

[55]unfledged birds

[56]shout down

[57]public theatres

[58]pens, the children's companies tended to present satirical plays, thus the actors are afraid of being satirised

[59]supported financially

[60]profession

[61]after their voices have broken

[62]incite

[63]plot

[64]i.e. the boys gained the advantage; could be a reference to the sign on the Globe theatre which showed Hercules bearing the world

[65]grimaces

[66]miniature

[67]proper accompaniment

[68]behaviour

| Hamlet | I am but mad north-north-west:[69] when the wind is | 380 |
| | southerly I know a hawk from a handsaw.[70] | |

Enter Polonius.

Polonius	Well be with you, gentlemen!	
Hamlet	Hark you, Guildenstern; and you too; at each ear a hearer: that great baby you see there is not yet out of his swaddling clouts.[71]	
Rosencrantz	Happily[72] he's the second time come to them; for they say an old man is twice a child.	
Hamlet	I will prophesy he comes to tell me of the players; mark it. You say right, sir; o' Monday morning; 'twas so indeed.	
Polonius	My lord, I have news to tell you.	390
Hamlet	My lord, I have news to tell you. When Roscius[73] was an actor in Rome, –	
Polonius	The actors are come hither, my lord.	
Hamlet	Buzz, buzz![74]	
Polonius	Upon my honour, –	
Hamlet	Then came each actor on his ass, –	
Polonius	The best actors in the world, either for tragedy, comedy, history, pastoral, pastoral-comical, historical-pastoral, tragical-historical, tragical-comical-historical-pastoral, scene individable, or poem unlimited: Seneca[75] cannot be too heavy, nor Plautus[76] too light. For the law of writ and the liberty,[77] these are the only men.	400
Hamlet	O Jephthah, judge of Israel,[78] what a treasure hadst thou!	
Polonius	What a treasure had he, my lord?	
Hamlet	Why –	
	One fair daughter and no more,	
	The which he loved passing well.	410
Polonius	[Aside] Still on my daughter.	
Hamlet	Am I not i' the right, old Jephthah?	
Polonius	If you call me Jephthah, my lord, I have a daughter that I love passing well.	
Hamlet	Nay, that follows not.	
Polonius	What follows, then, my lord?	
Hamlet	Why,	
	As by lot, God wot.[79]	
	And then, you know,	
	It came to pass, as most like it was. –	420
	The first row of the pious chanson[80] will show you more; for look where my abridgment[81] comes.	

[69] I am only a little bit mad – since he is only mad when the wind blows from one point on the compass

[70] heron

[71] clothes in which a baby is wrapped

[72] perhaps

[73] famous Roman comic actor

[74] expression of derision for stale news

[75] famous Roman tragic dramatist

[76] famous Roman comic dramatist

[77] plays written according to the laws of classical drama and plays free from rules

[78] title of a popular ballad; Jephthah promised God to sacrifice the first thing he met after his victory over the Ammonities. The first person he met was his own daughter whom he had to sacrifice (Book of Judges)

[79] knows

[80] the first stanza of the religious song

[81] cutting short

Enter four or five Players.

82bearded
83challenge
84young boys played the
   parts of women
85thick sole on a shoe for
   added height
86not legal
87a gold chain was stamped
   with the king's head
   around which there was
   a ring. If a crack reached
   as far as this ring it was
   no longer legal currency.
   Hamlet is referring to a
   crack in the young boy's
   changing voice. If a boy
   actor's voice broke he
   could no longer take the
   women's parts in the plays
   and is unvalued, like the
   coin.
88the French were expert
   in the art of falconry, but
   Hamlet critises their over-
   eagerness
89an expensive delicacy,
   therefore not popular, not
   appreciated generally
90constructed
91simplicity
92art
93spicy salad, i.e. saucy line
94convict
95Æneas, the hero of Virgil's
   Æneid, told the story of
   the fall of Troy to Dido,
   Queen of Carthage
96King of Troy

97son of Achilles, one of
   the men who hid in the
   wooden horse. He killed
   Priam to avenge his
   father's death
98the tiger – supposed to be
   bred in Hyrcanna, south of
   the Caspian Sea.
99the wooden horse of Troy
100red (heraldic term)
101outlined (heraldic term)

First Player
Hamlet

You are welcome, masters; welcome, all. I am glad
to see thee well: welcome, good friends. O, my old
friend! Thy face is valanced82 since I saw thee last:
com'st thou to beard83 me in Denmark? What! my
young lady and mistress!84 By'r lady, your ladyship
is nearer heaven than when I saw you last, by the al-
titude of a chopine.85 Pray God, your voice, like a
piece of uncurrent86 gold, be not cracked within
   the   430
ring.87 Masters, you are all welcome. We'll e'en to't
like French falconers, fly at anything we see:88 we'll
have a speech straight. Come, give us a taste of
your quality; come, a passionate speech.
What speech, my good lord?
I heard thee speak me a speech once, but it was
never acted; or, if it was, not above once; for the
play, I remember, pleased not the million; 'twas
caviare89 to the general: but it was – as I received it,
and others, whose judgments in such matters cried
   in   440
the top of mine – an excellent play, well digested90 in
the scenes, set down with as much modesty91
as cunning.92 I remember one said there were no
sallets93 in the lines to make the matter savoury, nor
no matter in the phrase that might indict94 the
author of affectation; but called it an honest method,
as wholesome as sweet, and by very much more
handsome than fine. One speech in it I chiefly loved;
'twas Æneas' tale to Dido;95 and thereabout of it
especially, where he speaks of Priam's96 slaughter. If
   it   450
live in your memory, begin at this line: let me see, let
me see:
The rugged Pyrrhus97 like the Hyrcanian beast,98
'Tis not so, it begins with Pyrrhus: –
The rugged Pyrrhus, he, whose sable arms
Black as his purpose, did the night resemble
When he lay couched in the ominous horse,99
Hath now this dread and black complexion smear'd
With heraldry more dismal; head to foot
Now is he total gules,100 horridly trick'd101   460
With blood of fathers, mothers, daughters, sons,
Bak'd and impasted with the parching streets,
That lend a tyrannous and damned light
To their vile murders: roasted in wrath and fire,

	And thus o'er-sized with coagulate gore,[102]
	With eyes like carbuncles,[103] the hellish Pyrrhus
	Old grandsire Priam seeks.
	So proceed you.
Polonius	'Fore God, my lord, well spoken; with good accent
	and good discretion.
First Player	Anon, he finds him 470

Striking too short at Greeks; his antique sword,
Rebellious to his arm,[104] lies where it falls,
Repugnant to command. Unequal match'd,
Pyrrhus at Priam drives; in rage strikes wide;
But with the whiff and wind of his fell[105] sword
The unnerved father falls. Then senseless Ilium,[106]
Seeming to feel this blow, with flaming top
Stoops to his base, and with a hideous crash
Takes prisoner Pyrrhus' ear: For lo! his sword,
Which was declining on the milky[107] head   480
Of reverend Priam, seem'd i' the air to stick:
So, as a painted[108] tyrant, Pyrrhus stood
And like a neutral[109] to his will and matter,
Did nothing.
But, as we often see, against[110] some storm,
A silence in the heavens, the rack[111] stand still,
The bold winds speechless and the orb[112] below
As hush as death, anon the dreadful thunder
Doth rend the region; so, after Pyrrhus' pause,
Aroused vengeance sets him new a-work;   490
And never did the Cyclops'[113] hammers fall
On Mars's[114] armour, forg'd for proof eterne,[115]
With less remorse than Pyrrhus' bleeding sword
Now falls on Priam.
Out, out, thou strumpet, Fortune! All you gods,
In general synod,[116] take away her power;
Break all the spokes and fellies[117] from her wheel,
And bowl the round nave[118] down the hill of heaven,
As low as to the fiends!

Polonius	This is too long.	500
Hamlet	It shall to the barber's, with your beard. Prithee, say	
	on: he's for a jig or a tale of bawdry, or he sleeps.	
	Say on; come to Hecuba.[119]	
First Player	But who, O! who had seen the mobled[120] queen	
Hamlet	'The mobled queen?' –	
Polonius	That's good; 'mobled queen' is good.	
First Player	Run barefoot up and down, threat'ning the flames	
	With bisson rheum;[121] a clout[122] upon that head	
	Where late the diadem [123] stood; and, for a robe,	
	About her lank and all o'er-teemed loins,[124]	510

Footnotes:
[102]smeared with dried blood
[103]precious red stones
[104]not obeying his arm
[105]cruel
[106]Troy
[107]white
[108]like a picture of a tyrant
[109]indifferent
[110]before
[111]accumulation of clouds
[112]earth
[113]one-eyed giants who helped forge the armour for Mars
[114]the god of war
[115]everlasting protection
[116]council
[117]outer wooden rim of wheel
[118]hub
[119]Queen of Troy, wife of Priam
[120]muffled
[121]blinding tears
[122]cloth
[123]crown
[124]exhausted from bearing children

A blanket, in the alarm of fear caught up;
Who this had seen, with tongue in venom steep'd
'Gainst Fortune's state would treason have
*   pronounc'd.'*
But if the gods themselves did see her then,
'When she saw Pyrrhus make malicious sport
In mincing with his sword her husband's limbs,
The instant burst of clamour that she made –
Unless things mortal move them not at all –

125 milky

Would have made milch[125] the burning eyes of
*   heaven,*
And passion in the gods.   520

Polonius	Look! wh'er he has not turned his colour and has tears in's eyes. Prithee, no more.
Hamlet	'Tis well; I'll have thee speak out the rest soon. Good my lord, will you see the players well be-stowed?[126] Do you hear, let them be well used; for they are the abstracts[127] and brief chronicles of the time: after your death you were better have a bad epitaph than their ill report while you live.

126 lodged

127 summary

128 as deserved

129 an oath; by God's little
    body – a reference to the
    Eucharist

Polonius	My lord, I will use them according to their desert.[128]
Hamlet	God's bodikins,[129] man, much better. Use every man 530 after his desert, and who should 'scape whipping? Use them after your own honour and dignity: the less they deserve, the more merit is in your bounty. Take them in.
Polonius	Come, sirs.
Hamlet	Follow him, friends: we'll hear a play to-morrow.

[Exit Polonius, with all the Players but the First.
Dost thou hear me, old friend; can you play *The*
Murder of Gonzago?

First Player	Ay, my lord.
Hamlet	We'll ha't to-morrow night. You could, for a need, 540 study a speech of some dozen or sixteen lines, which I would set down and insert in't, could you not?
First Player	Ay, my lord.
Hamlet	Very well. Follow that lord; and look you mock him not.

[Exit First Player.
[*To Rosencrantz and Guildenstern.*] My good friends,
I'll leave you till night; you are welcome to Elsinore.

Rosencrantz	Good my lord!

[Exeunt Rosencrantz and Guildenstern.

Hamlet	Ay, so, God be wi' ye! Now I am alone. 550 O! what a rogue and peasant slave am I! Is it not monstrous that this player here,

But in a fiction, in a dream of passion,
Could force his soul so to his own conceit[130]
That from her working all his visage wann'd,[131]
Tears in his eyes, distraction in's aspect,
A broken voice, and his whole function suiting
With forms to his conceit? and all for nothing!
For Hecuba!
What's Hecuba to him or he to Hecuba   560
That he should weep for her? What would he do
Had he the motive and the cue for passion
That I have? He would drown the stage with tears,
And cleave[132] the general ear with horrid speech,
Make mad the guilty and appal the free, [133]
Confound the ignorant, and amaze indeed
The very faculties of eyes and ears.
Yet I,
A dull and muddy-mettled[134] rascal, peak,[135]
Like John-a-dreams,[136] unpregnant[137] of my cause,   570
And can say nothing; no, not for a king,
Upon whose property and most dear life
A damn'd defeat was made. Am I a coward?
Who calls me villain? breaks my pate[138] across?
Plucks off my beard and blows it in my face?
Tweaks me by the nose? gives me the lie i' the throat,
As deep as to the lungs? Who does me this?
Ha!
Swounds,[139] I should take it, for it cannot be
But I am pigeon-liver'd,[140] and lack gall[141]   580
To make oppression bitter, or ere this
I should have fatted all the region kites[142]
With this slave's offal.[143] Bloody, bawdy villain!
Remorseless, treacherous, lecherous, kindless villain!
O! vengeance!
Why, what an ass am I! This is most brave
That I, the son of a dear father murder'd,
Prompted to my revenge by heaven and hell,
Must, like a whore, unpack my heart with words,
And fall a-cursing, like a very drab,[144]   590
A scullion![145] Fie upon't! foh!
About, my brain! I have heard,
That guilty creatures, sitting at a play,
Have by the very cunning of the scene
Been struck so to the soul that presently
They have proclaim'd their malefactions;[146]
For murder, though it have no tongue, will speak
With most miraculous organ. I'll have these players
Play something like the murder of my father

[130]thought, idea, imagination
[131] turned pale

[132]split open
[133]i.e. free from guilt

[134]dull spirited
[135]mope
[136]nick-name for a dreamy good-for-nothing
[137] unprepared

[138]head

[139]an oath; by God's wounds
[140]cowardly; a pigeon was considered weak
[141]bitter substance secreted by the liver
[142]birds of prey
[143]remains

[144]prostitute
[145]kitchen-maid

[146]evil deeds

147 flinch

Before mine uncle. I'll observe his looks;   600
I'll tent him to the quick: if he but blench[147]
I know my course. The spirit that I have seen
May be the devil: and the devil hath power
To assume a pleasing shape; yea, and perhaps
Out of my weakness and my melancholy –
As he is very potent with such spirits –
Abuses me to damn me. I'll have grounds

148 directly relevant, i.e.
more definite

More relative[148] than this. The play's the thing
Wherein I'll catch the conscience of the king.

[Exit.

Scene Analysis

The scene begins with the king welcoming Rosencrantz and Guildenstern. The king's *"hasty sending"* suggests trouble. He speaks of Hamlet's *"transformation"*. The queen calls him *"My too much changed son"*. She thinks the cause is *"His father's death, and our o'erhasty marriage"*. The king senses that it is more than the death of his father that is troubling Hamlet and he is suspicious of Hamlet's behaviour.

> *"...What it should be,*
> *More than his father's death, that thus hath put him*
> *So much from the understanding of himself,*
> *I cannot dream of."*

Both the king and queen hope that because Rosencrantz and Guildenstern were childhood friends with Hamlet they might be able to *"glean"* something from him. Rosencrantz and Guildenstern pledge their service to the throne.

Having announced the return of the ambassadors to Norway, Polonius claims to have discovered *"The very cause of Hamlet's lunacy"*. The news from Norway is good. Fortinbras has vowed to his uncle never again to take up arms against Denmark. He simply requests a safe passage through Denmark en route to Poland.

Polonius, full of his own importance, leads up to his news about Hamlet:

> *"... to expostulate*
> *What majesty should be, what duty is,*
> *Why day is day, night night, and time is time,*
> *Were nothing but to waste night, day, and time."*

It is ironic that Polonius of all people should proclaim that:

> *"... brevity is the soul of wit"*.

He states that he will be brief and bluntly affirms:

> *"Your noble son is mad"*.

The queen is impatient at Polonius' garrulity and peremptorily orders him to speak *"More matter, with less art"*. However Polonius continues playing around with words, enjoying the effect of his announcement.

> *"... and now remains*
> *That we find out the cause of this effect,*
> *Or rather say, the cause of this defect,*
> *For this effect defective comes by cause."*

Polonius reads a love letter from Hamlet to Ophelia. He wishes to be praised for forbidding Ophelia to encourage Hamlet:

> *"... what might you,*
> *Or my dear Majesty, your queen here, think,*
> *If I had play'd the desk or table-book,*
> *Or given my heart a winking, mute and dumb,*
> *Or look'd upon this love with idle sight;*
> *What might you think?"*

Polonius presumes that it is a simple matter of deduction to conclude that the rejected Hamlet:

> *"Fell into a sadness, then into a fast,*
> *Thence to a watch, thence into a weakness,*
> *Thence to a lightness; and by this declension*
> *Into the madness wherein now he raves".*

The king defers to Polonius:

> *"How may we try it further?"*

and Polonius suggests that while Hamlet is walking alone in the lobby he will *"loose"* Ophelia so that they may observe the encounter.

All the talk of Hamlet before his arrival heightens the dramatic effect of his entrance. When he appears he is reading a book, which does not give the impression that he is ready for action. Polonius approaches Hamlet who hails him as a fishmonger. Polonius interprets this as a sign that Hamlet is *"far gone"* but in fact Hamlet's words are very significant. Hamlet knows well that Polonius is fishing for information, that he is a go-between for the king. Hamlet questions the honesty of Polonius and cynically proclaims the dishonesty of the world:

> *"...to be honest, as this world goes, is to be one man picked out of ten thousand."*

His reference to Ophelia shows his disillusionment with love:

> *"...conception is a blessing; but not as your daughter may conceive."*

Though this be madness, yet there is method in't.

(Polonius, Act 2, Scene II)

Hamlet bandies words with Polonius, deliberately misunderstanding his:

> *"What is the matter, my lord?"*

His remarks about old men are cutting and insulting and Polonius is forced to acknowledge to himself:

> *"Though this be madness, yet there is method in't."*

When Polonius leaves, Hamlet is approached by Rosencrantz and Guildenstern. He receives his friends in a friendly enough fashion until he realises that they are not being honest with him. He knows that they have been sent for and in the name of their past friendship he asks them to be *"even and direct"* with him. Hamlet explains to his friends why they were sent for and in so doing reveals the state of his feelings. For him the earth is *"a sterile promontory"*. The air is *"a foul and pestilent congregation of vapours"*. He is disillusioned with the universe and with mankind. Knowing that Hamlet will be pleased to see the players who are on their way, Rosencrantz smiles when Hamlet proclaims *"Man delights not me"*. He fails to grasp Hamlet's meaning, that the splendour of the universe, the magnificence of man, no longer touches him. Hamlet gives a clear indication to Rosencrantz and Guildenstern that the king and queen are wrong to think that he is mad: *"I am but mad north-north-west"*. He ridicules Polonius in front of Rosencrantz and Guildenstern and again makes pointed remarks about his daughter. Hamlet associates Polonius with the biblical character Jephthah who sacrificed his daughter – a striking analogy, as we have just heard Polonius promise to use Ophelia to obtain the truth of Hamlet's madness.

Hamlet welcomes the players, asks for a passionate speech and quotes part of the speech of Æneas' tale to Dido, which the First Player continues. It is a speech full of gory details of a terrible slaughter. The player is so moved by the grief of the queen for her slaughtered husband that he has tears in his eyes. Hamlet confers alone with the First Player and asks him to play *The Murder of Gonzago*, with a speech of twelve to sixteen lines inserted by Hamlet and the player agrees. Once alone Hamlet compares the player's passion for the unknown Hecuba to his own *"motive and the cue for passion"* and he thinks that in comparison he is *"A dull and muddy-mettled rascal"*. He wonders desperately *"Am I a coward?"* and he concludes that he must be *"pigeon-liver'd"*. Then he thinks that the spirit he saw may have been the devil or the result of his own weakness and melancholy. He wishes to have grounds *"More relative than this"*. He intends that the players will enact the murder of his father. If he sees the king flinch *"I know my course"*. His determination to avenge his father is strengthened. Hamlet's last words look forward to the importance of the play in *Act 3*:

> *"... the play's the thing*
> *Wherein I'll catch the conscience of the king."*

REVISION

> *"nor the exterior nor the inward man*
> *Resembles that it was."*   *(Claudius, Act 2, Scene II)*

Polonius sends Reynaldo to Paris to spy on Laertes. Ophelia rejects Hamlet's strange behaviour and dutifully reports to her father. Polonius believes that he is mad for love and plans to have the king overhear Hamlet's meeting with Ophelia. Claudius sends for Rosencrantz and Guildenstern to try to find out the cause of Hamlet's behaviour but Hamlet knows that they have been summoned to court to spy on him. Fortinbras has agreed not to invade Denmark and requests permission to march through Denmark en route to Poland. A company of players arrives and Hamlet arranges a performance of a play, *The Murder of Gonzago*, in order to *"catch the conscience of the king"*.

Points To Note

1. Hamlet does not reappear until the middle of the second scene. His absence creates an impression of inactivity.

2. We see how world-weary Hamlet has become from his description of his disposition to Rosencrantz and Guildenstern.

3. Hamlet despises *"tedious old fools"* like Polonius, just as he despises Rosencrantz and Guildenstern for their hypocrisy.

4. Hamlet's anguish at his mother's lack of grief is clearly seen in the choice of a tragic speech which describes a queen's terrible grief for her slaughtered husband.

5. By the end of *Act 2*, Hamlet has thought of a plan to entrap the king and prove his guilt.

Revision Assignment

Discuss the development of the action between the end of *Act 1* and the end of *Act 2*. Has Hamlet made any progress? Have your impressions of him as a character changed in any way?

Act 3
Scene I

A Room in the Castle.
Enter King, Queen, Polonius, Ophelia,
Rosencrantz and Guildenstern.

King	And can you, by no drift of circumstance,[1]
	Get from him why he puts on this confusion,
	Grating so harshly all his days of quiet
	With turbulent and dangerous lunacy?
Rosencrantz	He does confess he feels himself distracted;
	But from what cause he will by no means speak.
Guildenstern	Nor do we find him forward to be sounded,[2]
	But, with a crafty madness, keeps aloof,
	When we would bring him on to some confession
	Of his true state. 10
Queen	Did he receive you well?
Rosencrantz	Most like a gentleman.
Guildenstern	But with much forcing of his disposition.
Rosencrantz	Niggard[3] of question, but of our demands
	Most free in his reply.
Queen	Did you assay[4] him
	To any pastime?
Rosencrantz	Madam, it so fell out that certain players
	We o'er-raught[5] on the way; of these we told him,
	And there did seem in him a kind of joy
	To hear of it: they are about the court,
	And, as I think, they have already order 20
	This night to play before him.
Polonius	'Tis most true;
	And he beseech'd me to entreat your Majesties
	To hear and see the matter.
King	With all my heart; and it doth much content me
	To hear him so inclin'd.
	Good gentlemen, give him a further edge,[6]
	And drive his purpose on to these delights.
Rosencrantz	We shall, my lord.
	[Exeunt Rosencrantz and Guildenstern.
King	Sweet Gertrude, leave us too;
	For we have closely[7] sent for Hamlet hither,
	That he, as 'twere by accident, may here 30
	Affront Ophelia.
	Her father and myself, lawful espials,[8]
	Will so bestow[9] ourselves, that, seeing, unseen,

[1]course of conversation

[2]willing to be questioned

[3]sparing

[4]tempt

[5]overtook

[6]encouragement

[7]privately

[8]spies
[9]place

	We may of their encounter frankly judge,
	And gather by him, as he is behav'd,
	If't be the affliction of his love or no
	That thus he suffers for.
Queen	I shall obey you.
	And for your part, Ophelia, I do wish
	That your good beauties be the happy cause
	Of Hamlet's wildness; so shall I hope your virtues 40
	Will bring him to his wonted[10] way again,
	To both your honours.
Ophelia	Madam, I wish it may.

[Exit Queen.

Polonius	Ophelia, walk you here. Gracious, so please you,
	We will bestow ourselves. [To Ophelia] Read on
	this book;
	That show of such an exercise may colour
	Your loneliness.[11] We are oft to blame in this,
	'Tis too much prov'd, that with devotion's visage
	And pious action we do sugar o'er
	The devil himself.
King	[Aside] O! 'tis too true;
	How smart a lash that speech doth give my
	conscience! 50
	The harlot's cheek, beautied with plastering art,
	Is not more ugly to the thing that helps it
	Than is my deed to my most painted word:
	O heavy burden!
Polonius	I hear him coming; let's withdraw, my lord.

[Exeunt King and Polonius.

Enter Hamlet.

Hamlet	To be, or not to be: that is the question:
	Whether 'tis nobler in the mind to suffer
	The slings and arrows of outrageous fortune,
	Or to take arms against a sea of troubles,
	And by opposing end them? To die: to sleep; 60
	No more; and, by a sleep to say we end
	The heart-ache and the thousand natural shocks
	That flesh is heir to. 'Tis a consummation[12]
	Devoutly to be wish'd. To die, to sleep;
	To sleep: perchance to dream. Ay, there's the rub;[13]
	For in that sleep of death what dreams may come,
	When we have shuffled off this mortal coil,[14]
	Must give us pause. There's the respect
	That makes calamity of so long life;
	For who would bear the whips and scorns of time, 70
	The oppressor's wrong, the proud man's contumely,[15]

[10]usual

[11]give a plausible reason for being alone

[12]conclusion

[13]obstacle (a bowling term)

[14]the troubles of life

[15]offensive language

The pangs of disprized[16] love, the law's delay,   ¹⁶ → [16]
The insolence of office, and the spurns
That patient merit of the unworthy takes,
When he himself might his quietus[17] make
With a bare bodkin?[18] Who would fardels[19] bear,
To grunt and sweat under a weary life,
But that the dread of something after death,
The undiscover'd country, from whose bourn[20]
No traveller returns, puzzles the will,   80
And makes us rather bear those ills we have
Than fly to others that we know not of?
Thus conscience[21] does make cowards of us all;
And thus the native hue of resolution
Is sicklied o'er with the pale cast of thought,
And enterprises of great pith[22] and moment
With this regard, their currents turn awry,[23]
And lose the name of action. Soft you now!
The fair Ophelia! Nymph, in thy orisons[24]
Be all my sins remember'd.   90

Ophelia	Good my lord,
	How does your honour for this many a day?
Hamlet	I humbly thank you; well, well, well.
Ophelia	My lord, I have remembrances of yours,
	That I have longed long to re-deliver;
	I pray you, now receive them.
Hamlet	No, not I;
	I never gave you aught.
Ophelia	My honour'd lord, you know right well you did;
	And, with them, words of so sweet breath compos'd
	As made the things more rich: their perfume lost,
	Take these again; for to the noble mind 100
	Rich gifts wax poor when givers prove unkind.
	There, my lord.
Hamlet	Ha, ha! are you honest?
Ophelia	My lord!
Hamlet	Are you fair?
Ophelia	What means your lordship?
Hamlet	That if you be honest and fair, your honesty should admit no discourse[25] to your beauty.
Ophelia	Could beauty, my lord, have better commerce than with honesty? 110
Hamlet	Ay, truly; for the power of beauty will sooner transform honesty from what it is to a bawd than the force of honesty can translate beauty into his likeness. This was sometime a paradox,[26] but now the time gives it proof. I did love thee once.

Marginal glosses:
[16] unvalued
[17] full discharge (legal term for acquittal)
[18] dagger
[19] burdens
[20] boundary
[21] has two meanings; moral judgment or consciousness; understanding
[22] importance
[23] turn events from their proper course
[24] prayers
[25] communication
[26] contrary to opinion (in this context)

27engraft
28stem

29fairly honest

Ophelia	Indeed, my lord, you made me believe so.
Hamlet	You should not have believed me; for virtue cannot so inoculate27 our old stock28 but we shall relish of it. I loved you not.
Ophelia	I was the more deceived. 120
Hamlet	Get thee to a nunnery. Why wouldst thou be a breeder of sinners? I am myself indifferent honest;29 but yet I could accuse me of such things that it were better my mother had not borne me. I am very proud, revengeful, ambitious; with more offences at my beck than I have thoughts to put them in, imagination to give them shape, or time to act them in. What should such fellows as I do crawling between heaven and earth? We are arrant knaves, all; believe none of us. Go thy ways to a nunnery. Where's your 130 father?
Ophelia	At home, my lord.
Hamlet	Let the doors be shut upon him, that he may play the fool nowhere but in's own house. Farewell.
Ophelia	O! help him, you sweet heavens.
Hamlet	If thou dost marry, I'll give thee this plague for thy dowry: be thou as chaste as ice, as pure as snow, thou shalt not escape calumny. Get thee to a nunnery, go; farewell. Or, if thou wilt needs marry, marry a fool; for wise men know well enough what 140 monsters30 you make of them. To a nunnery, go; and quickly too. Farewell.
Ophelia	O heavenly powers, restore him!
Hamlet	I have heard of your paintings too, well enough; God hath given you one face, and you make yourselves another. You jig, you amble, and you lisp, and nickname God's creatures, and make your wantonness your ignorance. Go to, I'll no more on't; it hath made me mad. I say, we will have no more marriages; those that are married already, all but one, shall live; 150 the rest shall keep as they are. To a nunnery, go.

30it was a popular
conception of the time
that men deceived by
women grew horns and
were thus easily identified
as cuckolds

[Exit.

| Ophelia | O! what a noble mind is here o'erthrown: |

The courtier's, soldier's, scholar's, eye, tongue, sword;
The expectancy and rose of the fair state,
The glass of fashion and the mould of form,
The observed of all observers, quite, quite down!
And I, of ladies most deject and wretched,
That suck'd the honey of his music vows,
Now see that noble and most sovereign reason,
Like sweet bells jangled, out of tune and harsh;   160

That unmatch'd form and feature of blown youth
Blasted with ecstasy. [31] O! woe is me,   [31] madness
To have seen what I have seen, see what I see!

Re-enter King and Polonius.

King   Love! his affections do not that way tend;
Nor what he spake, though it lack'd form a little,
Was not like madness. There's something in his soul
O'er which his melancholy sits on brood; [32]   [32] hatch
And, I do doubt, the hatch and the disclose
Will be some danger; which for to prevent,
I have, in quick determination,   *170*
Thus set it down: he shall with speed to England,
For the demand of our neglected tribute:[33]   [33] money paid to the king
Haply the seas, and countries different
With variable objects, shall expel
This something-settled matter in his heart,
Whereon his brains still beating, puts him thus
From fashion of himself. What think you on't?

Polonius   It shall do well: but yet do I believe
The origin and commencement of his grief
Sprung from neglected love. How now, Ophelia!   *180*
You need not tell us what Lord Hamlet said;
We heard it all. My lord, do as you please;
But, if you hold it fit, after the play,
Let his queen mother all alone entreat him
To show his griefs: let her be round[34] with him;   [34] blunt
And I'll be plac'd, so please you, in the ear
Of all their conference. If she find him not,[35]   [35] if she does not find out
To England send him, or confine him where   what is the matter
Your wisdom best shall think.

King   It shall be so:
Madness in great ones must not unwatch'd go.   *190*
                     [Exeunt.

Scene Analysis

At the beginning of the scene Claudius is surrounded by all who are on his side. The king tries to find out the reason for Hamlet's *"turbulent and dangerous lunacy"* but Rosencrantz and Guildenstern explain that Hamlet will not be *"sounded"*. It is ironic, in view of Hamlet's plan, that Claudius is pleased that Hamlet has welcomed the players. It is also extremely ironic that the queen would be glad to think that love for Ophelia is the cause of Hamlet's madness. Polonius tells Ophelia to read a book:

*"That show of such an exercise may colour
Your loneliness."*

He is fully aware of the hypocrisy of his instructions and his comment:

*"'Tis too much prov'd, that with devotion's visage
And pious action we do sugar o'er
The devil himself."*

provokes a guilty response in Claudius:

"How smart a lash that speech doth give my conscience!'

To be, or not to be: that is the question   (Hamlet, Act 3, Scene I)

Since Hamlet is about to test the conscience of Claudius, our sense of expectation at the play's outcome is increased with the awareness that Claudius has a conscience which is capable of smarting. Claudius and Polonius hide as Hamlet approaches, soliloquising. He is tormented, torn with indecision as to whether it is better:

*"...to suffer
The slings and arrows of outrageous fortune,*

Or to take arms against a sea of troubles,
And by opposing end them".

Death would be *"a consummation /Devoutly to be wish'd"* but even death for him, he realises, would not bring peace:

"For in that sleep of death what dreams may come,
When we have shuffled off this mortal coil,
Must give us pause."

He understands that in fact it is the dread of what is to come in the next life that makes man *"fardels bear"*. He realises that resolution is weakened by too much thought, action prevented by too much consideration of an enterprise. Just then he sees Ophelia and when she wishes to return his letters he denies having given them. Ophelia does not understand his questions:

"Ha, ha! are you honest?"

"Are you fair?"

He speaks a paradox:

"...for the power of beauty will sooner transform honesty from what it is to a bawd than the force of honesty can translate beauty into his likeness."

He taunts Ophelia, first proclaiming, *"I did love thee once"*, then stating *"I loved you not"*. His dismissal of Ophelia is harsh:

"Get thee to a nunnery. Why wouldst thou be a breeder of sinners?"

The violence of his rejection of Ophelia is an indication of his pain. Hamlet rejects Ophelia because he associates her with his mother. His bitter words to Ophelia are an attack on women in general. However chaste Ophelia is, she is already condemned unfairly by Hamlet:

"... be thou as chaste as ice, as pure as snow, thou shalt not escape calumny."

His words to Ophelia are the angry expression of disgust at his mother's lust. His condemnation of women is harsh and brutal:

"...You jig, you amble, and you lisp, and nickname God's creatures, and make your wantonness your ignorance."

and he believes that women make monsters of men.

Claudius astutely realises that Hamlet's harsh and bitter words are not the words of a man in love. He recognises that:

"...what he spake, though it lack'd form a little,
Was not like madness."

Get thee to a nunnery.

(Hamlet, Act 3, Scene I)

Yet he understands the dangerous nature of Hamlet's melancholy:

"...There's something in his soul
O'er which his melancholy sits on brood;
And, I do doubt, the hatch and the disclose
Will be some danger"

and he decides to send Hamlet to England at once. Polonius proposes that after the play the queen should see Hamlet alone and that he should be within earshot.

Scene II

A Hall in the Castle
Enter Hamlet and certain players

Hamlet	Speak the speech, I pray you, as I pronounced it to you, trippingly[1] on the tongue; but if you mouth it, as many of your players do, I had as lief[2] the town-crier spoke my lines. Nor do not saw[3] the air too much with your hand, thus; but use all gently; for in the very torrent, tempest, and – as I may say – whirl-wind of passion, you must acquire and beget a temperance,[4] that may give it smoothness. O! it offends me to the soul to hear a robustious[5] periwig-pated[6] fellow tear a passion to tatters, to very rags, to split 10 the ears of the groundlings,[7] who, for the most part are capable of nothing but inexplicable dumbshows and noise: I would have such a fellow whipped for o'er-doing Termagant;[8] it out-herods Herod:[9] pray you, avoid it.
First Player	I warrant your honour.
Hamlet	Be not too tame neither, but let your own discretion be your tutor: suit the action to the word, the word to the action; with this special observance, that you o'erstep not the modesty of nature; for anything so 20 overdone is from the purpose of playing, whose end, both at the first, and now, was, and is, to hold, as 'twere, the mirror up to nature; to show virtue her own feature, scorn her own image, and the very age and body of the time his form and pressure.[10] Now, this overdone, or come tardy[11] off, though it make the unskilful laugh, cannot but make the judicious grieve; the censure of which one must, in your allow-ance, o'erweigh a whole theatre of others. O! there

[1] easily

[2] I'd rather

[3] make a jerky movement like sawing

[4] moderation

[5] boisterous

[6] wearing wigs

[7] those who paid one penny to stand in the pit of theatre

[8] a mythical god

[9] tyrannical king of Israel (Termagant and Herod would be typical boisterous roles)

[10] the shape and impression of the society of the time

[11] slowly, badly

be players that I have seen play, and heard others   30
praise, and that highly, not to speak it profanely,
that, neither having the accent of Christians nor the
gait of Christian, pagan, nor man, have so strutted
and bellowed that I have thought some of nature's
journeymen[12] had made men and not made them
well, they imitated humanity so abominably.

First Player   I hope we have reformed that indifferently[13] with us.

Hamlet   O! reform it altogether. And let those that play your
clowns speak no more than is set down for them;
for there be of them that will themselves laugh, to   40
set on some quantity of barren[14] spectators to
laugh too, though in the mean time some necessary
question of the play be then to be considered; that's
villanous, and shows a most pitiful ambition in the fool
that uses it. Go, make you ready.   *[Exeunt Players.*

Enter Polonius, Rosencrantz and Guildenstern.

How now, my lord! will the King hear this piece of
work?

Polonius   And the Queen too, and that presently.

Hamlet   Bid the players make haste.

[Exit Polonius.

Will you two help to hasten them?   50

Rosencrantz }
Guildenstern } We will, my lord.

[Exeunt Rosencrantz and Guildenstern.

Hamlet   What, ho! Horatio!

Enter Horatio.

Horatio   Here, sweet lord, at your service.

Hamlet   Horatio, thou art e'en as just a man
As e'er my conversation cop'd[15] withal.

Horatio   O! my dear lord!

Hamlet   Nay, do not think I flatter;
For what advancement may I hope from thee,
That no revenue hast but thy good spirits
To feed and clothe thee? Why should the poor be
    flatter'd?
No; let the candied[16] tongue lick absurd pomp,   60
And crook the pregnant[17] hinges of the knee
Where thrift[18] may follow fawning. Dost thou hear?
Since my dear soul was mistress of her choice
And could of men distinguish, her election
Hath seal'd thee for herself; for thou hast been
As one, in suffering all, that suffers nothing,

[12]workers not yet masters of their trade

[13]fairly well

[14]i.e. barren of wits, stupid

[15]met

[16]i.e. sugared with flattery
[17]ready (to bend)
[18]gain

A man that Fortune's buffets and rewards
Hast ta'en with equal thanks; and bless'd are those
Whose blood and judgment are so well comingled
That they are not a pipe for Fortune's finger   70
To sound what stop[19] she please. Give me that man
That is not passion's slave, and I will wear him
In my heart's core, ay, in my heart of heart,
As I do thee. Something too much of this.
There is a play to-night before the King;
One scene of it comes near the circumstance
Which I have told thee of my father's death:
I prithee,[20] when thou seest that act afoot,
Even with the very comment of thy soul
Observe my uncle. If his occulted[21] guilt   80
Do not itself unkennel[22] in one speech,
It is a damned ghost that we have seen,
And my imaginations are as foul
As Vulcan's stithy.[23] Give him heedful note:
For I mine eyes will rivet to his face,
And after we will both our judgments join
In censure of his seeming.[24]

Horatio   Well, my lord:
If he steal[25] aught the whilst this play is playing,
And 'scape detecting, I will pay the theft.

Hamlet   They are coming to the play; I must be idle:[26]   90
Get you a place.

*Danish march. A Flourish.
Enter King, Queen, Polonius,
Ophelia, Rosencrantz, Guildenstern, and Others*

King   How fares our cousin Hamlet?

Hamlet   Excellent, i' faith; of the chameleon's dish: [27] I eat
the air, promise-crammed; you cannot feed
capons[28] so.

King   I have nothing with this answer, Hamlet; these
words are not mine.

Hamlet   No, nor mine now. *[To Polonius]* My lord, you
played once i' the university, you say?

Polonius   That did I, my lord, and was accounted a good
actor.   100

Hamlet   And what did you enact?

Polonius   I did enact Julius Caesar: I was kill'd i' the Capitol;
Brutus killed me.

Hamlet   It was a brute part of him to kill so capital a calf
there. Be the players ready?

[19]note

[20]beg

[21]hidden
[22]driven from his lair,
revealed

[23]Vulcan's forge; In Roman
mythology, Vulcan was the
metal worker of the gods

[24]appearance

[25]hide

[26]i.e. act like a fool

[27]the lizard can survive a
long time without food,
and was thought to live
on air
[28]fowl specially fattened
for table

Rosencrantz	Ay, my lord; they stay upon your patience.
Queen	Come hither, my good Hamlet, sit by me.
Hamlet	No, good mother, here's metal more attractive.[29]
Polonius	*[To the King.]* O ho! do you mark that?
Hamlet	Lady, shall I lie in your lap? *110*

[Lying down at Ophelia's feet.

Ophelia	No, my lord.
Hamlet	I mean, my head upon your lap?[30]
Ophelia	Ay, my lord.
Hamlet	Do you think I meant country matters?
Ophelia	I think nothing, my lord.
Hamlet	That's a fair thought to lie between maids' legs.
Ophelia	What is, my lord?
Hamlet	Nothing.
Ophelia	You are merry, my lord.
Hamlet	Who, I? *120*
Ophelia	Ay, my lord.
Hamlet	O God, your only jig-maker. What should a man do but be merry? For, look you, how cheerfully my mother looks, and my father died within's two hours.
Ophelia	Nay, 'tis twice two months, my lord.
Hamlet	So long? Nay, then, let the devil wear black, for I'll have a suit of sables.[31] O heavens! die two months ago, and not forgotten yet? Then there's hope a great man's memory may outlive his life half a year; but, by'r lady, he must build churches then, or else *130* shall he suffer not thinking on, with the hobby-horse, [32] whose epitaph is, 'For, O! for, O! the hobby-horse is forgot.'

Hautboys[33] play. The dumb-show enters.
Enter a King and a Queen, very lovingly; the Queen embracing him, and he her. She kneels, and makes show of protestation unto him. He takes her up, and declines his head upon her neck; lays him down upon a bank of flowers: she, seeing him asleep, leaves him. Anon comes in a fellow, takes off his crown, kisses it, and pours poison in the King's ears, and exit. The Queen returns, finds the King dead, and makes passionate action. The Poisoner, with some two or three Mutes, comes in again, seeming to lament with her. The dead body is carried away. The Poisoner wooes the Queen with gifts; she seems loath and unwilling awhile, but in the end accepts his love.

[Exeunt.

[29] something more magnetic; i.e. Ophelia

[30] quite an acceptable custom of gallantry

[31] luxurious furs, usually worn by men of wealth, and not suited to mourning

[32] small figure of a horse made of cloth and wood, worn by a dancer around the waist

[33] high pitched wooden instruments

Ophelia	What means this, my lord?
Hamlet	Marry, this is miching mallecho;[34] it means mischief.
Ophelia	Belike this show imports[35] the argument of the play.

Enter Prologue.

Hamlet	We shall know by this fellow: the players cannot keep counsel; they'll tell all.
Ophelia	Will he tell us what this show meant?
Hamlet	Ay, or any show that you will show him. Be not you 140 ashamed to show, he'll not shame to tell you what it means.
Ophelia	You are naught, you are naught.[36] I'll mark the play.

Prologue	*For us and for our tragedy,*
	Here stooping to your clemency,
	We beg your hearing patiently.
Hamlet	Is this a prologue, or the posy of a ring? [37]
Ophelia	'Tis brief, my lord.
Hamlet	As woman's love.

Enter two Players, King and Queen.

P. King	*Full thirty times hath Phoebus' cart[38] gone round* 150
	Neptune's[39] salt wash and Tellus'[40] orbed ground,
	And thirty dozen moons with borrow'd sheen
	About the world have times twelve thirties been,
	Since love our hearts and Hymen[41] did our hands
	Unite commutual in most sacred bands.
P. Queen	*So many journeys may the sun and moon*
	Make us again count o'er ere love be done!
	But, woe is me! you are so sick of late,
	So far from cheer and from your former state,
	That I distrust you. Yet, though I distrust, 160
	Discomfort you, my lord, it nothing must;
	For women's fear and love hold quantity,[42]
	In neither aught, or in extremity.[43]
	Now, what my love is, proof hath made you know;
	And as my love is siz'd, my fear is so.[44]
	Where love is great, the littlest doubts are fear:
	Where little fears grow great, great love grows there.
P. King	*Faith, I must leave thee, love, and shortly too;*
	My operant[45] powers their functions leave to do:
	And thou shalt live in this fair world behind, 170
	Honour'd, belov'd; and haply one as kind
	For husband shalt thou –
P. Queen	*O! confound the rest;*
	Such love must needs be treason in my breast:
	In second husband let me be accurst;
	None wed the second but who kill'd the first.

---

[34]skulking wickedness
[35]indicates

[36]of no worth; Ophelia realises that what Hamlet says is improper

[37]short verse inscribed on a ring

[38]Phoebus Apollo was the sun god, who drove through the sky in a chariot
[39]Roman god of the sea
[40]the earth god
[41]Greek god who personified marriage and fertility

[42]are balanced
[43]both are either nothing or excessive

[44]i.e. my fear is the same size as my love

[45]active

[46]a bitter herb; bitterness

Hamlet	[*Aside*] Wormwood, wormwood.[46]
P. Queen	The instances that second marriage move,
	Are base respects of thrift, but none of love;
	A second time I kill my husband dead,
	When second husband kisses me in bed. 180
P. King	I do believe you think what now you speak;
	But what we do determine oft we break.
	Purpose is but the slave to memory,
	Of violent birth, but poor validity;
	Which now, like fruit unripe, sticks on the tree,
	But fall unshaken when they mellow be.
	Most necessary 'tis that we forget
	To pay ourselves what to ourselves is debt;
	What to ourselves in passion we propose,
	The passion ending, doth the purpose lose. 190
	The violence of either grief or joy
	Their own enactures with themselves destroy:
	Where joy most revels grief doth most lament,
	Grief joys, joy grieves, on slender accident.

[47]ever

	This world is not for aye,[47] nor 'tis not strange,
	That even our love should with our fortunes change;
	For 'tis a question left us yet to prove
	Whether love lead fortune or else fortune love.
	The great man down, you mark his favourite flies;
	The poor advanc'd makes friends of enemies. 200
	And hitherto doth love on fortune tend,
	For who not needs shall never lack a friend;
	And who in want a hollow friend doth try

[48]ripens him into

	Directly seasons[48] him his enemy.
	But, orderly to end where I begun,
	Our wills and fates do so contrary run
	That our devices still are overthrown,
	Our thoughts are ours, their ends none of our own:
	So think thou wilt no second husband wed;
	But die thy thoughts when thy first lord is dead. 210
P. Queen	Nor earth to me give food, nor heaven light!
	Sport and repose lock from me day and night!
	To desperation turn my trust and hope!

[49]the fare of an anchorite (hermit)

	An anchor's cheer[49] in prison be my scope!
	Each opposite that blanks the face of joy
	Meet what I would have well, and it destroy!
	Both here and hence pursue me lasting strife,
	If, once a widow, ever I be wife!
Hamlet	If she should break it now!
P. King	'Tis deeply sworn. Sweet, leave me here awhile; 220
	My sprits grow dull, and fain I would beguile
	The tedious day with sleep. [*Sleeps.*

P. Queen	*Sleep rock thy brain;*
	And never come mischance between us twain!
	[*Exit.*
Hamlet	Madam, how like you this play?
Queen	The lady doth protest too much, methinks.
Hamlet	O! but she'll keep her word.
King	Have you heard the argument? Is there no offence in't?
Hamlet	No, no, they do but jest, poison in jest;
	no offence i' the world. 230
King	What do you call the play?
Hamlet	The Mouse-trap.[50] Marry, how? Tropically.[51] This
	play is the image of a murder done in Vienna:
	Gonzago is the duke's name; his wife, Baptista. You
	shall see anon; 'tis a knavish piece of work: but
	what of that? Your Majesty, and we that have free
	souls,
	it touches us not: let the galled jade[52] wince,
	our withers[53] are unwrung. [54]

Enter Player as Lucianus.

	This is one Lucianus, nephew to the King.
Ophelia	You are a good chorus, my lord.
Hamlet	I could interpret between you and your love, if I 240
	could see the puppets dallying.
Ophelia	You are keen, my lord, you are keen.
Hamlet	It would cost you a groaning to take off my edge.
Ophelia	Still better, and worse.
Hamlet	So you must take your husbands. Begin, murderer;
	pox, leave thy damnable faces, and begin. Come;
	the croaking raven doth bellow for revenge.
Lucianus	*Thoughts black, hands apt, drugs fit, and time*
	agreeing;
	Confederate season,[55] else no creature seeing; 250
	Thou mixture rank, of midnight weeds collected,
	With Hecate's[56] ban thrice blasted, thrice infected,
	Thy natural magic and dire property,
	On wholesome life usurp immediately.
	[*Pours the poison into the Sleeper's ears.*
Hamlet	He poisons him i' the garden for's estate. His
	name's Gonzago; the story is extant,[57] and writ in
	very choice Italian. You shall see anon how the
	murderer gets the love of Gonzago's wife.
Ophelia	The King rises.
Hamlet	What! frighted with false fire? 260
Queen	How fares my lord?
Polonius	Give o'er the play.

[50]the title of the play is *The Murder of Gonzago* but Hamlet calls it *The Mouse-Trap* since it is a trap to catch Claudius

[51]a trope is a figure of speech; figuratively

[52]sore old horse

[53]shoulder bones of a horse

[54]not strained

[55]time conspiring

[56]Greek goddess associated with witchcraft

[57]now existent, i.e. not destroyed

58unhurt deer

59in the actor's hat
60turn infidel
61large rosettes
62pattern obtained by
  slashing
63pack (of hounds)
64the principal actors in
  the company shared the
  profits
65Damon was a devoted
  friend of Pythias in a
  Greek legend
66Roman god of power (a
  reference to the dead
  king)
67peacock (reference to
  Claudius)

68by God!

69disturbed

70cleansing the system
71anger

72order

| King | Give me some light. Away! |
| All | Lights, lights, lights! |

[Exeunt all except Hamlet and Horatio.

Hamlet	Why, let the stricken deer go weep,
	The hart ungalled 58 play;
	For some must watch, while some must sleep:
	So runs the world away.
	Would not this, sir, and a forest of feathers,59 if the
	rest of my fortunes turn Turk60 with me, with two 270
	Provincial roses61 on my razed62 shoes, get me a
	fellowship in a cry63 of players, sir?
Horatio	Half a share.64
Hamlet	A whole one, I.
	For thou dost know, O Damon65 dear,
	This realm dismantled was
	Of Jove66 himself; and now reigns here
	A very, very – pajock.67
Horatio	You might have rhym'd.
Hamlet	O good Horatio! I'll take the ghost's word for a 280
	thousand pound. Didst perceive?
Horatio	Very well, my lord.
Hamlet	Upon the talk of the poisoning?
Horatio	I did very well note him.
Hamlet	Ah, ha! Come, some music! Come, the recorders!
	For if the King like not the comedy,
	Why, then, belike he likes it not, perdy.68
	Come, some music!

Re-enter Rosencrantz and Guildenstern.

Guildenstern	Good my lord, vouchsafe me a word with you.
Hamlet	Sir, a whole history. 290
Guildenstern	The King, sir, –
Hamlet	Ay, sir, what of him?
Guildenstern	Is, in his retirement, marvellous distempered.69
Hamlet	With drink, sir,?
Guildenstern	No, my lord, rather with choler.
Hamlet	Your wisdom should show itself more richer to
	signify this to his doctor; for, for me to put him to
	his purgation70 would perhaps plunge him into far
	more choler.71
Guildenstern	Good my lord, put your discourse into some 300
	frame,72 and start not so wildly from my affair.
Hamlet	I am tame, sir; pronounce.
Guildenstern	The Queen, your mother, in most great affliction of
	spirit, hath sent me to you.
Hamlet	You are welcome.

Guildenstern	Nay, good my lord, this courtesy is not of the right breed. If it shall please you to make me a whole-some answer, I will do your mother's command-ment; if not, your pardon and my return shall be the end of my business. *310*
Hamlet	Sir, I cannot.
Guildenstern	What, my lord?
Hamlet	Make you a wholesome answer: my wit's diseased. But, sir, such answer as I can make, you shall com-mand; or, rather, as you say, my mother. Therefore no more, but to the matter: my mother, you say, –
Rosencrantz	Then, thus she says: your behaviour hath struck her into amazement and admiration.[73]
Hamlet	O wonderful son, that can so astonish a mother! But is there no sequel at the heels of this mother's *320* admiration? Impart.
Rosencrantz	She desires to speak with you in her closet ere you go to bed.
Hamlet	We shall obey, were she ten times our mother. Have you any further trade with us?
Rosencrantz	My lord, you once did love me.
Hamlet	So I do still, by these pickers and stealers.[74]
Rosencrantz	Good my lord, what is your cause of distemper? You do surely bar the door upon your own liberty, if you deny your griefs to your friend. *330*
Hamlet	Sir, I lack advancement.
Rosencrantz	How can that be when you have the voice of the King himself for your succession in Denmark?
Hamlet	Ay, sir, but 'While the grass grows'[75] the proverb is something musty.[76]

Enter Players, with recorders.

	O! the recorders: let me see one. To withdraw with you: why do you go about to recover the wind of me,[77] as if you would drive me into a toil?[78]
Guildenstern	O! my lord, if my duty be too bold, my love is too unmannerly?[79] *340*
Hamlet	I do not well understand that. Will you play upon this pipe?
Guildenstern	My lord, I cannot.
Hamlet	I pray you.
Guildenstern	Believe me, I cannot.
Hamlet	I do beseech you.
Guildenstern	I know no touch of it, my lord.
Hamlet	'Tis as easy as lying; govern these ventages[80] with your finger and thumb, give it breath with your mouth, and it will discourse most eloquent music. *350* Look you, these are the stops.

[73]wonder

[74]hands

[75]...the horse starves
[76]old; because it is a well known proverb, Hamlet does not bother to finish it

[77]a hunting term; the wind blows the scent of the hunter to the hunted animal
[78]trap
[79]he excuses himself by saying that it is his love which makes him unmannerly

[80]finger stops

⁸¹range

⁸²small wooden bar that holds strings tight; Hamlet puns on fret in the sense of irritate

⁸³infectious evil

⁸⁴Roman emperor noted for his cruelty; he had his own mother killed

⁸⁵rebuked
⁸⁶to put a seal on them would be to turn the words into actions

Guildenstern	But these cannot I command to any utterance of harmony; I have not the skill.
Hamlet	Why, look you now, how unworthy a thing you make of me. You would play upon me; you would seem to know my stops; you would pluck out the heart of my mystery; you would sound me from my lowest note to the top of my compass;[81] and there is much music, excellent voice, in this little organ, yet cannot you make it speak. 'Sblood! do you think I am easier 360 to be played on than a pipe? Call me what instrument you will, though you can fret[82] me, you cannot play upon me.

Enter Polonius.

	God bless you, sir!
Polonius	My lord, the Queen would speak with you, and presently.
Hamlet	Do you see yonder cloud that's almost in shape of a camel?
Polonius	By the mass, and 'tis like a camel, indeed.
Hamlet	Methinks it is like a weasel. 370
Polonius	It is backed like a weasel.
Hamlet	Or like a whale?
Polonius	Very like a whale.
Hamlet	Then I will come to my mother by and by. *[Aside]* They fool me to the top of my bent. *[Aloud]* I will come by and by.
Polonius	I will say so.

[Exit.

Hamlet	By and by is easily said. Leave me, friends.

[Exeunt all but Hamlet.

'Tis now the very witching time of night,
When churchyards yawn, and hell itself breathes
out   380
Contagion[83] to this world: now could I drink hot blood,
And do such bitter business as the day
Would quake to look on. Soft! now to my mother.
O heart! lose not thy nature; let not ever
The soul of Nero[84] enter this firm bosom;
Let me be cruel, not unnatural;
I will speak daggers to her, but use none;
My tongue and soul in this be hypocrites;
How in my words soever she be shent,[85]
To give them seals[86] never, my soul, consent!   390

[Exit.

Scene Analysis

The scene begins with Hamlet instructing the players as to how to speak their lines. His advice is good advice and shows a knowledge of drama and acting. He is calm and self-possessed, despite the coming ordeal of testing the reaction of Claudius. Hamlet asks Horatio's help in observing the king's reactions during the play. He respects Horatio as:

> "A man that Fortune's buffets and rewards
> Hast ta'en with equal thanks".

As soon as the king and queen enter he resumes his antic disposition, answering the king flippantly, indulging in puns with Polonius and talking nonsense to Ophelia. When Ophelia remarks on his merriment he observes sarcastically:

> "What should a man do but be merry? For, look you, how cheerfully my mother looks, and my father died within's two hours."

From Ophelia's reminder that it is *"twice two months"* we realise how much time has passed since the appearance of the ghost.

Before the play itself there is the dumb-show which is an exact imitation of what happened in the orchard. Nobody speaks except Hamlet and Ophelia and the suspense is heightened before the play itself is performed. The style of the play is archaic and it is somewhat dull but it touches on the themes of the drama. The opening dialogue between the Player King and Queen enacts Hamlet's interpretation of the loving relationship between his mother and father. The Player Queen expresses Hamlet's very sentiments:

> "The instances that second marriage move,
> Are base respects of thrift, but none of love;"

I do believe you think what now you speak;
But what we do determine oft we break.   (Player King, Act 3, Scene II)

You are naught, you are naught. I'll mark the play.

(Ophelia, Act 3, Scene II)

Hamlet probes his mother's reaction, asking pointedly:

> *"Madam, how like you this play?"*

Gertrude of course cannot accept the sentiments of the queen and answers:

> *"The lady doth protest too much, methinks."*

Hamlet, as Ophelia points out, is as good as a chorus. He explains:

> *"This play is the image of a murder done in Vienna".*

It is in fact the very image of a murder done in Elsinore except that in the Gonzago play the murderer is nephew of the king. When Lucianus enters and actually pours the poison into the ears of the sleeping king, Claudius hurriedly leaves and the play is interrupted. Hamlet has not publicly denounced the king as a murderer but Claudius has recognized the re-enactment of the murder and there is an underlying threat in the implication that this king is to be killed by his nephew.

Hamlet planned the play to convince himself of the truth of the ghost's accusation. The play successfully confirms the guilt of Claudius and Hamlet is prepared to *"take the ghost's word for a thousand pound"*. When Rosencrantz and Guildenstern arrive to impart the queen's request to see Hamlet he will not give them *"a wholesome answer"*. He scathingly points out that he cannot since his *"wit's diseased"*. However Hamlet's wit is sharp enough to see through Rosencrantz and Guildenstern:

> *"You would play upon me; you would seem to know my stops; you would pluck out the heart of my mystery;"*

Hamlet knows *"They fool me to the top of my bent"*. Polonius will agree to anything Hamlet says and Hamlet shows him up as a fool willing to swear that a cloud is in the shape of a camel, a weasel, a whale.

There is an air of expectancy as Hamlet prepares to confront his mother. He is inspired to action by the atmosphere of the night. His desire for revenge is stirred:

> *"...now could I drink hot blood,*
> *And do such bitter business as the day*
> *Would quake to look on."*

He has to remind his heart:

> *"...lose not thy nature".*

This scene marks an important point in the plot as Hamlet's purpose is renewed and the action moves forward.

Scene III

A Room in the Castle
Enter King, Rosencrantz; and Guildenstern.

King   I like him not, nor stands it safe with us
              To let his madness range. Therefore prepare you;
              I your commission will forthwith dispatch,
              And he to England shall along with you.
              The terms of our estate[1] may not endure
              Hazard so dangerous as doth hourly grow
              Out of his lunacies.

Guildenstern   We will ourselves provide.
              Most holy and religious fear it is
              To keep those many many bodies safe
              That live and feed upon your Majesty.   10

Rosencrantz   The single and peculiar[2] life is bound
              With all the strength and armour of the mind
              To keep itself from noyance;[3] but much more
              That spirit upon whose weal[4] depend and rest
              The lives of many. The cease[5] of majesty
              Dies not alone, but, like a gulf doth draw
              What's near it with it; it is a massy[6] wheel,
              Fix'd on the summit of the highest mount,
              To whose huge spokes ten thousand lesser things
              Are mortis'd[7] and adjoin'd; which, when it falls,   20
              Each small annexment,[8] petty consequence,
              Attends the boisterous ruin. Never alone
              Did the king sigh, but with a general groan.

King   Arm you, I pray you, to this speedy voyage;
              For we will fetters[9] put upon this fear,
              Which now goes too free-footed.

Rosencrantz }
Guildenstern }
                                          We will haste us.
                        [Exeunt Rosencrantz and Guildenstern.

                        Enter Polonius.

Polonius   My lord, he's going to his mother's closet:
              Behind the arras[10] I'll convey myself
              To hear the process. I'll warrant she'll tax him home;
              And, as you said, and wisely was it said,   30
              'Tis meet that some more audience than a mother,
              Since nature makes them partial, should o'erhear
              The speech, of vantage.[11] Fare you well, my liege:
              I'll call upon you ere you go to bed
              And tell you what I know.

[1] my position as king

[2] individual

[3] injury
[4] well-being
[5] death

[6] massive

[7] joined
[8] something joined on

[9] iron chains

[10] tapestry

[11] from an advantageous position

King   Thanks, dear my lord.

                                         [Exit Polonius.

O! my offence is rank, it smells to heaven;

It hath the primal eldest curse[12] upon't;

A brother's murder! Pray can I not,

Though inclination be as sharp as will:

My stronger guilt defeats my strong intent;   *40*

And, like a man to double business bound,

I stand in pause where I shall first begin,

And both neglect. What if this cursed hand

Were thicker than itself with brother's blood,

Is there not rain enough in the sweet heavens

To wash it white as snow? Whereto serves mercy

But to confront the visage of offence?

And what's in prayer but this two-fold force,

To be forestalled, ere we come to fall,

Or pardon'd, being down? Then, I'll look up;   *50*

My fault is past. But, O! what form of prayer

Can serve my turn? 'Forgive me my foul murder?'

That cannot be; since I am still possess'd

Of those effects for which I did the murder,

My crown, mine own ambition, and my queen.

May one be pardon'd and retain the offence?

In the corrupted currents of this world

Offence's gilded[13] hand may shove by justice,

And oft 'tis seen the wicked prize itself

Buys out the law; but 'tis not so above;   *60*

There is no shuffling,[14] there the action lies

In his true nature, and we ourselves compell'd

Even to the teeth and forehead of our faults

To give in evidence. What then? What rests?

Try what repentance can: what can it not?

Yet what can it, when one can not repent?

O wretched state! O bosom black as death!

O limed[15] soul, that struggling to be free

Art more engaged! Help, angels! Make assay[16]

Bow, stubborn knees; and heart with strings of steel *70*

Be soft as sinews of the new-born babe.

All may be well.   *[Retires and kneels.*

                 Enter Hamlet.

Hamlet   Now might I do it pat, now he is praying;

And now I'll do't: and so he goes to heaven;

And so am I reveng'd. That would be scann'd:

A villain kills my father; and for that,

I, his sole son, do this same villain send

To heaven.

[12] i.e. the curse of Cain who killed his brother Abel

[13] covered with gold

[14] trickery

[15] snared – a reference to trapping birds with bird lime
[16] attempt

Why, this is hire and salary, not revenge.
He took my father grossly, full of bread,   80
With all his crimes broad blown,[17] as flush[18] as May;
And how his audit[19] stands who knows save heaven?
But in our circumstance and course of thought
'Tis heavy with him. And am I then reveng'd,
To take him in the purging of his soul,
When he is fit and season'd[20] for his passage?
No.
Up, sword, and know thou a more horrid hent;[21]
When he is drunk asleep, or in his rage,
Or in the incestuous pleasure of his bed,   90
At gaming, swearing, or about some act
That has no relish of salvation in't;
Then trip him, that his heels may kick at heaven,
And that his soul may be as damn'd and black
As hell, whereto it goes. My mother stays:
This physic[22] but prolongs thy sickly days.
                                                    [Exit.
                                    [The King rises and advances.

King   My words fly up, my thoughts remain below:
Words without thoughts never to heaven go.
                                                    [Exit.

[17]in full bloom
[18]full of life
[19]account

[20]ready

[21]occasion

[22]medicine, i.e. prayer

Scene Analysis

The sense of momentum created by the crisis of the play scene is maintained as this scene begins with Claudius taking immediate action to have Hamlet removed from the court. When he has given Rosencrantz and Guildenstern their instructions, Polonius informs him that Hamlet is on the way to his mother's room. Claudius is very much disturbed by the play. He is aware of the enormity of his crime:

"O! my offence is rank, it smells to heaven".

He realises that he can expect no forgiveness:

"...since I am still possess'd
Of those effects for which I did the murder,
My crown, mine own ambition, and my queen."

He cannot repent and struggles deeper and deeper in his guilt. As he kneels and tries to pray, Hamlet enters and has the opportunity of striking the king from behind. He realises that this is his chance:

"Now might I do it pat, now he is praying;"

but Hamlet does not do it *"pat"*. He hesitates with the thought:

> *"...And am I then reveng'd,*
> *To take him in the purging of his soul*
> *When he is fit and season'd for his passage?"*

He decides that he will wait until Claudius:

> *"...is drunk asleep, or in his rage,*
> *Or in the incestuous pleasure of his bed,*
> *At gaming, swearing, or about some act*
> *That has no relish of salvation in't".*

Hamlet does not know that the king cannot pray and therefore can obtain no salvation.

Scene IV

The Queen's Apartment.
Enter Queen and Polonius.

Polonius	He will come straight. Look you lay home to him;
	Tell him his pranks have been too broad to bear with,
	And that your Grace hath screen'd and stood between
	Much heat and him. I'll silence me e'en here.
	Pray you, be round with him.
Hamlet	*[Within]* Mother, mother, mother!
Queen	I'll warrant you;
	Fear me not. Withdraw, I hear him coming.
	[Polonius hides behind the arras.

Enter Hamlet.

Hamlet	Now, mother, what's the matter?	
Queen	Hamlet, thou hast thy father much offended.	
Hamlet	Mother, you have my father much offended.	10
Queen	Come, come, you answer with an idle¹ tongue.	¹foolish
Hamlet	Go, go, you question with a wicked tongue.	
Queen	Why, how now, Hamlet!	
Hamlet	What's the matter now?	
Queen	Have you forgot me?	
Hamlet	No, by the rood,² not so:	²cross
	You are the queen, your husband's brother's wife;	
	And, – would it were not so! – you are my mother.	
Queen	Nay then, I'll set those to you that can speak.	
Hamlet	Come, come, and sit you down; you shall not budge;	

	You go not, till I set you up a glass
	Where you may see the inmost part of you. 20
Queen	What wilt thou do? thou wilt not murder me?
	Help, help, ho!
Polonius	[Behind] What, ho! help! help! help!
Hamlet	[Draws] How now! a rat? Dead, for a ducat,³ dead!
	[Makes a pass through the arras.
Polonius	[Behind] O! I am slain.
Queen	O me! what hast thou done?
Hamlet	Nay, I know not:
	Is it the King?
Queen	O! what a rash and bloody deed is this!
Hamlet	A bloody deed! almost as bad, good mother,
	As kill a king, and marry with his brother.
Queen	As kill a king! 30
Hamlet	Ay, lady, 'twas my word.
	[Lifts up the arras and discovers Polonius.
	[To Polonius] Thou wretched, rash, intruding fool,
	farewell!
	I took thee for thy better; take thy fortune;
	Thou find'st to be too busy is some danger.
	Leave wringing of your hands: peace! sit you down,
	And let me wring your heart; for so I shall
	If it be made of penetrable stuff,
	If damned custom have not braz'd⁴ it so
	That it is proof and bulwark⁵ against sense.⁶
Queen	What have I done that thou dar'st wag thy tongue
	In noise so rude against me? 40
Hamlet	Such an act
	That blurs the grace and blush of modesty,
	Calls virtue hypocrite, takes off the rose
	From the fair forehead of an innocent love
	And sets a blister⁷ there, makes marriage vows
	As false as dicers' ⁸ oaths; O! such a deed
	As from the body of contraction⁹ plucks
	The very soul, and sweet religion makes
	A rhapsody of words; heaven's face doth glow,¹⁰
	Yea, this solidity and compound mass,¹¹
	With tristful¹² visage, against the doom, 50
	Is thought-sick at the act.
Queen	Ay me! what act,
	That roars so loud and thunders in the index?¹³
Hamlet	Look here, upon this picture, and on this;
	The counterfeit presentment¹⁴ of two brothers.
	See, what a grace was seated on this brow;
	Hyperion's curls,¹⁵ the front¹⁶ of Jove himself,
	An eye like Mars,¹⁷ to threaten and command,

³ I'll bet a ducat (gold coin)

⁴ hardened with brass
⁵ fortification
⁶ feeling

⁷ perhaps a reference to the fact that prostitutes and adultresses were sometimes branded
⁸ gamblers
⁹ marriage contract
¹⁰ i.e. blush with shame
¹¹ the earth (which is compounded of four elements)
¹² sad
¹³ table of contents; prologue or introduction
¹⁴ picture
¹⁵ the golden curls of the sun god
¹⁶ forehead
¹⁷ the god of war

A station[18] like the herald Mercury[19]
New-lighted on a heaven-kissing hill,
A combination and a form indeed,   60
Where every god did seem to set his seal,
To give the world assurance of a man.
This was your husband. Look you now, what follows.
Here is your husband; like a mildew'd ear,
Blasting his wholesome brother. Have you eyes?
Could you on this fair mountain leave to feed,
And batten[20] on this moor? Ha! have you eyes?
You cannot call it love, for at your age
The hey-day in the blood is tame, it's humble,
And waits upon the judgment; and what judgment 70
Would step from this to this? Sense, sure, you have,
Else could you not have motion; but sure, that sense
Is apoplex'd;[21] for madness would not err,
Nor sense to ecstasy was ne'er so thrall'd[22]
But it reserv'd some quantity of choice,
To serve in such a difference. What devil was't
That thus hath cozen'd[23] you at hoodman-blind?[24]
Eyes without feeling, feeling without sight,
Ears without hands or eyes, smelling sans all,[25]
Or but a sickly part of one true sense   80
Could not so mope.[26]
O shame! where is thy blush? Rebellious hell,
If thou canst mutine[27] in a matron's bones,
To flaming youth let virtue be as wax,
And melt in her own fire: proclaim no shame
When the compulsive ardour gives the charge,
Since frost itself as actively doth burn,
And reason panders will.

Queen   O Hamlet! speak no more;
Thou turn'st mine eyes into my very soul;
And there I see such black and grained[28] spots   90
As will not leave their tinct.[29]

Hamlet   Nay, but to live
In the rank sweat of an enseamed[30] bed,
Stew'd in corruption, honeying and making love
Over the nasty sty, –

Queen   O! speak to me no more;
These words like daggers enter in mine ears;
No more, sweet Hamlet!

Hamlet   A murderer, and a villain;
A slave that is not twentieth part the tithe[31]
Of your precedent lord; a vice of kings;
A cutpurse[32] of the empire and the rule,

[18]stance
[19]messenger of the gods

[20]feed greedily

[21]paralysed
[22]enslaved

[23]deceived
[24]blind-man's buff
[25]without all (the senses)

[26]be stupid

[27]mutiny

[28]ingrained
[29]colour

[30]saturated with seam
(animal grease) sweaty

[31]tenth part

[32]thief

That from a shelf the precious diadem stole,   *100*
And put it in his pocket!

Queen   No more!

Hamlet   A king of shreds and patches,[33] –

[33]In Morality plays Vice was represented as a clown-figure dressed in motley

Enter Ghost.

Save me, and hover o'er me with your wings,
You heavenly guards! What would your gracious
    figure?

Queen   Alas! he's mad!

Hamlet   Do you not come your tardy son to chide,
That, laps'd in time and passion, lets go by
The important acting of your dread command?
O! say.

Ghost   Do not forget: this visitation
Is but to whet thy almost blunted purpose.   *110*
But, look! amazement on thy mother sits;
O! step between her and her fighting soul;

[34]imagination

Conceit[34] in weakest bodies strongest works:
Speak to her, Hamlet.

Hamlet   How is it with you, lady?

Queen   Alas! how is't with you,
That you do bend your eye on vacancy

[35]bodiless

And with the incorporal[35] air do hold discourse?
Forth at your eyes your spirits wildly peep;
And, as the sleeping soldiers in the alarm,

[36]lying flat
[37]outgrowths, i.e. the hair

Your bedded[36] hair, like life in excrements,[37]   *120*
Starts up and stands an end. O gentle son!
Upon the heat and flame of thy distemper
Sprinkle cool patience. Whereon do you look?

Hamlet   On him, on him! Look you, how pale he glares!
His form and cause conjoin'd, preaching to stones,
Would make them capable. Do not look upon me;
Lest with this piteous action you convert
My stern effects: then, what I have to do
Will want true colour; tears, perchance, for blood.

Queen   To whom do you speak this?   *130*

Hamlet   Do you see nothing there?

Queen   Nothing at all; yet all that is I see.

Hamlet   Nor did you nothing hear?

Queen   No, nothing but ourselves.

Hamlet   Why, look you there! look, how it steals away;

[38]usual dress

My father, in his habit[38] as he liv'd;
Look! where he goes, even now, out at the portal.
                                        [Exit Ghost.

Queen	This is the very coinage[39] of your brain:	[39]invention
	This bodiless creation ecstasy	
	Is very cunning in.	
Hamlet	Ecstasy!	
	My pulse, as yours, doth temperately keep time, 140	
	And makes as healthful music. It is not madness	
	That I have utter'd: bring me to the test,	
	And I the matter will re-word, which madness	
	Would gambol from. Mother, for love of grace,	
	Lay not that flattering unction[40] to your soul,	[40]ointment
	That not your trespass but my madness speaks;	
	It will but skin and film the ulcerous place,	
	Whiles rank corruption, mining[41] all within,	[41]i.e.undermining
	Infects unseen. Confess yourself to heaven;	
	Repent what's past; avoid what is to come; 150	
	And do not spread the compost[42] on the weeds	[42]fertiliser
	To make them ranker. Forgive me this my virtue;	
	For in the fatness of these pursy[43] times	[43]bloated
	Virtue itself of vice must pardon beg,	
	Yea, curb and woo,[44] for leave to do him good.	[44]bow and scrape
Queen	O Hamlet! thou has cleft[45] my heart in twain.	[45]split
Hamlet	O! throw away the worser part of it,	
	And live the purer with the other half.	
	Good night; but go not to mine uncle's bed;	
	Assume a virtue, if you have it not. 160	
	That monster, custom, who all sense doth eat,	
	Of habits devil, is angel yet in this,	
	That to the use of actions fair and good	
	He likewise gives a frock or livery,[46]	[46]clothes or uniform
	That aptly[47] is put on. Refrain to-night;	[47]easily
	And that shall lend a kind of easiness	
	To the next abstinence: the next more easy;	
	For use almost can change the stamp of nature,	
	And either curb the devil or throw him out	
	With wondrous potency. Once more, good night: 170	
	And when you are desirous to be bless'd,	
	I'll blessing beg of you. For this same lord,	
	[Pointing to Polonius.	
	I do repent: but heaven hath pleas'd it so,	
	To punish me with this, and this with me,	
	That I must be their scourge and minister.	
	I will bestow him,[48] and will answer well	[48]dispose
	The death I gave him. So, again, good night.	
	I must be cruel only to be kind:	
	Thus bad begins and worse remains behind.	
	One word more, good lady. 180	

49affectionate term
50reeky, filthy

51toad
52tomcat

53reference to an old fable
54experiments

55order

56hoisted, blown up
57bomb

58two clever plots meet
  head on

59chattering

Queen	What shall I do?

Hamlet   Not this, by no means, that I bid you do:
Let the bloat king tempt you again to bed;
Pinch wanton on your cheek; call you his mouse;49
And let him, for a pair of reechy50 kisses,
Or paddling in your neck with his damn'd fingers,
Make you to ravel all this matter out,
That I essentially am not in madness,
But mad in craft. 'Twere good you let him know;
For who that's but a queen, fair, sober, wise,
Would from a paddock,51 from a bat, a gib,52   190
Such dear concernings hide? who would do so?
No, in despite of sense and secrecy,
Unpeg the basket on the house's top,
Let the birds fly, and, like the famous ape,53
To try conclusions,54 in the basket creep,
And break your own neck down.

Queen   Be thou assur'd, if words be made of breath,
And breath of life, I have no life to breathe
What thou hast said to me.

Hamlet   I must to England; you know that?   200

Queen   Alack!
I had forgot: 'tis so concluded on.

Hamlet   There's letters seal'd, and my two school-fellows,
Whom I will trust as I will adders fang'd,
They bear the mandate;55 they must sweep my way,
And marshal me to knavery. Let it work;
For 'tis the sport to have the engineer
Hoist56 with his own petar:57 and it shall go hard
But I will delve one yard below their mines,
And blow them at the moon. O! 'tis most sweet,
When in one line two crafts58 directly meet.   210
This man shall set me packing;
I'll lug the guts into the neighbour room.
Mother, good night. Indeed this counsellor
Is now most still, most secret, and most grave,
Who was in life a foolish prating59 knave.
Come, sir, to draw toward an end with you.
Good night, mother.
          [Exeunt severally; Hamlet dragging in the body of Polonius.

Scene Analysis

Before Gertrude's meeting with her son, Polonius proceeds to give her advice on how to deal with Hamlet:

> *"...Look you lay home to him,*
> *Tell him his pranks have been too broad to bear with".*

After Polonius hides behind the arras, the queen begins to chastise Hamlet for offending his father but he turns the accusation back on her:

> *"Mother, you have my father much offended."*

He bitterly rejects her:

> *"You are the queen, your husband's brother's wife;*
> *And, – would it were not so! – you are my mother."*

The queen becomes afraid when Hamlet insists that she sit down so that he can:

> *"... set you up a glass*
> *Where you may see the inmost part of you."*

She shouts for help and is answered by Polonius. Hamlet immediately draws his sword and strikes through the arras. He supposes it is the king but on seeing the dead Polonius he dismisses him as a:

> *"... wretched, rash, intruding fool".*

Hamlet shows little feeling for the dead Polonius but he vents his feelings on his mother. Gertrude asks what she has done to incur such rudeness and Hamlet denounces her deed as:

> *"Such an act*
> *That blurs the grace and blush of modesty".*

He then compares his father:

> *"A combination and a form indeed,*
> *Where every god did seem to set his seal*
> *To give the world assurance of a man."*

and his uncle:

> *"... like a mildew'd ear,*
> *Blasting his wholesome brother."*

Hamlet's words are indeed daggers. He accuses her of being:

> *"Stew'd in corruption, honeying and making love*
> *Over the nasty sty".*

Be thou assur'd, if words be made of breath,
And breath of life, I have no life to breathe
What thou hast said to me.

(Gertrude, Act 3, Scene IV)

His bitter invective is interrupted as he sees the ghost of his father. As he speaks to it, the queen, who sees nothing, believes he is truly mad. Hamlet's feeling of guilt is conveyed by the question he asks the ghost:

> *"Do you not come your tardy son to chide,*
> *That, laps'd in time and passion, lets go by*
> *The important acting of your dread command?"*

The significance of the appearance of the ghost at this point in the action is clear. He has come

> *"to whet thy almost blunted purpose".*

The queen believes:

> *"This is the very coinage of your brain"*

but Hamlet earnestly pleads with his mother not to deceive herself:

> *"That not your trespass but my madness speaks".*

In fact the queen seems broken-hearted and Hamlet begs her to repent and reject his uncle's love. Hamlet informs his mother:

> *"That I essentially am not in madness,*
> *But mad in craft."*

Indeed Hamlet is one step ahead of the king and knowing well that Rosencrantz and Guildenstern are to betray him, intends to:

> *"...delve one yard below their mines,*
> *And blow them at the moon."*

Hamlet repents killing Polonius and sees it as a punishment from heaven, nevertheless he treats Polonius with scant respect:

> *"I'll lug the guts into the neighbour room."*

and dismisses Polonius as *"a foolish prating knave".*

REVISION

> *"What to ourselves in passion we propose,*
> *The passion ending, doth the purpose lose". (Hamlet, Act 3, Scene II)*

Rosencrantz and Guildenstern cannot discover the cause of Hamlet's strange behaviour. Polonius and the king eavesdrop on Hamlet's conversation with Ophelia in which he roughly rejects her love. Claudius is suspicious of Hamlet's seeming madness and decides to send him to England with Rosencrantz and Guildenstern. Hamlet asks the players to perform *The Murder of Gonzago*. Claudius is so disturbed that he rushes out during the performance thus confirming his guilt. Yet when Hamlet comes across Claudius alone, believing him to be praying he cannot make up his mind to kill the king. Polonius arranges for Gertrude to talk to Hamlet in her bedroom and hides behind the arras. Hamlet bitterly reproaches her and she cries for help which causes Polonius to shout out. Hamlet immediately draws his sword and stabs him to death. The ghost appears again to Hamlet *"to whet thy almost blunted purpose"*.

Points To Note

1. In *Scene I* we have a direct admission of guilt from Claudius.

2. The perfect opportunity for Hamlet to turn his resolution into action is provided in *Scene III*. Hamlet's failure to seize the opportunity marks the turning point of the play.

3. Hamlet strikes blindly at the figure behind the arras but in so doing he proves that he is capable of action.

4. The killing of Polonius is to have very important consequences in the subsequent development of plot.

5. Although the ghost is not seen by Gertrude this does not necessarily mean that he is intended as a figment of Hamlet's imagination. The Elizabethans accepted that a ghost could be visible to some and not to others.

Revision Assignment

Consider the ghost's accusation that Hamlet's purpose is blunted in the light of the events in *Act 3*.

Act 4
Scene I

A Room in the Castle.
Enter King, Queen, Rosencrantz, and Guildenstern.

King	There's matter[1] in these sighs, these profound heaves:
	You must translate: 'tis fit we understand them.
	Where is your son?
Queen	*[To Rosencrantz and Guildenstern]* Bestow this place on us[2] a little while.
	[Exeunt Rosencrantz and Guildenstern.
	Ah! my good lord, what have I seen to-night!
King	What, Gertrude? How does Hamlet?
Queen	Mad as the sea and wind, when both contend
	Which is the mightier. In his lawless fit,
	Behind the arras hearing something stir,
	Whips out his rapier, cries, 'A rat! a rat!' 10
	And, in his brainish apprehension, kills
	The unseen good old man.
King	O heavy deed!
	It had been so with us had we been there.
	His liberty is full of threats to all;
	To you yourself, to us, to every one.
	Alas! how shall this bloody deed be answer'd?
	It will be laid to us, whose providence[3]
	Should have kept short, restrain'd, and out of haunt,[4]
	This mad young man: but so much was our love,
	We would not understand what was most fit, 20
	But, like the owner of a foul disease,
	To keep it from divulging, let it feed
	Even on the pith of life. Where is he gone?
Queen	To draw apart the body he hath kill'd;
	O'er whom his very madness, like some ore[5]
	Among a mineral of metals base,
	Shows itself pure: he weeps for what is done.
King	O Gertrude! come away.
	The sun no sooner shall the mountains touch
	But we will ship him hence; and this vile deed 30
	We must, with all our majesty and skill,
	Both countenance[6] and excuse. Ho! Guildenstern!

Re-enter Rosencrantz and Guildenstern.

Friends both, go join you with some further aid:
Hamlet in madness hath Polonius slain,

[1] meaning

[2] leaves us to ourselves

[3] foresight
[4] company

[5] vein of gold

[6] support

And from his mother's closet hath he dragg'd him:
Go seek him out; speak fair, and bring the body
Into the chapel. I pray you, haste in this.
                    [Exeunt Rosencrantz and Guildenstern.
Come, Gertrude, we'll call up our wisest friends;
And let them know, both what we mean to do,
And what's untimely done: so, haply, slander,   40
Whose whisper o'er the world's diameter
As level as the cannon to his blank [7]
Transports his poison'd shot, may miss our name,
And hit the woundless[8] air. O! come away;
My soul is full of discord and dismay.   [Exeunt.

[7] as straight as the cannon fires at its target

[8] invulnerable

Scene Analysis

In this short scene the queen informs Claudius of the death of Polonius. She is true to her word not to betray Hamlet and tells Claudius that Hamlet is:

> *"Mad as the sea and wind, when both contend*
> *Which is the mightier."*

Claudius expresses no sorrow at the death of Polonius. His immediate concern is for himself:

> *"O heavy deed!*
> *It had been so with us had we been there."*

He is also concerned with the consequences of Polonius' death.

> *"Alas! how shall this bloody deed be answer'd?"*

Claudius knows that he cannot proclaim Hamlet a murderer and so he must appear to protect him. Nevertheless he is determined to *"ship him hence"*.

Scene II

Another Room in the Same.
Enter Hamlet.

[1] stowed away, hidden

Hamlet   Safely stowed.[1]
Rosencrantz
Guildenstern *[Within]* Hamlet! Lord Hamlet!
Hamlet   What noise? who calls on Hamlet? O! here they
                       come.

Enter Rosencrantz and Guildenstern.

Rosencrantz	What have you done, my lord, with the dead body?	
Hamlet	Compounded[2] it with dust, whereto 'tis kin.[3]	[2] mixed with
Rosencrantz	Tell us where 'tis, that we may take it thence	[3] related
	And bear it to the chapel.	
Hamlet	Do not believe it.	
Rosencrantz	Believe what? 10	
Hamlet	That I can keep your counsel and not mine own.	
	Besides, to be demanded of a sponge! what	
	replication[4]	[4] reply
	should be made by the son of a king?	
Rosencrantz	Take you me for a sponge, my lord?	
Hamlet	Ay, sir, that soaks up the King's countenance,[5] his	[5] favour
	rewards, his authorities. But such officers do the	
	King best service in the end: he keeps them, like an	
	ape an apple in the corner of his jaw; first mouthed,	
	to be last swallowed: when he needs what you have	
	gleaned, it is but squeezing you, and, sponge, you 20	
	shall be dry again.	
Rosencrantz	I understand you not, my lord.	
Hamlet	I am glad of it: a knavish speech sleeps in a foolish	
	ear. [6]	[6] Hamlet implies that Rosencrantz is too stupid to understand his sarcasm
Rosencrantz	My lord, you must tell us where the body is, and go	
	with us to the King.	[7] i.e. the king is not part of the body politic because he is not the rightful king
Hamlet	The body is with the King, but the King is not with	
	the body. [7] The King is a thing –	[8] Hamlet implies that Rosencrantz and Guildenstern are the king's hounds hunting him
Guildenstern	A thing, my lord!	
Hamlet	Of nothing: bring me to him. Hide fox,[8] and all after. 30	
	[Exeunt.	

Scene Analysis

Rosencrantz and Guildenstern encounter Hamlet who acts in a truly lunatic manner, hiding the body and running away. Hamlet accuses Rosencrantz of being a sponge:

"… that soaks up the King's countenance, his rewards, his authorities."

Rosencrantz protests that he doesn't understand Hamlet and Hamlet quite aptly replies that "a knavish speech sleeps in a foolish ear". Hamlet deliberately misunderstands Rosencrantz's request for Polonius' body. He replies:

"The body is with the King, but the King is not with the body".

This raises the whole issue of Claudius not being the rightful king, "not with the body", but just as Hamlet is about to develop his idea of what constitutes a king "The king is a thing", he is interrupted by the shocked protests of Guildenstern, who interprets Hamlet's words literally and who objects to the idea of the king being referred to as a thing. But Hamlet intended to say *"a thing of nothing"* to indicate the insignificance of the king. Hamlet delights in taunting Rosencrantz and Guildenstern. They have been sent to find the body of Polonius and he challenges them to a game of hide and seek:

> *"Hide fox, and all after."*

Scene III

Another Room in the Same.
Enter King, attended.

King	I have sent to seek him, and to find the body.
	How dangerous is it that this man goes loose!
	Yet must not we put the strong law on him:
	He's loved of the distracted[1] multitude,
	Who like not in their judgment, but their eyes;
	And where 'tis so, the offender's scourge[2] is weigh'd,
	But never the offence. To bear all smooth and even,
	This sudden sending him away must seem
	Deliberate pause:[3] diseases, desperate grown,
	By desperate appliance[4] are reliev'd, *10*
	Or not at all.

[1] confused

[2] punishment

[3] carefully considered
[4] remedy

Enter Rosencrantz.

	How now! what hath befall'n?
Rosencrantz	Where the dead body is bestow'd, my lord,
	We cannot get from him.
King	But where is he?
Rosencrantz	Without, my lord; guarded, to know your pleasure.
King	Bring him before us.
Rosencrantz	Ho, Guildenstern! bring in my lord.

Enter Hamlet and Guildenstern.

King	Now, Hamlet, where's Polonius?
Hamlet	At supper.
King	At supper! Where?
Hamlet	Not where he eats, but where he is eaten: a certain *20*
	convocation of politic worms[5] are e'en at him. Your
	worm is your only emperor for diet: we fat all crea-
	tures else to fat us, and we fat ourselves for mag-
	gots: your fat king and your lean beggar is but
	variable service;[6] two dishes, but to one table:
	that's the end.

[5] politic = shrewd; this could be a reference to the Diet of Worms in 1521 before which Luther defended his doctrines
[6] different courses

King	Alas, alas!
Hamlet	A man may fish with the worm that hath eat of a king, and eat of the fish that hath fed of that worm.
King	What dost thou mean by this? 30
Hamlet	Nothing, but to show you how a king may go a progress through the guts of a beggar.
King	Where is Polonius?
Hamlet	In heaven; send thither to see: if your messenger find him not there, seek him i' the other place your- self. But, indeed, if you find him not within this month, you shall nose him as you go up the stairs into the lobby.
King	*[To some Attendants]* Go seek him there.
Hamlet	He will stay till you come. 40

[Exeunt Attendants.

King	Hamlet, this deed, for thine especial safety, Which we do tender,[7] as we dearly grieve For that which thou hast done, must send thee hence With fiery quickness; therefore prepare thyself; The bark is ready, and the wind at help, The associates tend, and every thing is bent For England.
Hamlet	For England!
King	Ay, Hamlet.
Hamlet	Good.
King	So is it, if thou knew'st our purposes.
Hamlet	I see a cherub that sees them. But, come; for England! Farewell, dear mother. 50
King	Thy loving father, Hamlet.
Hamlet	My mother: father and mother is man and wife, man and wife is one flesh, and so, my mother. Come, for England! *[Exit.*
King	Follow him at foot; tempt him with speed aboard: Delay it not, I'll have him hence to-night. Away! for everything is seal'd and done That else leans on the affair: pray you, make haste.

[Exeunt Rosencrantz and Guildenstern.

And, England, if my love thou hold'st at aught,–
As my great power thereof may give thee sense, 60
Since yet thy cicatrice[8] looks raw and red
After the Danish sword, and thy free awe
Pays homage to us, – thou mayst not coldly set
Our sovereign process, which imports at full,[9]
By letters conjuring to that effect,
The present death of Hamlet. Do it, England;
For like the hectic[10] in my blood he rages,
And thou must cure me. Till I know 'tis done,
Howe'er my haps,[11] my joys were ne'er begun. *[Exit.*

[7] value

[8] scar

[9] signifies completely

[10] fever

[11] whatever may happen

Scene Analysis

In Scene III Claudius is surrounded by his attendants. He realises that he must proceed carefully as Hamlet is loved by the people of Denmark. Hamlet is being treated like a prisoner but he boldly confronts the king and in an answer to the king's question as to the whereabouts of Polonius he replies flippantly *"At supper."* He then points out how:

> *"...a king may go a progress through the guts of a beggar"*

a pointed and grim reminder to the king of the inevitability of death and decay. The king does not understand his sombre riddles:

> *'A man may fish with the worm that hath eat of a king, and eat of the fish that hath fed of that worm."*

Hamlet's wit at the expense of Polonius' corpse is grim:

> *"He will stay till you come"*.

The king informs Hamlet that for his own safety he must go to England. Hamlet calmly replies *"Good"*. Claudius' rejoinder is threatening *"So is it, if thou knew'st our purposes"* but Hamlet shows remarkable self-possession and tells Claudius, *"see a cherub that sees them"*. Hamlet takes his leave of the king by saluting him scathingly as his mother:

> *"My mother: father and mother is man and wife, man and wife is one flesh, and so, my mother."*

The king's final words to himself reveal that he has planned the death of Hamlet in England.

Scene IV

A Plain in Denmark.
Enter Fortinbras, a Captain, and Soldiers, marching.

Fortinbras	Go, captain, from me greet the Danish king;
	Tell him that, by his licence,[1] Fortinbras
	Claims the conveyance[2] of a promis'd march
	Over his kingdom. You know the rendezvous.
	If that his Majesty would aught with us,
	We shall express our duty in his eye,[3]
	And let him know so.
Captain	
	I will do't, my lord.
Fortinbras	
	Go softly on.

[Exeunt Fortinbras and Soldiers.

[1] permission
[2] escort
[3] presence

Enter Hamlet, Rosencrantz, Guildenstern &c.

Hamlet	Good sir, whose powers are these?
Captain	They are of Norway, sir. 10
Hamlet	How purpos'd, sir, I pray you?
Captain	Against some part of Poland.
Hamlet	Who commands them, sir?
Captain	The nephew to old Norway, Fortinbras.
Hamlet	Goes it against the main of Poland, sir,
	Or for some frontier?
Captain	Truly to speak, and with no addition,[4]
	We go to gain a little patch of ground
	That hath in it no profit but the name.
	To pay five ducats, five, I would not farm it; 20
	Nor will it yield to Norway or the Pole
	A ranker rate, should it be sold in fee.[5]
Hamlet	Why, then the Polack never will defend it.
Captain	Yes, 'tis already garrison'd.
Hamlet	Two thousand souls and twenty thousand ducats
	Will not debate the question of this straw:
	This is the imposthume[6] of much wealth and peace,
	That inward breaks, and shows no cause without
	Why the man dies. I humbly thank you, sir.
Captain	God be wi' you, sir. 30
	[Exit.
Rosencrantz	Will't please you go, my lord?
Hamlet	I'll be with you straight. Go a little before.
	[Exeunt all except Hamlet.
	How all occasions do inform against me;
	And spur my dull revenge! What is a man,
	If his chief good and market of his time
	Be but to sleep and feed? A beast, no more.
	Sure he that made us with such large discourse,[7]
	Looking before and after, gave us not
	That capability and god-like reason
	To fust[8] in us unus'd. Now, whether it be
	Bestial oblivion, or some craven[9] scruple 40
	Of thinking too precisely on the event,
	A thought, which, quarter'd, hath but one part
	wisdom,
	And ever three parts coward, I do not know
	Why yet I live to say 'This thing's to do;'
	Sith I have cause and will and strength and means
	To do't. Examples gross as earth exhort me:
	Witness this army of such mass and charge,[10]
	Led by a delicate and tender prince,
	Whose spirit, with divine ambition puff'd,

[4] exaggeration

[5] as a freehold, giving total possession

[6] abcess

[7] understanding

[8] go mouldy
[9] cowardly

[10] numbers and expense

[11]unforeseen consequences

Makes mouths at the invisible event[11]   50
Exposing what is mortal and unsure
To all that fortune, death and danger, dare,
Even for an egg-shell. Rightly to be great
Is not to stir without great argument,
But greatly to find quarrel in a straw
When honour's at the stake. How stand I then,
That have a father kill'd, a mother stain'd,
Excitements of my reason and my blood,
And let all sleep, while, to my shame, I see
The imminent death of twenty thousand men,   60
That, for a fantasy and trick of fame,
Go to their graves like beds, fight for a plot

[12]the area is so small that the numbers in the army are too great to fight on it
[13]sufficient to contain

Whereon the numbers cannot try the cause,[12]
Which is not tomb enough and continent[13]
To hide the slain? O! from this time forth,
My thoughts be bloody, or be nothing worth!

[Exit.

Scene Analysis

There is a complete change of scene as Hamlet meets up with the captain of Fortinbras' army and his soldiers who are marching to Poland. The encounter seems of little dramatic interest since it hardly advances the action but Hamlet sees it as a significant spur to his *"dull revenge"*. The courage and daring of Fortinbras is a measure by which Hamlet judges himself. He ponders the example of an army which is prepared to:

> *"... death and danger, dare,*
> *Even for an egg-shell"*.

He wonders:

> *"... How stand I then,*
> *That have a father kill'd, a mother stain'd,*
> *Excitements of my reason and my blood,*
> *And let all sleep"*.

Hamlet knows that man is no better than a beast:

> *"If his chief good and market of his time*
> *Be but to sleep and feed"*.

He does not know why he cannot act:

> *"... whether it be*
> *Bestial oblivion, or some craven scruple*
> *Of thinking too precisely on the event"*.

He examines his scruples and realises that they are only one quarter wise but three quarters cowardly. Hamlet assesses the facts coldly and realises that he has *"cause and will and strength and means"*. He even finds justification in revenge against Claudius because he *"a father kill'd, a mother stain'd"*.

Hamlet's encounter with Fortinbras' army awakens in him a sense of shame, but also a new sense of assertiveness. He ends his meditation on a note of resolution and determination:

> *"...O! from this time forth,*
> *My thoughts be bloody, or be nothing worth!"*

Scene V

Elsinore. A Room in the Castle.
Enter Queen, Horatio, and a Gentleman.

Queen	I will not speak with her.
Gentleman	She is importunate,[1] indeed distract:
	Her mood will needs be pitied.
Queen	What would she have?
Gentleman	She speaks much of her father; says she hears
	There's tricks i' the world; and hems, and beats her heart;
	Spurns enviously[2] at straws; speaks things in doubt,
	That carry but half sense: her speech is nothing,
	Yet the unshap'd use of it doth move
	The hearers to collection;[3] they aim at it,[4]
	And botch the words up fit to their own thoughts: 10
	Which, as her winks, and nods, and gestures yield them,
	Indeed would make one think there might be thought,
	Though nothing sure, yet much unhappily.
Horatio	'Twere good she were spoken with, for she may strew
	Dangerous conjectures in ill-breeding minds.
Queen	Let her come in.

> *[Exit Gentleman.*

[Aside] To my sick soul, as sin's true nature is,
Each toy[5] seems prologue to some great amiss:
So full of artless jealousy[6] is guilt
It spills itself in fearing to be spilt.[7]   20

Re-enter Gentleman, with Ophelia.

[1] persistent

[2] angrily

[3] infer meaning
[4] they guess at it

[5] trivial thing

[6] uncontrolled suspicion

[7] it gives itself away because of its fear of being discovered

Ophelia	Where is the beauteous Majesty of Denmark?
Queen	How now, Ophelia!
Ophelia	[Sings] How should I your true love know

> From another one?
> By his cockle hat[8] and staff,
> And his sandal shoon.

| Queen | Alas! sweet lady, what imports this song? |
| Ophelia | Say you? Nay, pray you, mark. |

> [Sings] He is dead and gone, lady,
> He is dead and gone;   30
> At his head a grass-green turf,
> At his heels a stone.

O, ho!

| Queen | Nay, but Ophelia, – |
| Ophelia | Pray you, mark. |

[Sings] White his shroud as the mountain snow, –

Enter King.

| Queen | Alas! look here, my lord. |
| Ophelia | |

> [Sings] Larded[9] with sweet flowers;
> Which bewept to the grave did go
> With true-love showers.

King	How do you, pretty lady? 40
Ophelia	Well, God 'ild[10] you! They say the owl was a baker's daughter.[11] Lord! we know what we are, but know not what we may be. God be at your table!
King	Conceit[12] upon her father.
Ophelia	Pray you, let's have no words of this; but when they ask you what it means, say you this:

> [Sings]To-morrow is Saint Valentine's day,
> All in the morning betime,
> And I a maid at your window,
> To be your Valentine: 50
> Then up he rose and donn'd his clothes,
> And dupp'd[13] the chamber door;
> Let in the maid, that out a maid
> Never departed more.

| King | Pretty Ophelia! |
| Ophelia | Indeed, la! without an oath, I'll make an end on't: |

> [Sings] By Gis[14] and by Saint Charity,
> Alack, and fie for shame!
> Young men will do't, if they come to't;   60
> By Cock[15] they are to blame.
> Quoth she, 'Before you tumbled me,
> You promis'd me to wed:'

[8] hat with a shell on it worn by pilgrims of St. James at Compostella; lovers very often went on pilgrimage

[9] strewn

[10] reward

[11] there is a legend of a baker's daughter who was turned into an owl because she scolded her mother for giving Christ too much bread

[12] thinking about

[13] opened

[14] Jesus

[15] God (Ophelia has promised to sing her song without an oath and so will not use the name of God)

	He answers:
	'So would I ha' done, by yonder sun,
	An thou hadst not come to my bed.'
King	How long hath she been thus?
Ophelia	I hope all will be well. We must be patient: but I can

	not choose but weep, to think they should lay him i'
	the cold ground. My brother shall know of it: and so 70
	I thank you for your good counsel. Come, my coach!
	Good night, ladies; good night, sweet ladies, good
	night, good night. [Exit.
King	Follow her close; give her good watch, I pray you.
	[Exit Horatio.

O! this is the poison of deep grief; it springs
All from her father's death. O Gertrude, Gertrude!
When sorrows come, they come not single spies,[16]   16scouts
But in battalions. First, her father slain;
Next, your son gone; but he most violent author
Of his own just remove: the people muddied,   80
Thick and unwholesome in their thoughts and
  whispers,
For good Polonius' death; and we have done but
  greenly,[17]   17foolishly
In hugger-mugger[18] to inter him: poor Ophelia   18secretly and hastily
Divided from herself and her fair judgment,
Without the which we are pictures, or mere beasts:
Last, and as much containing as all these,
Her brother is in secret come from France,
Feeds on his wonder, keeps himself in clouds,
And wants not buzzers[19] to infect his ear   19gossips
With pestilent speeches of his father's death;   90
Wherein necessity, of matter beggar'd,[20]   20destitute of facts
Will nothing stick our person to arraign[21]   21accuse
In ear and ear. O my dear Gertrude! this,
Like to a murdering-piece,[22] in many places   22small cannon
Gives me superfluous[23] death. [A noise within.   23unnecessary because he is
                                                                                    already being attacked

| Queen | Alack! what noise is this? |

Enter an Attendant.

King	Where are my Switzers?[24] Let them guard the door.
	What is the matter?

24Swiss bodyguards

Gentleman	Save yourself, my lord;

The ocean, overpeering of his list,[25]   25boundary
Eats not the flats with more impetuous haste
Than young Laertes, in a riotous head,[26]   100   26with a riotous force
O'erbears your officers. The rabble call him lord;
And, as the world were now but to begin,

Antiquity forgot, custom not known,
The ratifiers and props of every word,
They cry, 'Choose we; Laertes shall be king!'
Caps, hands, and tongues, applaud it to the clouds,
'Laertes shall be king, Laertes king!'

Queen   How cheerfully on the false trail they cry!
O! this is counter,[27] you false Danish dogs!

King   The doors are broke.   110

[*Noise within.*

Enter Laertes, armed; Danes following.

Laertes   Where is the king? Sirs, stand you all without.
Danes   No, let's come in.
Laertes   I pray you, give me leave.
Danes   We will, we will.

[*They retire without the door.*

Laertes   I thank you: keep the door. O thou vile king!
Give me my father.
Queen   Calmly, good Laertes.
Laertes   That drop of blood that's calm proclaims me bastard,[28]
Cries cuckold to my father, brands the harlot
Even here, between the chaste unsmirched brow
Of my true mother.   120
King   What is the cause, Laertes,
That thy rebellion looks so giant-like?
Let him go, Gertrude: do not fear our person:
There's such divinity doth hedge[29] a king,
That treason can but peep to what it would,
Acts little of his will.[30] Tell me, Laertes,
Why thou art thus incens'd. Let him go, Gertrude.
Speak, man.
Laertes   Where is my father?
King   Dead.
Queen   But not by him.
King   Let him demand his fill.
Laertes   How came he dead? I'll not be juggled with.   130
To hell, allegiance! Vows, to the blackest devil!
Conscience and grace, to the profoundest pit!
I dare damnation. To this point I stand,
That both the worlds I give to negligence,[31]
Let come what comes; only I'll be reveng'd
Most throughly for my father.
King   Who shall stay[32] you?
Laertes   My will, not all the world:
And, for my means, I'll husband[33] them so well,
They shall go far with little.
King   Good Laertes,
If you desire to know the certainty   140

[27] hunting term referring to the hound following the scent in the opposite direction to his prey

[28] Laertes maintains that if he were calm he would not be his father's son, hence a bastard

[29] surround

[30] performs little that treason desires

[31] indifference

[32] prevent

[33] use economically

	Of your dear father's death, is't writ in your revenge,	
	That, swoopstake,[34] you will draw both friend and foe	[34]in a clean sweep
	Winner and loser?	
Laertes	None but his enemies.	
King	Will you know them then?	
Laertes	To his good friends thus wide I'll ope my arms;	
	And like the kind life-rendering pelican,[35]	[35]refers to the legendary belief that the pelican feeds her young with her own blood
	Repast[36] them with my blood.	
King	Why, now you speak	[36]feed
	Like a good child, and a true gentleman.	
	That I am guiltless of your father's death,	
	And am most sensibly in grief for it, *150*	
	It shall as level[37] to your judgment pierce	[37]plain
	As day does to your eye.	
Danes	*[within]* Let her come in.	
Laertes	How now! what noise is that?	

Re-enter Ophelia.

	O heat, dry up my brains! tears seven times salt,	
	Burn out the sense and virtue of mine eye!	
	By heaven, thy madness shall be paid by weight,	
	Till our scale turn the beam.[38] O rose of May!	[38]weigh down the bar of the balance
	Dear maid, kind sister, sweet Ophelia!	
	O heavens! is't possible a young maid's wits *160*	
	Should be as mortal as an old man's life?	
	Nature is fine in love, and where 'tis fine	
	It sends some precious instance[39] of itself	[39]example
	After the thing it loves.	
Ophelia	*[Sings]* They bore him barfac'd on the bier;	
	Hey non nonny, nonny, hey nonny;	
	And in his grave rain'd many a tear; –	
	Fare you well, my dove!	
Laertes	Hadst thou thy wits, and didst persuade revenge,	
	It could not move thus. *170*	
Ophelia	You must sing, 'A-down a-down, and you call him	
	a-down-a.' O how the wheel becomes it! It is the	
	false steward that stole his master's daughter.	
Laertes	This nothing's more than matter.	
Ophelia	There's rosemary, that's for remembrance; pray,	
	love, remember: and there is pansies, that's for	[40]yellow-flowered herb; symbol of flattery and deceit
	thoughts.	
Laertes	A document in madness, thoughts and	[41]wild plant, symbol of disloyalty
	remembrance fitted.	
Ophelia	There's fennel[40] for you, and columbines;[41] there's *180*	[42]yellow-flowered herb; symbol of repentance
	rue[42] for you; and here's some for me; we may call it	[43]rue was known as the herb of grace
	herb of grace[43] o' Sundays. O! you may wear your	
	rue with a difference. There's a daisy;[44] I would give	[44]symbol of faithlessness

[45] symbol of faithfulness

[46] charm

[47] head

[48] share

[49] indirect

[50] i.e. with guilt

[51] coat of arms
[52] ceremony

you some violets,[45] but they withered all when my
father died. They say he made a good end, –
[Sings] For bonny sweet Robin is all my joy.

Laertes Thought and affliction, passion, hell itself,
She turns to favour[46] and to prettiness.

Ophelia [Sings]   And will he not come again?
And will he not come again?   190
No, no, he is dead;
Go to thy death-bed,
He never will come again.
His beard was as white as snow
All flaxen was his poll;[47]
He is gone, he is gone,
And we cast away moan:
God ha'mercy on his soul!
And of all Christian souls! I pray God. God be wi' ye!
[Exit.

Laertes Do you see this, O God?   200

King Laertes, I must commune[48] with your grief,
Or you deny me right. Go but apart,
Make choice of whom your wisest friends you will,
And they shall hear and judge 'twixt you and me.
If by direct or by collateral[49] hand
They find us touch'd,[50] we will our kingdom give,
Our crown, our life, and all that we call ours,
To you in satisfaction; but if not,
Be you content to lend your patience to us,
And we shall jointly labour with your soul   210
To give it due content.

Laertes   Let this be so:
His means of death, his obscure funeral,
No trophy, sword, nor hatchment[51] o'er his bones,
No noble rite, nor formal ostentation,[52]
Cry to be heard, as 'twere from heaven to earth,
That I must call't in question.

King   So you shall;
And, where the offence is, let the great axe fall.
I pray you go with me.   [Exeunt.

Scene Analysis

In this scene we are presented with the consequences of the death of Polonius. From what the gentleman tells the queen, we learn that Ophelia is distracted by the death of her father:

> *"She is importunate, indeed distract:*
> *Her mood will needs be pitied."*

Ophelia's entrance gives a new dramatic impetus to the play. Her madness shocks and its stark reality counterpoints Hamlet's antic disposition. Ophelia is pathetic as she sings her sad song and the king realises *"this is the poison of deep grief"*. Claudius is apprehensive about the arrival of Laertes *"in secret come from France"*. His fears are confirmed by the report of the gentleman who tells that:

> *"...The rabble call him lord;*
> *And, as the world were now but to begin...*
> *They cry 'Choose we; Laertes shall be king!' "*

The gentle entrance of Ophelia contrasts with the rude entrance of her brother who confronts the king threateningly, demanding:

> *"...O thou vile king!*
> *Give me my father."*

The king acknowledges Laertes's right to be angry:

> *"Let him demand his fill"*

and tries to reason with him that he should not fight friend and foe alike. The irate Laertes is deeply moved at the sight of his sister:

> *"O heat, dry up my brains! tears seven times salt,*
> *Burn out the sense and virtue of mine eye!"*

Ophelia distributes flowers and the flowers which she offers have a special significance. She gives rosemary and pansies signifying her remembrance and love for Hamlet. But she also offers fennel and columbine symbolising flattery and lechery, and rue and daisies signifying repentance, faithlessness. There are flowers of spring and love and there are flowers of grief and sorrow; death has withered the violets. Laertes now has double cause to grieve as he watches his mad sister leave, singing her poignant song of death. Claudius quickly assures Laertes that he shares his grief. Laertes demands to know the reason for his father's obscure burial and the king promises:

> *"And we shall jointly labour with your soul*
> *To give it due content."*

Good night, ladies; good night, sweet ladies, good night, good night.
(Ophelia, Act 4, Scene V)

Scene VI

Another Room in the Same.
Enter Horatio and a Servant.

Horatio	What are they that would speak with me?
Servant	Sailors, sir: they say, they have letters for you.
Horatio	Let them come in.

[Exit Servant.

I do not know from what part of the world
I should be greeted, if not from Lord Hamlet.

Enter Sailors.

1st Sailor	God bless you, sir.	
Horatio	Let him bless thee too.	
2nd Sailor	He shall, sir, an't please Him. There's a letter for you, sir;	
	– it comes from the ambassador that was bound	
	for England; – if your name be Horatio, as I am	10
	let to know it is.	
Horatio	*[Reads] Horatio, when thou shalt have overlooked*	

this,
give these fellows some means¹ to the King: ¹ access
they have letters for him. Ere we were two days
old at sea, a pirate of very war-like appointment
gave us chase. Finding ourselves too slow of
sail, we put on a compelled valour, in the grapple²   ² grappling irons hold
I boarded them: on the instant they got   together two ships
clear of our ship, so I alone became their
prisoner. They have dealt with me like thieves   20
of mercy, but they knew what they did; I am to
do a good turn for them. Let the King have the
letters I have sent; and repair thou to me with as
much haste as thou wouldst fly death. I have
words to speak in thine ear will make thee
dumb; yet are they much too light
for the bore³ of the matter. These good   ³ i.e.bore of a gun, caliber;
fellows will bring thee where I am. Rosencrantz   the matter is so important
and Guildenstern hold their course for England: that Hamlet's words are
of them I have much to tell thee. Farewell.   30   inadequate
He that thou knowest thine,
HAMLET

Come, I will give you way for these your letters;
And do't the speedier, that you may direct me
To him from whom you brought them.   *[Exeunt.*

Scene Analysis

This brief scene serves to fill us in on Hamlet's whereabouts. From Hamlet's letter to Horatio we learn that Hamlet has fallen into the hands of pirates who in fact have dealt kindly with him. He asks Horatio to deliver letters to the king and then to come to him. *Scene VI* is dramatically important as it informs us that Hamlet will return to Denmark.

Scene VII

Another Room in the Same.
Enter King and Laertes.

King
Now must your conscience my acquittance seal,
And you must put me in your heart for friend,
Sith you have heard, and with a knowing ear,
That he, which hath your noble father slain,
Pursu'd my life.

Laertes
It well appears: but tell me
Why you proceeded not against these feats,
So crimeful and so capital in nature,
As by your safety, wisdom, all things else,
You mainly were stirr'd up.

King
O! for two special reasons;
Which may to you, perhaps, seem much unsinew'd,[1] *10*
But yet to me they are strong. The Queen, his mother,
Lives almost by his looks, and for myself, –
My virtue or my plague, be it either which, –
She's so conjunctive[2] to my life and soul,
That, as the star moves not but in his sphere,
I could not but by her. The other motive,
Why to a public count[3] I might not go,
Is the great love the general gender[4] bear him;
Who, dipping all his faults in their affection,
Would, like the spring that turneth wood to stone, *20*
Convert his gyves[5] to graces; so that my arrows,
Too slightly timber'd for so loud a wind,
Would have reverted to my bow again,
And not where I had aim'd them.

Laertes
And so have I a noble father lost;
A sister driven into desperate terms,
Whose worth, if praises may go back again,
Stood challenger on mount of all the age
For her perfections. But my revenge will come.

[1] weak

[2] closely united

[3] account, trial
[4] common people

[5] fetters, i.e. crimes

King	Break not your sleeps for that; you must not think	30
	That we are made of stuff so flat and dull	
	That we can let our beard be shook with danger	
	And think it pastime. You shortly shall hear more;	
	I lov'd your father, and we love ourself,	
	And that, I hope, will teach you to imagine, –	

Enter a Messenger.

	How now! what news?	
Messenger	Letters, my lord, from Hamlet:	
	This to your Majesty; this to the Queen.	
King	From Hamlet! who brought them?	
Messenger	Sailors, my lord, they say; I saw them not:	
	They were given me by Claudio, he receiv'd them	40
	Of him that brought them.	
King	Laertes, you shall hear them.	
	Leave us.	

[Exit Messenger.

[Reads] High and Mighty, you shall know I am set naked[6] *on your kingdom. To-morrow shall I beg leave to see your kingly eyes; when I shall, first asking your pardon thereunto, recount the occasions of my sudden and more strange return.*

> [6] destitute

HAMLET

	What should this mean? Are all the rest come back?	
	Or is it some abuse and no such thing?	
Laertes	Know you the hand?	50
King	'Tis Hamlet's character.[7] 'Naked,'	
	And in a postscript here, he says, 'alone.'	
	Can you advise me?	

> [7] handwriting

Laertes	I'm lost in it, my lord. But let him come:	
	It warms the very sickness in my heart,	
	That I shall live and tell him to his teeth,	
	'Thus diddest thou.'	
King	If it be so, Laertes,	
	As how should it be so? how otherwise?	
	Will you be rul'd by me?	
Laertes	Ay, my lord;	
	So you will not o'er-rule me to a peace.	60
King	To thine own peace. If he be now return'd,	
	As checking[8] at his voyage, and that he means	
	No more to undertake it, I will work him	
	To an exploit, now ripe in my device,	
	Under the which he shall not choose but fall;	
	And for his death no wind of blame shall breathe,	
	But even his mother shall uncharge the practice[9]	
	And call it accident.	

> [8] term of falconry – a falcon checks when it breaks off its flight

> [9] exonerate the plot

10instrument

11total accomplishments

12ribbon, decoration

13dark clothing

14incorporated
15sharing one body i.e. they
    seemed like half horse and
    half man
16imagining

17ornament

18fencers

Laertes		My lord, I will be rul'd;
	The rather, if you could devise it so	
	That I might be the organ.[10]	70
King		It falls right.
	You have been talked of since your travel much,	
	And that in Hamlet's hearing, for a quality	
	Wherein, they say, you shine; your sum of parts[11]	
	Did not together pluck such envy from him	
	As did that one; and that, in my regard,	
	Of the unworthiest siege.	
Laertes		What part is that, my lord?
King	A very riband[12] in the cap of youth,	
	Yet needful too; for youth no less becomes	
	The light and careless livery that it wears	
	Than settled age his sables and his weeds,[13]	80
	Importing health and graveness. Two months since	
	Here was a gentleman of Normandy:	
	I've seen myself, and serv'd against, the French,	
	And they can well on horseback; but this gallant	
	Had witchcraft in't, he grew unto his seat,	
	And to such wondrous doing brought his horse,	
	As he had been incorps'd[14] and demi-natur'd[15]	
	With the brave beast; so far he topp'd my thought,	
	That I, in forgery[16] of shapes and tricks,	
	Come short of what he did.	90
Laertes		A Norman was't?
King	A Norman.	
Laertes	Upon my life, Lamord.	
King		The very same.
Laertes	I know him well; he is the brooch[17] indeed	
	And gem of all the nation.	
King	He made confession of you,	
	And gave you such a masterly report	
	For art and exercise in your defence,	
	And for your rapier most especially,	
	That he cried out, 'twould be a sight indeed	
	If one could match you; the scrimers[18] of their	100
	nation,	
	He swore, had neither motion, guard, nor eye,	
	If you oppos'd them. Sir, this report of his	
	Did Hamlet so envenom with his envy	
	That he could nothing do, but wish and beg	
	Your sudden coming o'er, to play with him.	
	Now, out of this, –	
Laertes		What out of this, my lord?

King	Laertes, was your father dear to you?
	Or are you like the painting of a sorrow,
	A face without a heart?
Laertes	Why ask you this?
King	Not that I think you did not love your father, *110*
	But that I know love is begun by time,
	And that I see, in passages of proof,[19]
	Time qualifies the spark and fire of it.
	There lives within the very flame of love
	A kind of wick, or snuff, that will abate it,[20]
	And nothing is at a like goodness still,
	For goodness, growing to a plurisy,[21]
	Dies in his own too-much. That we would do,
	We should do when we would, for this 'would'
	changes,
	And hath abatements and delays as many *120*
	As there are tongues, are hands, are accidents;
	And then this 'should' is like a spendthrift[22] sigh,
	That hurts by easing. But, to the quick o' the ulcer
	Hamlet comes back; what would you undertake
	To show yourself your father's son in deed
	More than in words?
Laertes	To cut his throat i' the church.
King	No place, indeed, should murder sanctuarize;
	Revenge should have no bounds. But, good Laertes,
	Will you do this, keep close within your chamber.
	Hamlet, return'd, shall know you are come home; *130*
	We'll put on those shall praise your excellence,
	And set a double varnish on the fame
	The Frenchman gave you; bring you, in fine, together,
	And wager on your heads: he, being remiss,
	Most generous and free from all contriving,
	Will not peruse the foils; so that, with ease
	Or with a little shuffling, you may choose
	A sword unbated,[23] and, in a pass of practice[24]
	Requite him for your father.
Laertes	I will do't;
	And, for that purpose, I'll anoint my sword. *140*
	I bought an unction of a mountebank,[25]
	So mortal that but dip a knife in it,
	Where it draws blood no cataplasm[26] so rare,
	Collected from all simples[27] that have virtue
	Under the moon, can save the thing from death
	That is but scratch'd withal; I'll touch my point
	With this contagion, that, if I gall[28] him slightly,
	It may be death.

[19] incidents which prove

[20] a charred wick dims the flame of the candle

[21] excess; pleurisy, a lung disease, was attributed to too much of the humour of blood

[22] wasteful – because it was thought that sighing thinned the blood

[23] not blunted
[24] treacherous thrust

[25] one who sold medicines illegally

[26] poultice
[27] herbs

[28] hurt

King	Let's further think of this;
	Weigh what convenience both of time and means
	May fit us to our shape. If this should fail, *150*
	And that our drift look through our bad performance
	'Twere better not assay'd; therefore this project
	Should have a back or second, that might hold,
	If this should blast in proof.²⁹ Soft! let me see;
	We'll make a solemn wager on your cunnings:³⁰
	I ha't:
	When in your motion you are hot and dry, –
	As make your bouts more violent to that end, –
	And that he calls for drink, I'll have prepar'd him
	A chalice for the nonce,³¹ whereon but sipping, *160*
	If he by chance escape your venom'd stuck,
	Our purpose may hold there. But stay! what noise?

Enter Queen.

	How now, sweet Queen!
Queen	One woe doth tread upon another's heel,
	So fast they follow: your sister's drown'd, Laertes.
Laertes	Drown'd! O, where?
Queen	There is a willow grows aslant a brook,
	That shows his hoar³² leaves in the glassy stream;
	There with fantastic garlands did she come,
	Of crow-flowers, nettles, daisies, and long purples, *170*
	That liberal shepherds give a grosser name,
	But our cold maids do dead men's fingers call them:
	There, on the pendent boughs her coronet weeds
	Clambering to hang, an envious sliver broke,
	When down her weedy trophies and herself
	Fell in the weeping brook. Her clothes spread wide,
	And, mermaid-like, awhile they bore her up:
	Which time, she chanted snatches of old tunes,
	As one incapable³³ of her own distress,
	Or like a creature native³⁴ and indu'd³⁵ *180*
	Unto that element; but long it could not be
	Till that her garments, heavy with their drink,
	Pull'd the poor wretch from her melodious lay³⁶
	To muddy death.
Laertes	Alas! then, she is drown'd?
Queen	Drown'd, drowned.
Laertes	Too much of water hast thou, poor Ophelia,
	And therefore I forbid my tears; but yet
	It is our trick,³⁷ nature her custom holds,
	Let shame say what it will; when these are gone
	The woman will be out.³⁸ Adieu, my lord! *190*

Margin notes:

²⁹fail in the attempt – a cannon had to be tested in case it burst
³⁰skills

³¹occasion

³²silver-grey

³³unaware
³⁴belonging
³⁵endowed

³⁶song

³⁷habit
³⁸the womanly feeling will be gone; I will be a man again

> I have a speech of fire, that fain would blaze,
> But that this folly douts[39] it.   *[Exit.*   [39]extinguishes

King   Let's follow, Gertrude.
> How much I had to do to calm his rage!
> Now fear I this will give it start again;
> Therefore let's follow.   *[Exeunt.*

Scene Analysis

In this scene Claudius sets out to make peace with Laertes. He justifies his position to Laertes and is persuasive:

> *"Now must your conscience my acquittance seal*
> *And you must put me in your heart for friend".*

Their conversation is interrupted by a messenger bringing the letters from Hamlet informing the king of his unexpected return to Denmark alone. Claudius clearly states his intention of getting rid of Hamlet:

> *"...I will work him*
> *To an exploit, now ripe in my device,*
> *Under the which he shall not choose but fall"*

He contrives a plot which would make Hamlet's death appear above suspicion. He convinces Laertes that Hamlet envies him his excellent swordsmanship and so will agree to a fencing match in which Laertes is to kill Hamlet with an unbated sword. Laertes agrees to this and furthermore offers to poison the tip of the sword:

> *"...that, if I gall him slightly,*
> *It may be death."*

To make doubly sure of Hamlet's death, the king intends to have Hamlet's drink poisoned. This artful intrigue is offset by the pathetic account of Ophelia's death which is described sorrowfully and sensitively by Gertrude. The king, having succeeded in calming Laertes, now fears that his sister's death will stir him to anger again.

REVISION

> *"How all occasions do inform against me,*
> *And spur my dull revenge!"*   (Hamlet, Act 4, Scene IV)

The queen reports the death of Polonius to the king, who decides to send Hamlet to England accompanied by Rosencrantz and Guildenstern, who bear letters from Claudius demanding Hamlet's death. Laertes returns to Elsinore intending to avenge his father's death and is deeply grieved to find that Ophelia has become mad. Sailors bring letters from Hamlet to Horatio and the king announcing his return to Denmark. He escaped when the ship was attacked by pirates. Claudius deflects Laertes' anger and plots with him to kill Hamlet in a duelling match. Laertes will fight with an unbated, poison-tipped sword and as an extra precaution the king will poison Hamlet's drink. The queen relates the manner of Ophelia's death by drowning.

Points To Note

1. There is a sense of greater speed of action in the sequence of very short scenes in *Act 4.*

2. Hamlet submits to the king's plan to send him to England so he is not yet ready for action.

3. Hamlet's encounter with Fortinbras is extremely important as it provides him with a new incentive to action.

4. The lack of cause in Fortinbras' fight emphasises the very real cause for revenge which Hamlet has.

5. The obscure burial of Polonius makes us aware of the success of Claudius in covering up his death. Yet there is a feeling of discontent in Denmark *"the people muddied/Thick and unwholesome in their thoughts and whisper,/For good Polonius' death"*.

6. Laertes is now in the same position as Hamlet – if he does not avenge his father's death he is not a loyal son.

7. The alliance of Laertes with the king is a significant element in the plot as the king can now use Laertes to kill Hamlet.

Revision Assignment

Discuss the importance of *Act 4* in terms of plot and character motivation.

Act 5

Scene I

A Churchyard.
Enter two Clowns, with spades and mattock.

1st Clown   Is she to be buried in Christian burial, that wilfully seeks her own salvation?

2nd Clown   I tell thee, she is; and therefore make her grave straight: the crowner[1] hath sat on her, and finds it Christian burial.

1st Clown   How can that be, unless she drowned herself in her own defence?

2nd Clown   Why, 'tis found so.

1st Clown   It must be *se offendendo*;[2] it cannot be else. For here lies the point: if I drown myself wittingly it   *10* argues an act; and an act hath three branches; it is, to act, to do, and to perform: argal,[3] she drowned herself wittingly.

2nd Clown   Nay, but hear you, goodman delver, –

1st Clown   Give me leave. Here lies the water; good: here stands the man; good: if the man go to this water, and drown himself, it is, will he, nill he, he goes; mark you that? but if the water come to him, and drown him, he drowns not himself: argal, he that is not guilty of his own death shortens not his own life. *20*

2nd Clown   But is this law?

1st Clown   Ay, marry, is't; crowner's quest[4] law.

2nd Clown   Will you ha' the truth on't? If this had not been a gentlewoman she should have been buried out o' Christian burial.

1st Clown   Why, there thou sayest; and the more pity that great folk should have countenance[5] in this world to drown or hang themselves more than their even Christian.[6] Come, my spade. There is no ancient   *30* gentlemen but gardeners, ditchers, and grave-makers; they hold up Adam's profession.

2nd Clown   Was he a gentleman?

1st Clown   He was the first that ever bore arms.[7]

2nd Clown   Why, he had none.

1st Clown   What! art a heathen? How dost thou understand the Scripture? The Scripture says, Adam digged; could he dig without arms? I'll put another question to thee; if thou answerest me not to the purpose, confess thyself –

[1] coroner

[2] mistake for se defendo, the Latin legal term for self-defence

[3] mistake for ergo, Latin for therefore

[4] inquest

[5] permission

[6] fellow-Christian

[7] to have a coat of arms was the sign of a gentleman

2nd Clown	Go to.	40
1st Clown	What is he that builds stronger than either the mason, the shipwright, or the carpenter?	
2nd Clown	The gallows-maker; for that frame outlives a thou-sand tenants.	
1st Clown	I like thy wit well, in good faith; the gallows does well, but how does it well? it does well to those that do ill; now thou dost ill to say the gallows is built stronger than the church: argal, the gallows may do well to thee. To't again; come.	
2nd Clown	Who builds stronger than a mason, a shipwright, or a carpenter?	50
1st Clown	Ay, tell me that, and unyoke.[8]	
2nd Clown	Marry, now I can tell.	
1st Clown	To't.	
2nd Clown	Mass,[9] I cannot tell.	

Enter Hamlet and Horatio at a distance.

1st Clown	Cudgel thy brains no more about it, for your dull ass will not mend his pace with beating; and, when you are asked this question next, say, 'a grave-maker:' the houses that he makes last till doomsday. Go, get thee to Yaughan,[10] fetch me a stoup[11] of liquor.	60

[Exit 2nd Clown.

[1st Clown digs, and sings.]

> In youth, when I did love, did love,
> Methought it was very sweet,
> To contract, O! the time, for, ah! my behove,[12]
> O! methought there was nothing meet.[13]

Hamlet	Has this fellow no feeling of his business, that he sings at grave-making?	
Horatio	Custom hath made it in him a property of easiness.	
Hamlet	'Tis e'en so; the hand of little employment hath the daintier sense.[14]	
1st Clown	*[Sings]* But age, with his stealing steps,	70

> Hath claw'd me in his clutch,
> And hath shipped me intil the land,
> As if I had never been such.

[Throws up a skull.

Hamlet	That skull had a tongue in it, and could sing once; how the knave jowls[15] it to the ground, as if it were Cain's jaw-bone,[16] that did the first murder! This might be the pate of a politician,[17] which this ass now o'er-offices, one that would circumvent[18] God, might it not?	
Horatio	It might, my lord.	80

[8] finish work

[9] by the Mass!

[10] probably the name of the owner of the inn where the grave-digger is going to get the drink

[11] tankard

[12] benefit

[13] fit

[14] is more sensitive to

[15] knocks to the ground

[16] Cain was supposed to have used the jaw-bone of an ass to murder Abel

[17] i.e. a clever schemer

[18] get round

Hamlet	Or a courtier, which could say, 'Good morrow, sweet lord! How dost thou, good lord?' This might be my Lord Such-a-one, that praised my Lord Such-a-one's horse, when he meant to beg it, might it not?
Horatio	Ay, my lord.
Hamlet	Why, e'en so, and now my Lady Worm's; chapless,[19] and knocked about the mazzard[20] with a sexton's spade. Here's fine revolution, an we had the trick to see't. Did these bones cost no more the breeding but to play at loggats[21] with 'em? mine ache to think on't. *90*

[19]without the lower jaw
[20]head
[21]a game in which small pieces of wood were thrown at a stake

1st Clown	*[Sings]* A pick-axe, and a spade, a spade,
	            For and a shrouding sheet;
	        O! a pit of clay for to be made
	            For such a guest is meet.
	
	                    [Throws up another skull.

Hamlet	There's another; why may not that be the skull of a lawyer? Where be his quiddities[22] now, his quillets,[23] his cases, his tenures,[24] and his tricks? Why does he suffer this rude knave to knock him about the sconce[25] with a dirty shovel, and will not tell him *100* of his action of battery?[26] Hum! This fellow might be in's time a great buyer of land, with his statutes, his recognizances,[27] his fines,[28] his double vouchers,[29] his recoveries; is this the fine[30] of his fines, and the recovery of his recoveries, to have his fine pate full of fine dirt? Will his vouchers vouch him no more of his purchases, and double ones too, than the length and breadth of a pair of indentures?[31] The very conveyance of his lands will hardly lie in this box, and must the inheritor himself have no more, ha? *110*

[22]from the Latin quidditas; here used to mean subtle arguments
[23]fine distinctions
[24]legal term for holding land
[25]head
[26]assault
[27]bonds of security
[28]documents for transferring an estate from one owner to another
[29]guarantors
[30]end
[31]duplicate legal documents

Horatio	Not a jot more, my lord.
Hamlet	Is not parchment made of sheep-skins?
Horatio	Ay, my lord, and of calf-skins too.
Hamlet	They are sheep and calves which seek out assurance in that. I will speak to this fellow. Whose grave's this, sir?
lst Clown	Mine, sir, *[Sings]* O! a pit of clay for to be made For such a guest is meet.
Hamlet	I think it be thine, indeed; for thou liest in't. *120*
1st Clown	You lie out on't, sir, and therefore it is not yours; for my part, I do not lie in't, and yet it is mine.
Hamlet	Thou dost lie in't, to be in't and say it is thine: 'tis for the dead, not for the quick;[32] therefore thou liest.
1st Clown	'Tis a quick lie, sir; 'twill away again, from me to you.
Hamlet	What man dost thou dig it for?

[32]living

1st Clown	For no man, sir.
Hamlet	What woman, then?
1st Clown	For none, neither.
Hamlet	Who is to be buried in't? 130
1st Clown	One that was a woman, sir; but, rest her soul, she's dead.
Hamlet	How absolute the knave is! We must speak by the card, or equivocation[33] will undo us. By the Lord, Horatio, these three years I have taken note of it; the age is grown so picked that the toe of the peasant comes so near the heel of the courtier, he galls his kibe.[34] How long hast thou been a grave-maker?
1st Clown	Of all the days i' the year, I came to't that day that our last King Hamlet overcame Fortinbras. 140
Hamlet	How long is that since?
1st Clown	Cannot you tell that? Every fool can tell that; it was the very day that young Hamlet was born; he that is mad, and sent into England.
Hamlet	Ay, marry; why was he sent into England?
1st Clown	Why, because he was mad: he shall recover his wits there; or, if he do not, 'tis no great matter there.
Hamlet	Why?
1st Clown	'Twill not be seen in him there; there the men are as mad as he. 150
Hamlet	How came he mad?
1st Clown	Very strangely, they say.
Hamlet	How strangely?
Ist Clown	Faith, e'en with losing his wits.
Hamlet	Upon what ground?
1st Clown	Why, here in Denmark; I have been sexton here, man and boy, thirty years.
Hamlet	How long will a man lie i' the earth ere he rot?
1st Clown	Faith, if he be not rotten before he die,–as we have many pocky[35] corses now-a-days, that will 160 scarce hold the laying in, – he will last you some eight year or nine year; a tanner will last you nine year.
Hamlet	Why he more than another?
1st Clown	Why, sir, his hide is so tanned with his trade that he will keep out water a great while, and your water is a sore decayer of your whoreson dead body. Here's a skull now; this skull hath lain you i' the earth three-and-twenty years.
Hamlet	Whose was it?
1st Clown	A whoreson mad fellow's it was: whose do you 170 think it was?
Hamlet	Nay, I know not.

[33]ambiguous meaning

[34]sore on heel

[35]infected with pox; rotten

1st Clown	A pestilence on him for a mad rogue! a' poured a flagon of Rhenish on my head once. This same skull, sir, was Yorick's skull, the king's jester.
Hamlet	This!
1st Clown	E'en that.
Hamlet	Let me see. – *[Takes the skull]* – Alas! poor Yorick. I knew him, Horatio; a fellow of infinite jest, of most excellent fancy; he hath borne me on his 180 back a thousand times; and now, how abhorred in my imagination it is! My gorge[36] rises at it. Here hung those lips that I have kissed I know not how oft. Where be your gibes now, your gambols, your songs, your flashes of merriment, that were wont to set the table on a roar? Not one now, to mock your own grinning – quite chapfallen?[37] Now get you to my lady's chamber, and tell her, let her paint an inch thick, to this favour she must come; make her laugh at that. Prithee, Horatio, tell me one thing. 190
Horatio	What's that, my lord?
Hamlet	Dost thou think Alexander[38] looked o' this fashion i' the earth?
Horatio	E'en so.
Hamlet	And smelt so? pah!
	[Puts down the skull.
Horatio	E'en so, my lord.
Hamlet	To what base uses we may return, Horatio! Why may not imagination trace the noble dust of Alexander, till he find it stopping a bung-hole?[39]
Horatio	'Twere to consider too curiously, to consider so. 200
Hamlet	No, faith, not a jot; but to follow him thither with modesty enough, and likelihood to lead it; as thus: Alexander died, Alexander was buried, Alexander returneth into dust; the dust is earth; of earth we make loam,[40] and why of that loam, whereto he was converted, might they not stop a beer-barrel?

    Imperious Caesar, dead and turn'd to clay,
    Might stop a hole to keep the wind away:
    O! that that earth, which kept the world in awe,
    Should patch a wall to expel the winter's flaw. 210
But soft! but soft! aside: here comes the King.

Enter Priests, &c., in procession: the Corpse of Ophelia,
Laertes and Mourners following; King, Queen, their Trains, &c.

    The Queen, the courtiers: who is that they follow?
    And with such maimed[41] rites? This doth betoken
    The corse they follow did with desperate hand

[36] throat; his stomach turns

[37] jaw falling, crestfallen

[38] Alexander the Great, so called because he conquered the world

[39] hole in a beer barrel

[40] mixture of clay and sand used for plastering

[41] incomplete

42lie in hiding

43authority

44garlands

Fordo its own life; 'twas of some estate.
Couch42 we awhile, and mark.

[Retiring with Horatio.

Laertes What ceremony else?
Hamlet   That is Laertes.
A very noble youth: mark.
Laertes What ceremony else?
First Priest Her obsequies have been as far enlarg'd   220
As we have warrantise:43 her death was doubtful,
And, but that great command o'ersways the order,
She should in ground unsanctified have lodg'd
Till the last trumpet; for charitable prayers,
Shards, flints, and pebbles should be thrown on her;
Yet here she is allow'd her virgin crants,44
Her maiden strewments, and the bringing home
Of bell and burial.
Laertes Must there no more be done?
First Priest   No more be done:
We should profane the service of the dead,   230
To sing a requiem, and such rest to her
As to peace-parted souls.
Laertes   Lay her i' the earth;
And from her fair and unpolluted flesh
May violets spring! I tell thee, churlish priest,
A ministering angel shall my sister be,
When thou liest howling.
Hamlet   What! the fair Ophelia?
Queen Sweets to the sweet: farewell!

[Scattering flowers.

I hop'd thou shouldst have been my Hamlet's wife;
I thought thy bride-bed to have deck'd, sweet maid,
And not have strew'd thy grave.   240
Laertes   O! treble woe
Fall ten times treble on that cursed head
Whose wicked deed thy most ingenious sense
Depriv'd thee of. Hold off the earth awhile.
Till I have caught her once more in mine arms.

[Leaps into the grave.

Now pile your dust upon the quick and dead,
Till of this flat a mountain you have made,
To o'er-top old Pelion45 or the skyish head
Of blue Olympus.46
Hamlet [Advancing]   What is he whose grief
Bears such an emphasis, whose phrase of sorrow
Conjures the wandering stars, and makes them   250
   stand
Like wonder-wounded hearers? This is I,
Hamlet the Dane.

[Leaps into the grave.

45mountain in Thessaly,
   Greece
46mountain in Thessaly
   which was the abode
   of the gods. In Greek
   Mythology, two giants
   piled Pelion on Ossa (see
   note 50) and Ossa on
   Mount Olympus to try to
   reach heaven

Laertes	The devil take thy soul!
	[Grapples with him.
Hamlet	Thou pray'st not well.
	I prithee, take thy fingers from my throat;
	For though I am not splenetive[47] and rash
	Yet have I in me something dangerous,
	Which let thy wisdom fear. Hold off thy hand!
King	Pluck them asunder.
Queen	Hamlet! Hamlet!
All	Gentlemen, —
Horatio	Good my lord, be quiet.

[47]quick to anger

[The Attendants part them, and they come out of the grave.

Hamlet	Why, I will fight with him upon this theme	260
	Until my eyelids will no longer wag.	
Queen	O my son, what theme?	
Hamlet	I lov'd Ophelia: forty thousand brothers	
	Could not, with all their quantity of love,	
	Make up my sum. What wilt thou do for her?	
King	O! he is mad, Laertes.	
Queen	For love of God, forbear him.	
Hamlet	'Swounds, show me what thou'lt do:	
	Woo't[48] weep, woo't fight, woo't fast, woo't tear	
	thyself?	
	Woo't drink up eisel,[49] eat a crocodile?	270
	I'll do't. Dost thou come here to whine?	
	To outface me with leaping in her grave?	
	Be buried quick with her, and so will I:	
	And, if thou prate of mountains, let them throw	
	Millions of acres on us, till our ground,	
	Singeing his pate against the burning zone,	
	Make Ossa[50] like a wart! Nay, an thou'lt mouth,	
	I'll rant as well as thou.	
Queen	This is mere madness:	
	And thus a while the fit will work on him;	
	Anon, as patient as the female dove,	280
	When that her golden couplets[51] are disclos'd,	
	His silence will sit drooping.	
Hamlet	Hear you, sir;	
	What is the reason that you use me thus?	
	I lov'd you ever: but it is no matter;	
	Let Hercules himself do what he may,	
	The cat will mew and dog will have his day. [Exit.	
King	I pray you, good Horatio, wait upon him.	
	[Exit Horatio.	
	[To Laertes] Strengthen your patience in our last	
	night's speech;	

[48]wilt thou

[49]vinegar

[50]mountain in Thessaly

[51]the dove lays eggs which produce golden furred young

We'll put the matter to the present push.
Good Gertrude, set some watch over your son.   *290*
This grave shall have a living[52] monument:
An hour of quiet shortly shall we see;
Till then, in patience our proceeding be.   *[Exeunt.*

[52]enduring

Scene Analysis

The tragic implications of the scene in the graveyard are relieved for a time by the two clowns whose jokes and antics provide a touch of light relief. They discuss Ophelia's death with absolute indifference. The first clown cannot understand how Ophelia can be given a Christian burial if she drowned herself. The first clown is wittier than the second. He has some knowledge of the law but gets the terminology wrong, thus striking a humorous note. He likes to talk in riddles:

> *"What is he that builds stronger than either the mason, the shipwright, or the carpenter?"*

As Hamlet approaches he hears the first grave-digger singing and is shocked:

> *"Has this fellow no feeling of his business, that he sings at grave-making?"*

One that was a woman, sir; but, rest her soul, she's dead.   *(1st Clown, Act 5, Scene I)*

He is also shocked when the grave-digger unceremoniously throws up a skull *"to play at loggats"*.

Hamlet is forcefully struck by the realisation that the importance of one's role in life is reduced to nothingness in death. The first clown quips with Hamlet about the grave and again we see Hamlet's wit in his punning with the grave-digger:

> *"Thou dost lie in 't, to be in 't and say it is thine: 'tis for the dead, not for the quick; therefore thou liest."*

The first clown enjoys playing on words. He is not digging the grave for a man or a woman but *"One that was a woman"*. Not realising to whom he is speaking, the clown talks about Hamlet *"he that is mad, and sent into England"*. The grave-digger throws up the skull of Yorick, the court jester who has been dead for twenty-three years. Hamlet is moved by the memory of the jester who *"hath borne me on his back a thousand times"* and concludes:

> *"To what base uses we may return, Horatio?"*

Hamlet's thoughts on death are interrupted by the arrival of the funeral party. Hamlet is shocked and grieved when he realises that the grave has in fact been dug for *"the fair Ophelia"*. Because Ophelia's manner of death was *"doubtful"*, the funeral rites are minimal. The queen scatters flowers over Ophelia and reinforces the tragedy of Ophelia's death with her words:

> *"I hop'd thou shouldst have been my Hamlet's wife;*
> *I thought thy bride-bed to have deck'd, sweet maid,*
> *And not have strew'd thy grave."*

Laertes, beside himself with grief, leaps into the grave to hold Ophelia's body in his arms again. This jolts Hamlet into confronting Laertes and declaring:

> *"I lov'd Ophelia: forty thousand brothers*
> *Could not, with all their quantity of love,*
> *Make up my sum."*

Neither the king nor queen recognise that Hamlet's grief is genuine. The king intervenes:

> *"O! he is mad, Laertes."*

The queen dismisses Hamlet's words as *"mere madness"*. Hamlet is puzzled at Laertes' aggressiveness:

> *"What is the reason that you use me thus?*
> *I lov'd you ever."*

The king asks Laertes to be patient yet awhile.

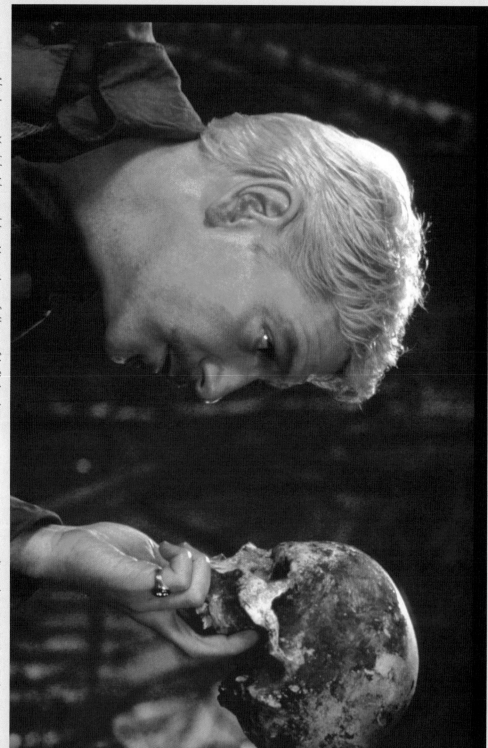

Alas! poor Yorick. I knew him, Horatio; a fellow of infinite jest

(Hamlet, Act 5, Scene I)

Scene II

A Hall in the Castle.
Enter Hamlet and Horatio.

Hamlet	So much for this, sir: now shall you see the other;
	You do remember all the circumstance?
Horatio	Remember it, my lord?
Hamlet	Sir, in my heart there was a kind of fighting
	That would not let me sleep; methought I lay
	Worse than the mutines in the bilboes.[1] Rashly,
	And prais'd be rashness for it, let us know,
	Our indiscretion sometimes serves us well
	When our deep plots do pall;[2] and that should teach us
	There's a divinity that shapes our ends, 10
	Rough-hew them how we will.
Horatio	That is most certain.
Hamlet	Up from my cabin,
	My sea-gown scarf'd about me, in the dark
	Grop'd I to find out them, had my desire,
	Finger'd their packet, and, in fine, withdrew
	To mine own room again; making so bold –
	My fears forgetting manners, to unseal
	Their grand commission; where I found, Horatio,
	O royal knavery! an exact command,
	Larded[3] with many several sorts of reasons 20
	Importing Denmark's health, and England's too,
	With, ho! such bugs and goblins in my life,[4]
	That, on the supervise, no leisure bated,[5]
	No, not to stay the grinding of the axe,
	My head should be struck off.
Horatio	Is't possible?
Hamlet	Here's the commission: read it at more leisure.
	But wilt thou hear me how I did proceed?
Horatio	I beseech you.
Hamlet	Being thus benetted round with villanies,–
	Ere I could make a prologue to my brains 30
	They had begun the play. I sat me down,
	Devis'd a new commission, wrote it fair;
	I once did hold it, as our statists[6] do,
	A baseness to write fair, and labour'd much
	How to forget that learning; but, sir, now
	It did me yeoman's service.[7] Wilt thou know
	The effect of what I wrote?
Horatio	Ay, good my lord.

[1] mutineers in irons

[2] fail

[3] enriched

[4] such bugbears and imaginary terrors in my being allowed to live

[5] on reading it, without wasting time

[6] statesmen

[7] faithful service, a yeoman was a royal servant or a small freeholder, and so was respected

[8] like a comma, linking their
friendship
[9] as clauses of great
importance; also a pun
on asses in which case 'of
great charge' = with heavy
burdens
[10] time for confession

[11] in control

[12] signed it
[13] sealed it

Hamlet   An earnest conjuration from the King,
As England was his faithful tributary,
As love between them like the palm should flourish, *40*
As peace should still her wheaten garland wear,
And stand a comma 'tween their amities,[8]
And many such-like 'As'es of great charge,[9]
That, on the view and knowing of these contents,
Without debatement further, more or less,
He should the bearers put to sudden death,
Not shriving-time[10] allow'd.

Horatio   How was this seal'd?

Hamlet   Why, even in that was heaven ordinant.[11]
I had my father's signet in my purse,
Which was the model of that Danish seal;   *50*
Folded the writ up in form of the other,
Subscrib'd[12] it, gave't the impression,[13] plac'd it
   safely,
The changeling never known. Now, the next day
Was our sea-fight, and what to this was sequent
Thou know'st already.

Horatio   So Guildenstern and Rosencrantz go to't.

Hamlet   Why, man, they did make love to this employment;
They are not near my conscience; their defeat
Does by their own insinuation grow.
'Tis dangerous when the baser nature comes   *60*
Between the pass and fell-incensed points
Of mighty opposites.

Horatio   Why, what a king is this!

Hamlet   Does it not, thinks't thee, stand me now upon –
He that hath kill'd my king and whor'd my mother,
Popp'd in between the election and my hopes,
Thrown out his angle for my proper life,
And with such cozenage[14] – is't not perfect
   conscience
To quit him with this arm? And is't not to be damn'd
To let this canker of our nature come
In further evil?   *70*

Horatio   It must be shortly known to him from England
What is the issue of the business there.

Hamlet   It will be short: the interim is mine;
And a man's life's no more than to say 'One.'[15]
But I am very sorry, good Horatio,
That to Laertes I forgot myself;
For, by the image of my cause, I see
The portraiture of his: I'll count his favours:
But, sure, the bravery[16] of his grief did put me
Into a towering passion.   *80*

[14] trickery

[15] what is said when the first
hit is made in a duel

[16] bravado

Horatio	Peace! who comes here?

Enter Osric.

Osric   Your lordship is right welcome back to Denmark.

Hamlet   I humbly thank you, sir. *[Aside to Horatio.]* Dost
know this water-fly?

Horatio   *[Aside to Hamlet]* No, my good lord.

Hamlet   *[Aside to Horatio]* Thy state is the more gracious;
for 'tis a vice to know him. He hath much land, and
fertile: let a beast be lord of beasts, and his crib[17]
shall stand at the king's mess:[18] 'Tis a chough;[19] but
as I say, spacious in the possession of dirt.   90

Osric   Sweet lord, if your lordship were at leisure, I should
impart a thing to you from his Majesty.

Hamlet   I will receive it, sir, with all diligence of spirit. Your
bonnet to his right use; 'tis for the head.

Osric   I thank your lordship, 'tis very hot.

Hamlet   No, believe me, 'tis very cold; the wind is northerly.

Osric   It is indifferent cold, my lord, indeed.

Hamlet   But yet, methinks, it is very sultry and hot for my
complexion.[20]

Osric   Exceedingly, my lord; it is very sultry, as 'twere, I   100
cannot tell how. But, my lord, his Majesty bade me
signify to you that he has laid a great wager on your
head. Sir, this is the matter, –

Hamlet   I beseech you, remember –

[Hamlet moves him to put on his hat.

Osric   Nay, good my lord; for mine ease, in good faith. Sir,
here is newly come to court Laertes; believe me, an
absolute gentleman, full of most excellent differ-
ences,[21] of very soft society[22] and great showing;
indeed, to speak feelingly of him, he is the card or
calendar[23] of gentry, for you shall find in him the   110
continent[24] of what part a gentleman would see.

Hamlet   Sir, his definement suffers no perdition[25] in you;
though, I know, to divide him inventorially,[26] would
dizzy the arithmetic of memory, and yet but yaw[27]
neither, in respect of his quick sail. But, in the verity
of extolment, I take him to be a soul of great
article;[28] and his infusion[29] of such dearth[30] and
rareness, as, to make true diction of him,[31] his sem-
blable is his mirror;[32] and who else would trace him,
his umbrage,[33] nothing more.   120

Osric   Your lordship speaks most infallibly of him.

Hamlet   The concernancy,[34] sir? Why do we wrap the gentleman in our more rawer breath?

Osric   Sir?

[17]feeding trough
[18]table
[19]jackdaw

[20]constitution

[21]distinctions
[22]refined manners
[23]model
[24]embodiment
[25]his definition suffers no loss
[26]to make a detailed list of his qualities
[27]roll from side to side

[28]importance
[29]natural endowment
[30]value
[31]to give a true description of him
[32]his only likeness is his own reflection in the mirror
[33]shadow
[34]relevance

35 Horatio is impatient
because Osric does not
understand Hamlet's
meaning

Horatio	Is't not possible to understand in another tongue?[35] You will do't, sir, really.
Hamlet	What imports the nomination of this gentleman?
Osric	Of Laertes?
Horatio	His purse is empty already; all's golden words are spent.	130
Hamlet	Of him, sir.
Osric	I know you are not ignorant –
Hamlet	I would you did, sir; in faith, if you did, it would not much approve me. Well, sir.
Osric	You are not ignorant of what excellence Laertes is –
Hamlet	I dare not confess that, lest I should compare with him in excellence; but, to know a man well, were to know himself.
Osric	I mean, sir, for his weapon; but in the imputation laid on him by them, in his meed[36] he's unfellowed.	140
Hamlet	What's his weapon?
Osric	Rapier and dagger.
Hamlet	That's two of his weapons; but, well.
Osric	The King, sir, hath wagered with him six Barbary[37] horses; against the which he has imponed,[38] as I take it, six French rapiers and poniards,[39] with their assigns[40], as girdle,[41] hangers,[42] and so: three of the carriages,[43] in faith, are very dear to fancy,[44] very responsive to the hilts,[45] most delicate carriages, and of very liberal conceit.[46]	150
Hamlet	What call you the carriages?
Horatio	I knew you must be edified by the margent,[47] ere you had done.
Osric	The carriages, sir, are the hangers.
Hamlet	The phrase would be more german[48] to the matter, if we could carry cannon by our sides; I would it might be hangers till then. But, on; six Barbary horses against six French swords, their assigns, and three liberal-conceited carriages; that's the French bet against the Danish. Why is this 'imponed,' as you call it?	160
Osric	The King, sir, hath laid, that in a dozen passes between yourself and him, he shall not exceed you three hits; he hath laid on twelve for nine, and it would come to immediate trial, if your lordship would vouchsafe the answer.
Hamlet	How if I answer no?
Osric	I mean, my lord, the opposition of your person in trial.
Hamlet	Sir, I will walk here in the hall; if it please his Majesty,	170

36 merit

37 from the Barbary states of
North Africa
38 pledged
39 small daggers
40 fittings
41 belt
42 straps
43 as Hamlet implies, this is
simply an affected word
for hangers
44 imaginatively designed
45 corresponding (in design)
to the hilts.
46 very elaborate design
47 marginal, i.e. an
explanatory comment
48 appropriate

	'tis the breathing time of day with me; let the foils be brought, the gentleman willing, and the King hold his purpose, I will win for him an I can; if not, I will gain nothing but my shame and the odd hits.
Osric	Shall I re-deliver you so?
Hamlet	To this effect, sir; after what flourish your nature will.
Osric	I commend my duty to your lordship.
Hamlet	Yours, yours. [Exit Osric.] He does well to commend it himself; there are no tongues else for's turn.
Horatio	This lapwing runs away with the shell on his 180 head.[49]
Hamlet	He did comply with his dug[50] before he sucked it. Thus has he, and many more of the same bevy,[51] that I know the drossy[52] age dotes on, only got the tune of the time and outward habit of encounter, a kind of yesty[53] collection which carries them through and through the most fond and winnowed[54] opinions; and do but blow them to their trial, the bubbles are out.

Enter a Lord.

Lord	My lord, his Majesty commended him to you by young Osric, who brings back to him, that you 190 attend him in the hall; he sends to know if your pleasure hold to play with Laertes, or that you will take longer time.
Hamlet	I am constant to my purposes; they follow the King's pleasure: if his fitness speaks,[55] mine is ready; now, or whensoever, provided I be so able as now.
Lord	The King, and Queen, and all are coming down.
Hamlet	In happy time.[56]
Lord	The Queen desires you to use some gentle entertainment[57] to Laertes before you fall to play. 200
Hamlet	She well instructs me. [Exit Lord.
Horatio	You will lose this wager, my lord.
Hamlet	I do not think so; since he went into France, I have been in continual practice; I shall win at the odds. But thou wouldst not think how ill all's here about my heart; but it is no matter.
Horatio	Nay, good my lord,–
Hamlet	It is but foolery; but it is such a kind of gain-giving[58] as would perhaps trouble a woman.
Horatio	If your mind dislike anything, obey it; I will forestal210 their repair[59] hither, and say you are not fit.
Hamlet	Not a whit, we defy augury;[60] there's a special providence in the fall of a sparrow.[61] If it be now, 'tis not to come; if it be not to come, it will be now; if it be

[49] newly hatched; implies that Osric is silly and precocious
[50] paid compliments to his mother's breast; implies that Osric is ridiculously flattering
[51] company; a flock of birds
[52] worthless
[53] frothy, i.e. superficial
[54] well-sifted, selected

[55] if he says he is ready

[56] at an opportune time

[57] act courteously

[58] misgiving
[59] coming
[60] omens
[61] ref. to Ch. 12 St. Matthew "Are not two sparrows sold for a farthing? And one of them shall not fall on the ground without your Father knowing".

not now, yet it will come: the readiness is all. Since
no man has aught of what he leaves, what is't to
leave betimes?[62] Let be.

Enter King, Queen, Laertes, Lords, Osric,
and Attendants with foils, &c.

King	Come, Hamlet, come, and take this hand from me.
	[The King puts the hand of Laertes into that of Hamlet.
Hamlet	Give me your pardon, sir; I've done you wrong;
	But pardon't, as you are a gentleman. 220
	This presence knows,
	And you must needs have heard how I am punish'd
	With sore distraction. What I have done,
	That might your nature, honour and exception
	Roughly awake, I here proclaim was madness.
	Was't Hamlet wrong'd Laertes? Never Hamlet:
	If Hamlet from himself be ta'en away,
	And when he's not himself does wrong Laertes,
	Then Hamlet does it not; Hamlet denies it.
	Who does it then? His madness. If't be so, 230
	Hamlet is of the faction that is wrong'd;
	His madness is poor Hamlet's enemy.
	Sir, in this audience,
	Let my disclaiming from a purpos'd evil
	Free me so far in your most generous thoughts,
	That I have shot mine arrow o'er the house,
	And hurt my brother.

63in my natural feelings, i.e.
on a personal level

Laertes	I am satisfied in nature,[63]
	Whose motive, in this case, should stir me most
	To my revenge; but in my terms of honour
	I stand aloof, and will no reconcilement, 240
	Till by some elder masters, of known honour,
	I have a voice and precedent of peace,

64unstained

	To keep my name ungor'd.[64] But till that time,
	I do receive your offer'd love like love,
	And will not wrong it.
Hamlet	I embrace it freely;
	And will this brother's wager frankly play.
	Give us the foils. Come on.
Laertes	Come, one for me.
Hamlet	I'll be your foil, Laertes; in mine ignorance
	Your skill shall, like a star i' the darkest night,

65contrast brilliantly

	Stick fiery[65] off indeed. 250
Laertes	You mock me, sir.
Hamlet	No, by this hand.
King	Give them the foils, young Osric. Cousin Hamlet,
	You know the wager?

Hamlet	Very well, my lord;
	Your Grace hath laid the odds o' the weaker side.
King	I do not fear it; I have seen you both;
	But since he is better'd, we have therefore odds.
Laertes	This is too heavy; let me see another.
Hamlet	This likes me well. These foils have all a length?
Osric	Ay, my good lord.

[They prepare to play.

King   Set me the stoups of wine upon that table.   260
         If Hamlet gives the first or second hit,
         Or quit in answer of the third exchange,
         Let all the battlements their ordnance fire;
         The King shall drink to Hamlet's better breath;
         And in the cup an union[66] shall he throw,
         Richer than that which four successive kings
         In Denmark's crown have worn. Give me the cups;
         And let the kettle[67] to the trumpet speak,
         The trumpet to the cannoneer without,
         The cannons to the heavens, the heavens to earth, 270
         'Now the King drinks to Hamlet!' Come, begin;
         And you, the judges, bear a wary eye.

[66]pearl; it was a custom for the king to drop a jewel into a cup as a present for a subject who was invited to drink from this cup
[67]kettle drum

| Hamlet | Come on, sir. |
| Laertes | Come. my lord. |

[They play.

Hamlet	One.
Laertes	No.
Hamlet	Judgment.
Osric	A hit, a very palpable hit.
Laertes	Well; again.
King	Stay; give me drink. Hamlet, this pearl[68] is thine;
	Here's to thy health. Give him the cup.

[Trumpets sound; and cannon shot off within.

[68]the king is complimenting Hamlet by passing him the cup into which he has dropped the pearl

Hamlet	I'll play this bout first; set it by awhile.
	Come. – *[They play.]* Another hit; what say you?
Laertes	A touch, a touch, I do confess.
King	Our son shall win. 280
Queen	He's fat,[69] and scant of breath.
	Here, Hamlet, take my napkin,[70] rub thy brows;
	The Queen carouses to thy fortune, Hamlet.

[69]i.e. out of condition
[70]handkerchief

Hamlet	Good madam!
King	Gertrude, do not drink.
Queen	I will, my lord; I pray you, pardon me.
King	*[Aside]* It is the poison'd cup! it is too late.
Hamlet	I dare not drink yet, madam; by and by.
Queen	Come, let me wipe thy face.
Laertes	My lord, I'll hit him now.
King	I do not think't.

Laertes	[Aside] And yet 'tis almost 'gainst my conscience.
Hamlet	Come, for the third, Laertes. You but dally; 290
	I pray you, pass with your best violence.
	I am afeard you make a wanton[71] of me.
Laertes	Say you so? come on. [They play.
Osric	Nothing, neither way.
Laertes	Have at you now.

[Laertes wounds Hamlet, then in
scuffling, they change rapiers, and
Hamlet wounds Laertes.

King	Part them! they are incens'd.
Hamlet	Nay, come, again.

[The Queen falls.

Osric	Look to the Queen there, ho!
Horatio	They bleed on both sides. How is it, my lord?
Osric	How is it, Laertes?
Laertes	Why, as a woodcock to mine own springe,[72] Osric;
	I am justly kill'd with mine treachery. 300
Hamlet	How does the Queen?
King	She swounds[73] to see them bleed.
Queen	No, no, the drink, the drink, – O my dear Hamlet!
	The drink, the drink; I am poison'd. [Dies.
Hamlet	O villany! Ho! let the door be lock'd:
	Treachery! seek it out. [Laertes falls.
Laertes	It is here, Hamlet. Hamlet, thou art slain;
	No medicine in the world can do thee good;
	In thee there is not half an hour of life;
	The treacherous instrument is in thy hand,
	Unbated and envenom'd. The foul practice 310
	Hath turn'd itself on me; lo! here I lie,
	Never to rise again. Thy mother's poison'd.
	I can no more. The King, the King's to blame.
Hamlet	The point envonom'd too! –
	Then, venom, to thy work. [Stabs the King.
All	Treason! treason!
King	O! yet defend me, friends; I am but hurt.
Hamlet	Here, thou incestuous, murderous, damned Dane,
	Drink off this potion; – is thy union[74] here?
	Follow my mother. 320

[King dies.

Laertes	He is justly serv'd;
	It is a poison temper'd[75] by himself.
	Exchange forgiveness with me, noble Hamlet:
	Mine and my father's death come not upon thee,
	Nor thine on me! [Dies.
Hamlet	Heaven make thee free of it! I follow thee.
	I am dead, Horatio. Wretched Queen, adieu!

Margin notes:

[71] spoilt child; Hamlet realises that Laertes is not fighting at his best

[72] snare; woodcocks were sometimes used to decoy birds to a trap but they often went too near the trap and so were themselves ensnared

[73] swoons

[74] a reference to the pearl, but also refers to the union in death of Claudius and Gertrude

[75] mixed

You that look pale and tremble at this chance,
That are but mutes or audience to this act,
Had I but time, – as this fell sergeant, Death,
Is strict in his arrest, – O! I could tell you –   330
But let it be. Horatio, I am dead;
Thou liv'st; report me and my cause aright
To the unsatisfied.

Horatio   Never believe it;
I am more an antique Roman[76] than a Dane:
Here's yet some liquor left.

> [76] the ancient Romans committed suicide when they lost what they most valued

Hamlet   As thou'rt a man,
Give me the cup: let go; by heaven, I'll have't.
O God! Horatio, what a wounded name,
Things standing thus unknown, shall live behind me.
If thou didst ever hold me in thy heart,
Absent thee from felicity[77] awhile,   340
And in this harsh world draw thy breath in pain,
To tell my story.

> [77] happiness (of death)

                                  [March afar off, and shot within.

Hamlet   What warlike noise is this?
Osric   Young Fortinbras, with conquest come from Poland,
To the ambassadors of England gives
This warlike volley.

Hamlet   O! I die, Horatio;
The potent poison quite o'er-crows[78] my spirit:
I cannot live to hear the news from England,
But I do prophesy the election lights
On Fortinbras; he has my dying voice;
So tell him, with the occurrents, more and less,[79]   350
Which have solicited.[80] – The rest is silence.   *[Dies.*

> [78] triumphs over

> [79] greater and lesser occurrences
> [80] prompted me to

Horatio   Now cracks a noble heart. Good night, sweet prince,
And flights of angels sing thee to thy rest!
Why does the drum come hither?   *[March within.*

Enter Fortinbras, the English Ambassadors, and Others.

Fortinbras   Where is this sight?
Horatio   What is it ye would see?
If aught of woe or wonder, cease your search.
Fortinbras   This quarry[81] cries on havoc.[82] O proud death!
What feast is toward in thine eternal cell,
That thou so many princes at a shot
So bloodily hast struck?   360
1st Ambassador   The sight is dismal;
And our affairs from England come too late:
The ears are senseless that should give us hearing,
To tell him his commandment is fulfill'd,

> [81] heap of dead bodies of deer after a hunt
> [82] the cry havoc meant to kill without mercy – Fortinbras, seeing all the bodies realises that there has been a general slaughter

That Rosencrantz and Guildenstern are dead.
Where should we have our thanks?

Horatio   Not from his mouth,
Had it the ability of life to thank you:
He never gave commandment for their death.
But since, so jump upon this bloody question,
You from the Polack wars, and you from England,
Are here arriv'd, give order that these bodies   *370*
High on a stage be placed to the view;
And let me speak to the yet unknowing world
How these things came about: so shall you hear
Of carnal, bloody, and unnatural acts,
Of accidental judgments, casual slaughters;
Of deaths put on by cunning and forc'd cause,
And, in this upshot, purposes mistook
Fall'n on the inventors' heads; all this can I
Truly deliver.

Fortinbras   Let us haste to hear it,
And call the noblest to the audience.   *380*
For me, with sorrow I embrace my fortune;
I have some rights of memory in this kingdom,
Which, now to claim, my vantage doth invite me.

Horatio   Of that I shall have also cause to speak,
And from his mouth whose voice will draw on
                    more[83]
But let this same be presently perform'd,
Even while men's minds are wild, lest more mischance
On plots and errors happen.

Fortinbras   Let four captains
Bear Hamlet, like a soldier, to the stage;
For he was likely, had he been put on,   *390*
To have prov'd most royally: and, for his passage,
The soldiers' music, and the rites of war
Speak loudly for him.
Take up the bodies: such a sight as this
Becomes the field, but here shows much amiss.
Go, bid the soldiers shoot.

                        [A dead march. Exeunt, bearing off the
                        bodies; after which a peal of ordnance
                        is shot off.

[83]whose voice will influence
more people

Scene Analysis

From Hamlet's conversation with Horatio we learn all that happened on the voyage to England – how he intercepted the letters ordering his death, changed the content so that in fact Rosencrantz and Guildenstern should be put to death and how he sealed it with his father's signet. Hamlet acted decisively to save his own life and has no scruples about causing the death of Rosencrantz and Guildenstern. His conscience is untroubled:

> *"... their defeat*
> *Does by their own insinuation grow."*

His purse is empty already; all's golden words are spent.   *(Horatio, Act 5, Scene II)*

In fact, Hamlet is not wrestling with his conscience any more and asks Horatio if he may not now kill Claudius with a clear conscience. However he does regret his behaviour to Laertes because he understands the motivation for Laertes' behaviour.

And in the cup an union shall he throw,
Richer than that which four successive kings
In Denmark's crown have worn.

(King, Act 5, Scene II)

The introduction of Osric is a reminder of the shallowness of court life which Hamlet despises. Osric comes to inform Hamlet about the wager which the king has made on the duelling match. Osric, instead of coming straight to the point, indulges in flattery. He speaks in affected jargon and does not dare to contradict Hamlet, who shows him up to be a fool. Hamlet accepts the challenge without hesitation:

> *"...I will win for him an I can; if not, I will gain nothing but my shame and the odd hits."*

Yet he confesses to Horatio:

> *"But thou wouldst not think how ill all's here about my heart."*

Nevertheless Hamlet will not allow Horatio to cancel the duel. He is prepared to accept his fate. He now believes:

> *"the readiness is all".*

Hamlet greets Laertes courteously. His apology to Laertes is noble and sincere. He excuses himself on the grounds that it was not Hamlet who acted badly but *"His madness"*. Laertes seems prepared to accept Hamlet's apology but reserves the right to have his honour satisfied. The impending sense of doom which broods over the final act is heightened when the king orders the stoups of wine to be set out on the table. Hamlet fights with skill and appears to be winning. The dramatic tension rises as Gertrude drinks from the poisoned cup and almost at the same moment Laertes wounds Hamlet. Then Hamlet wounds Laertes with the same poisoned sword. The king pretends that Gertrude has just fainted but with her dying breath she tells that it was the drink. The dying Laertes exposes the plot *"The King, the King's to blame,"* whereupon Hamlet stabs the king with the same envenomed sword. Hamlet and Laertes exchange forgiveness and Hamlet asks Horatio to *"report me and my cause aright"*. He begs Horatio not to drink the poison:

> *"Absent thee from felicity awhile,*
> *And in this harsh world draw thy breath in pain,*
> *To tell my story."*

Before he dies Hamlet gives his blessing to Fortinbras as his successor. The play ends with the arrival of Fortinbras and his soldiers with the English ambassadors who report that Rosencrantz and Guildenstern are dead. Horatio will fulfil Hamlet's request to:

> *"... speak to the yet unknowing world*
> *How these things came about:"*

and Hamlet is borne *"like a soldier to the stage."*

I embrace it freely;
And will this brother's wager frankly play.

(Hamlet, Act 5, Scene II)

REVISION

"There's a divinity that shapes our ends,
Rough-hew them how we will."   *(Hamlet, Act V, Scene II)*

Hamlet talks to the two grave-diggers who are digging Ophelia's grave. Hamlet and Laertes fight in Ophelia's grave and have to be parted. Hamlet tells Horatio how he stole Claudius' sealed letters and substituted orders for the death of Rosencrantz and Guildenstern. Osric arrives with the challenge for the duel between Hamlet and Laertes. Laertes wounds Hamlet with the poisoned sword but in the scuffle the swords are exchanged and Hamlet wounds Laertes with the same poisoned sword. During the fight, Gertrude drinks the poisoned wine which Claudius had intended for Hamlet. Laertes reveals the king's villainy before he dies. Hamlet stabs Claudius with the poisoned sword and forces him to drink the remaining wine. Although Horatio wants to die alongside his friend, Hamlet begs him to live to clear his name. Before he dies, Hamlet names Fortinbras as his successor. The English ambassadors report the death of Rosencrantz and Guildenstern and Fortinbras orders that Hamlet be buried like a soldier.

Points To Note

1. The tension of the previous act is momentarily broken as the grave-diggers indulge in jokes about their trade. Yet underlying the humour is the constant awareness of death.

2. Ophelia's death is part of Hamlet's tragedy. It is the consequence of his failure to kill Claudius.

3. Hamlet fights with skill and courage and in the end does not hesitate to do what he knows to be justified.

4. Before he dies Hamlet settles the matter of the succession so that Denmark may flourish once more as a land of law and order.

Revision Assignment

Show how the Hamlet who returns from England is different from the Hamlet of the earlier acts of the play.

Part 3

FURTHER STUDY

The Plot

The legend of Hamlet can be traced to Saxo Grammaticus' *Danish History* compiled at the end of the twelfth century. According to the legend, Feng murdered his brother, King of Jutland, and married his queen, Gerutha. Prince Amleth, his nephew, feigned madness and Feng resolved to have him murdered in England. Having changed Feng's instructions for his execution, Amleth returned to Jutland a year later, where according to a promise his mother had made him, his funeral was being celebrated. Amleth set fire to the hall and killed Feng. He took the throne and lived a life of adventure.

The legend tells of Feng's attempt to trap Amleth by leaving him alone with a young woman. It also recounts how Amleth killed a courtier who was eavesdropping on his conversation with his mother, how he reproached his mother and won her over to his side, how he changed the king's message so that the two lords who accompanied him to England were put to death.

Shakespeare kept many elements of the legend in the plot of Hamlet but he transformed the old story, not by just changing the ending, but by exploring the human passions evoked by revenge. The Hamlet of the play is totally unlike Amleth, whose final act of revenge on the king is savage and vindictive. Shakespeare's Hamlet is a most sensitive and imaginative man, a man of reflection and refinement, a scholar and a poet. The plot is concerned with a son's revenge for the murder of his father, but it is enriched by an intricate development of themes, the vividness of the language and symbolism, and especially the dramatic complexity of the character of Hamlet.

Structure

Structurally, *Hamlet* follows the pattern of most tragedies – exposition, conflict and catastrophe.

In Act 1, the situation is expounded, out of which the conflict arises. Hamlet, deeply grieved by the death of his father and the over-hasty marriage of his mother to his uncle, learns from the ghost of his father that he was murdered by Claudius, who now rules Denmark. He promises swift vengeance.

Throughout the next three acts, we see the development and consequences of Hamlet's inner conflict. The turning point of the play comes in Act 3, Scene III. Hamlet's trap to prove Claudius's guilt has worked and Hamlet has the opportunity of killing Claudius when he is kneeling at prayer. He refrains and so initiates the catastrophe by killing Polonius in the mistaken assumption that it is Claudius. The action moves swiftly towards a resolution. Hamlet is sent to England, Ophelia's madness and death is described and Laertes returns seeking revenge.

The catastrophe begins in Act 5 with the burial of Ophelia. Hamlet achieves his revenge, but not before the queen, Laertes and he himself are claimed by death. The threads of the plot are gathered in with the information that Rosencrantz and Guildenstern are dead and the arrival of Fortinbras to succeed to the throne.

Themes

The Political Theme

The action of *Hamlet* centres around the court of Denmark and the political aspect of the play embodies many of the play's concerns. There is a *"strict and most observant watch"* and the spirit of the late king walks the battlements. Fortinbras, believing the state to be *"disjoint and out of frame"*, is preparing to attack. Horatio interprets the appearance of the ghost as a foreboding of war. Denmark is in danger and the ghost is a symptom of the political disturbance brought about by the murder of the rightful king.

According to Elizabethan belief, the king served under God as head of the body politic and the health of the body depended on the goodness of the king. A violation of any part of the natural order of things affected the rest. There was an inseparable link between king and state, between God and king. Claudius believes:

> *"There's such divinity doth hedge a king,*
> *That treason can but peep to what it would,*
> *Acts little of his will".*   (Act 4, Scene V)

This awareness of a mystical union between God, king and body politic is clearly reflected in the words of Guildenstern:

> *"Most holy and religious fear it is*
> *To keep those many many bodies safe*
> *That live and feed upon your Majesty".*   (Act 3, Scene III)

Laertes points out to Ophelia that Hamlet cannot *"Carve for himself"* because:

> *"on his choice depends*
> *The safety and the health of this whole state."*(Act 1, Scene III)

Rosencrantz too voices the Elizabethan belief that on the life of the king *"depend and rest/ The lives of many"*. He states that the king is the centre of *"a massy wheel"* and when it falls, everything else is destroyed. So if the king, who is the centre of the state, is corrupt, the state automatically becomes infected with this corruption:

> "Never alone
> Did the king sigh, but with a general groan". (Act 3, Scene III)

Because of the succession of a usurper king, Denmark has become a prison. It is closed and secretive; spying is encouraged. Hamlet is kept under close guard. Even Claudius is imprisoned in spirit, a *"limed soul"*; *"struggling to be free"*. Denmark is *"rotten"* because *"a vice of kings"* rules. The growing political unease in Denmark is evident from the fact that Laertes can win support so easily as he tries to stir up a rebellion against Claudius to avenge his father's death.

Hamlet is alienated from this corrupt political world of Denmark. Denmark was once a different place, ruled by a heroic and honourable king.

At the end of the play, political balance is restored. Before he dies, Hamlet approves the succession of Fortinbras so that Denmark can thrive once more.

The Theme of Corruption

Since a corrupt king results in a corrupt state, an aura of corruption permeates the play.

The court of Denmark is corrupt because the king is a murderer and the queen an adulteress. The courtiers accept without question their bland self-justification. Therefore the traditional positive values of kingship and marriage are undermined and Hamlet sees corruption spreading through Denmark. Corruption is significant only in relation to goodness and virtue and the contrasting values are underlined throughout the play.

Hamlet's ideal of kingship is embodied in his father *"So excellent a king"*. The attributes of the ideal king are contrasted with those of the usurper king. The rightful king is godlike, the usurper king beast-like, *"Hyperion to a satyr"*. For Hamlet, his father and his uncle represent the two extremes of good and evil, the ideal and the negation of it. The two kings are repeatedly contrasted so that we may see how goodness has been corrupted. An evil man is ruling Denmark and so all values are perverted. Love is corrupted to lust and friendship is corrupted by power. Hamlet asks Ophelia if she is honest and implies that she is not, since honesty is corrupted by beauty. Marriage vows have been corrupted and are *"As false as dicers' oaths"*. Hamlet's awareness of corruption extends to himself. He accuses himself of:

> "such things that it were better my mother had not
> borne me".   (Act 3, Scene I)

Throughout the play Hamlet struggles against evil and finally frees Denmark from its corruption by killing the usurper king.

The Theme of Revenge

In one sense, Hamlet's revenge is an attack on a corrupt world.

The theme of revenge is central to the plot and the effect of the awesome responsibility of revenge is central to the characterisation of Hamlet.

The theme of revenge in Shakespeare's *Hamlet* is complex. In its original form, the narrative was one of simple revenge and the avenger delayed because of external difficulties. But Hamlet's delay is due to an internal conflict between the impulse to avenge on the one hand and the unconscious repugnance to vengeance on the other.

The motif of revenge has many aspects in the play. Hamlet's revenge is motivated by the bond between father and son. Hamlet accepts the obligation of vengeance imposed by the ghost. He assumes that he ought to avenge his father, yet this instinctive impulse is inhibited by unconscious misgivings. Although he realises that he has every justification for revenge, the power of thought and conscience prevents him from murdering Claudius.

Hamlet's reply to the ghost's command is:

> *"Haste me to know't, that I, with wings as swift*
> *As meditation or the thoughts of love,*
> *May sweep to my revenge".*   (Act 1, Scene V)

Yet although the ghost finds him *"apt"*, the very words which Hamlet uses suggest other values. Vengeance, especially when it is justified, is relatively simple. The avenger acts to right a wrong. But for Hamlet, the command to revenge reveals insoluble complications, irreconcilable contradictions. What the ghost commands is impossible – *"Taint not thy mind"*. If Hamlet is to exact revenge, then the very act of vengeance will taint his mind. It is this consciousness which involves Hamlet in the soul-searching which delays action.

The situations of Hamlet and Laertes are very similar. Each must avenge his own father. Hamlet says:

> *"by the image of my cause, I see*
> *The portraiture of his".*   (Act 5, Scene II)

Yet the difference in the attitude of each to revenge is striking. When Laertes hears of his father's death he states:

> *"To this point I stand,*
> *That both the worlds I give to negligence,*

> Let come what comes, only I'll be reveng'd
> Most throughly for my father".   *(Act 4, Scene V)*

Laertes dares damnation, but Hamlet is troubled by *"the dread of something after death"*. Claudius asks Laertes a significant question:

> *"is't writ in your revenge,*
> *That, swoopstake, you will draw both friend and foe,*
> *Winner and loser?"*   *(ibid)*

In fact Claudius himself believes that *"Revenge should have no bounds"* and Laertes is prepared to defy all laws, deny all values in the pursuit of revenge:

> *"To hell allegiance! Vows, to the blackest devil!*
> *Conscience and grace, to the profoundest pit!"*   *(ibid)*

Laertes doesn't even act according to the ethics of the old revenge code. He is utterly unscrupulous and allows himself to be manipulated by Claudius. Laertes is corrupted by his thirst for vengeance whereas, in the end, Hamlet avenges his father nobly and bravely.

Likewise Fortinbras contrasts in every way with Hamlet though their situations are similar. Fortinbras is also the son of a dead king and at the beginning of the play he is fighting to right his father's losses. However Fortinbras' bid for revenge is unjustified and endangers the peace of Denmark. He puts himself at the head of a band of desperadoes and is prepared to fight without the knowledge or consent of his uncle, the reigning king of Norway. His desire for restitution is irresponsible. He is contravening:

> *"...a seal'd compact,*
> *Well ratified by law and heraldry".*   *(Act 1, Scene I)*

When his plan is thwarted by his uncle, Fortinbras diverts his energy into an attack on Poland *"to gain a little patch of ground"*.

Fortinbras is an obvious contrast to Hamlet as a man of action and daring enterprise. Yet we are made see the harmful effects of a revenge which exposes:

> *"what is mortal and unsure*
> *To all that fortune, death and danger dare,*
> *Even for an egg-shell".*   *(Act 4, Scene IV)*

Hamlet admires Fortinbras, yet he instinctively recognises:

> *"This is the imposthume of much wealth and peace,*
> *That inward breaks, and shows no cause without"*   *(ibid)*

The play depicts three sons, all concerned with avenging their fathers. Fortinbras tries to achieve revenge by force of arms but is persuaded to recognise the agreement between his father and King Hamlet. Laertes is violent and unscrupulous as an avenger. He is unrestrained by considerations of law or conscience in his revenge. Hamlet looks for certainty before taking action. He seeks to right a wrong without tainting his mind. When he does kill the king it is openly, not furtively, and after fighting honourably. The play raises many questions about the notion of revenge. Laertes and Fortinbras represent the threat of vengeance let loose. If we blame Hamlet for not rushing to take revenge then we are approving a code of revenge which is contrary to all civilised values. The ultimate consequences of a revenge beyond all control is presented in the image of Pyrrhus, smeared with gore, who hacks to pieces the aged and defenceless Priam in order to avenge his father. For one moment Pyrrhus stands, sword in hand:

> *"And like a neutral to his will and matter,*
> *Did nothing."*   *(Act 2, Scene II)*

This is a striking parallel image of Hamlet, sword in hand, with the kneeling Claudius at his mercy, but whereas Hamlet put his sword up, for Pyrrhus:

> *"Aroused vengeance sets him new a-work".*   *(ibid)*

In his raging fury Pyrrhus symbolises a remorseless and cruel avenger.

At the end of the play Fortinbras succeeds to the throne of Denmark, but he succeeds through right, not through force. Hamlet nominates Fortinbras as his successor, but his successor will nevertheless be by *"election"*. The principle of law and order is clearly endorsed.

The Theme of Love

It is his deep disgust over his mother's over-hasty incestuous marriage that disturbs Hamlet rather than the political disruption of Denmark. Nevertheless love and revenge are inextricably mixed in the play.

The ghost's call to revenge is an appeal to Hamlet's love:

> *"If thou didst ever thy dear father love –"*   *(Act 1, Scene V)*

Since Hamlet loved his father, the ghost's command cannot be ignored. Love is associated with remembrance. The ghost pleads *"remember me"*, and Hamlet responds passionately:

> *"Ay, thou poor ghost, while memory holds a seat*
> *In this distracted globe".*   *(ibid)*

But Gertrude chooses not to remember her dead husband and marries his brother less than a month after the funeral.

Hamlet's ideal of love is based on his father's love for his mother, a love which seems to continue beyond the grave. Despite the ghost's disappointment in Gertrude, he is loyal to his love and asks Hamlet to avenge his death without harming Gertrude. In the bedroom scene when Hamlet bitterly chastises his mother, the ghost intervenes. Hamlet recalls his father's love for his mother as gentle and caring:

> "...so loving to my mother
> That he might not beteem the winds of heaven
> Visit her face too roughly".   (Act 1, Scene II)

He recalls his mother's response as being more sensual:

> "... why, she would hang on him,
> As if increase of appetite had grown
> By what it fed on".   (ibid)

Throughout the play the ideal of love is set against its debasement – lust. The contamination of love through lust is conveyed in the antithesis of images:

> "But virtue, as it never will be mov'd,
> Though lewdness court it in a shape of heaven,
> So lust, though to a radiant angel link'd
> Will sate itself in a celestial bed,
> And prey on garbage".   (Act 1, Scene V)

The ghost pleads with Hamlet:

> "Let not the royal bed of Denmark be
> A couch for luxury and damned incest".   (ibid)

Love has been poisoned. Hamlet accuses his mother of:

> "Such an act
> That blurs the grace and blush of modesty,
> Calls virtue hypocrite, takes off the rose
> From the fair forehead of an innocent love
> And sets a blister there".   (Act 3, Scene IV)

Hamlet's view of love has been based on an ideal of love. His response to love is idealistic. The *"celestial"* Ophelia is his *"soul's idol"*. Hamlet's love for Ophelia before the death of his father, was honourable. It typified all the innocent pleasures of young love. Hamlet gave Ophelia *"rememberances"* and spoke:

> "words of so sweet breath compos'd".   (Act 3, Scene I)

However once Hamlet's ideal of love has been shattered by his mother's *"falling off"*, he denies the existence of true love, certain that all women share his mother's corruption. Remembrance is associated with love and so Hamlet refuses to remember his past tender relationship with Ophelia:

> "I never gave you aught".   (ibid)

Hamlet's love for Ophelia is destroyed by his association of love and lust. Disillusioned and resentful, Hamlet debases true love into something ugly. He warps Ophelia's innocence with his bitter insults which are reflected in the bawdy songs she sings in her madness. Because Hamlet no longer believes in love, all women are suspect of fickleness. Convinced that the human race is corrupt, Hamlet is convinced that man is incapable of true love:

> *"for virtue cannot so inoculate our old stock but we shall*
> *relish of it".*   *(ibid)*

In a bitter attempt to restrain Ophelia from becoming *"a breeder of sinners"*, he orders her harshly *"Get thee to a nunnery"*.

The theme of love is highlighted through the Player King in *The Murder of Gonzago*. He discusses love with his queen who protests that she could never love a second husband. But the Player King points out:

> *"That even our love should with our fortunes change". (Act 3, Scene II)*

The words of the Player Queen point to Gertrude's situation:

> *"A second time I kill my husband dead,*
> *When second husband kisses me in bed".*   *(ibid)*

Claudius does not believe in the endurance of love, stating:

> *"Time qualifies the spark and fire of it.*
> *There lives within the very flame of love*
> *A kind of wick, or snuff, that will abate it".*   *(Act 4, Scene VII)*

Although he claims he loves Gertrude, he betrays her by letting her drink the poison.

The only positive affirmation of love in the play is at Ophelia's funeral when Hamlet remembers the beauty of his love for Ophelia and declares:

> *"I lov'd Ophelia: forty thousand brothers*
> *Could not, with all their quantity of love,*
> *Make up my sum".*   *(Act 5, Scene I)*

Reason v Passion

In Hamlet's soliloquy in *Act 2, Scene II* he refers to man as *"the paragon of animals"*. Man is a perfect *"piece of work"*, because of his excellence in reason and faculty and action, in body and in mind.

Throughout the play Hamlet struggles between reason and passion. Hamlet reacts passionately to the ghost's command for revenge but the truth of the player's words is evident as Hamlet's purpose becomes lost:

> *"What to ourselves in passion we propose,*
> *The passion ending, doth the purpose lose".*   *(Act 3, Scene II)*

Hamlet's passion urges him to vengeance but his reason and conscience do not approve of murder.

Hamlet believes that *"the pale cast of thought"* weakens his power of action but in fact passion weakens his ability to act rationally. His actions are often impulsive and unpremeditated and he often acts on instinct rather than reason. On the spur of the moment he decides to assume an *"antic disposition"*, he asks for the playing of *The Murder of Gonzago* to trap Claudius when the players happen to arrive at Elsinore, and he promptly changes the king's sealed letter ordering his death in England.

Hamlet speaks of:

> *"the o'ergrowth of some complexion,*
> *Oft breaking down the pales and forts of reason"* *(Act 1, Scene IV)*

And Hamlet allows his passion to dominate his reason on many occasions. He allows his passion to take control in the scenes with Ophelia and his mother. Hamlet is aware of the danger of such passion and warns himself before visiting his mother:

> *"O heart! lose not thy nature; let not ever*
> *The soul of Nero enter this firm bosom;*
> *Let me be cruel not unnatural;".*   *(Act 3, Scene II)*

However Hamlet's passionate feelings provoke him to furious outbursts not just against others but against himself until reason causes him to stop.

> *"Fie upon 't! Foh!*
> *About, my brain!"*   *(Act 2, Scene II)*

Hamlet's passionate outbursts are destructive. As his emotions master him he becomes incapable of action or constructive thinking. Hamlet advises the players that they must not indulge in excessive emotion,

> *"for in the very torrent, tempest, and – as I may say –*
> *whirlwind of passion, you must acquire and beget a temperance,*
> *that may give it smoothness".*   *(Act 3, Scene II)*

Hamlet too must acquire a more temperate passion. The discussion by the Player King of the relation of passion and action is directly relevant to this important theme of the play. He points out that a purpose which is prompted by passion will die when the passion dies:

> *"Purpose is but the slave to memory,*
> *Of violent birth, but poor validity;...*

The violence of either grief or joy
Their own enactures with themselves destroy".   *(ibid)*

Hamlet seeks the right balance between passion and reason but he alternates between the two extremes of feeling and thought. Either he displays undisciplined emotion or he thinks *"too precisely on the event"*. Horatio has that balance. Hamlet pays tribute to Horatio, recognizing that his:

"blood and judgment are so well comingled
That they are not a pipe for Fortune's finger".   *(ibid)*

Conscious, perhaps, of his own weakness, Hamlet cries out:

"Give me that man
That is not passion's slave, and I will wear him
In my heart's core..."   *(ibid)*

In his last soliloquy in *Act 4, Scene IV*, Hamlet asserts the value of reason. Man possesses god-like reason so he should not be just like a beast:

"Sure he that made us with such large discourse,
Looking before and after, gave us not
That capability and god-like reason
To fust in us unus'd."   *(Act 4, Scene IV)*

But reason fails to show Hamlet how to rationalise the evil of murder and incest. When Hamlet accepts that reason is not enough he can come to terms with the situation. On the journey to England a series of fortunate circumstances save his life. Without having reasoned out a plan Hamlet acts and realises:

"Our indiscretion sometimes serves us well
When our deep plots do pall, and that should teach us
There's a divinity that shapes our ends,
Rough-hew them how we will".   *(Act 5, Scene II)*

This recalls the words of the Player King:

"Our wills and fates do so contrary run
That our devices still are overthrown,
Our thoughts are ours, their ends none of our own." (Act 3, Scene II)

Hamlet finally understands that human action is not always compatible with reason as he praises *"rashness"* for saving his life and can now say *"let be"*. Now Hamlet can rationally analyse his situation. He can justify his revenge and as his reason takes control he asks Horatio:

"He that hath kill'd my king and whor'd my mother,
Popp'd in between the election and my hopes,

> *Thrown out his angle for my proper life,*
> *And with such cozenage – is 't not perfect conscience*
> *To quit him with this arm?"*   (Act 5, Scene II)

He has also sent Rosencrantz and Guildenstern to their deaths but can see that:

> *"their defeat*
> *Does by their own insinuation grow".*   (ibid)

No longer troubled by reasoning doubts, no longer controlled by passion, Hamlet dies nobly.

The Theme of Hypocrisy

The court of Elsinore is a prison, a place of spying and watching, a world of hypocrisy and false appearances where:

> *"one may smile, and smile, and be a villain".*   (Act I, Scene V)

The people of Denmark have been deceived by the smiles. Claudius has assumed the throne *"by a forged process"*. The court accepts the appearance of rightful kingship. The queen is *"seeming-virtuous"*. Appearances are deceptive. Little is what it seems:

> *"In the corrupted currents of this world*
> *Offence's gilded hand may shove by justice".* (Act 3, Scene III)

The court appears to be a place of nobility and dignity but it is a place of lying and subterfuge. Claudius assumes an aspect of *"wisest sorrow"* for his dead brother whom he has in fact murdered. In a world of deception and treachery, hypocrisy is essential to survive. Claudius and Polonius are *"lawful espials"*. Characters deceive each other, spy on each other, conceal their true motives. Polonius sends Reynaldo to spy on his son. He constantly undertakes the role of spying or eavesdropping. He dies in the very act of spying. Rosencrantz and Guildenstern act as spies in the guise of friendship. Hamlet and Horatio watch the king in the play scene. Laertes persuades Ophelia that Hamlet's vows are false.

Polonius tells Ophelia to read a pious book for the sake of appearances. Hamlet tells his mother *"Assume a virtue, if you have it not"*. Everyone is wearing a disguise of some sort. Hamlet hides behind a mask of madness. His bitter quips challenge the hypocrisy which surrounds him. He declares *"I know not seems"*. He tells Horatio:

> *"No; let the candied tongue lick absurd pomp".*(Act 3, Scene II)

Hamlet's bitter asides attack Claudius's facade, but it is Polonius who speaks the words which cause Claudius to start guiltily:

> *"'Tis too much prov'd, that with devotion's visage*
> *And pious action we do sugar o'er*
> *The devil himself".*   (Act 3, Scene I)

Claudius recognises that in the next world he cannot sugar over the crime he has committed:

> *"but 'tis not so above,*
> *There is no shuffling, there the action lies*
> *In his true nature...".*   (Act 3, Scene III)

The secrecy and pretence in the court of Denmark hides the evil which Hamlet is trying to expose. Hamlet fights continually to strip off false appearances in order to see reality. He enlists the help of the actors:

> *"to hold, as 'twere, the mirror up to nature;"*   (Act 3, Scene II)

In fact, acting assumes a symbolic importance in the play. The actors play a part consciously but many other characters in the play act a part in order to conceal their real feelings. The play within the play focuses on false appearances. The Player King performs before King Claudius who in turn acts the part of the rightful king. Hamlet watches the play but he too is playing the role of the mad prince in order to deceive the court.

Duplicity and hypocrisy are an underlying feature of *Hamlet*. The other characters are content to accept the world as they find it, but Hamlet questions the relation between appearance and reality, action and motive, real character and outward behaviour. The discrepancy between appearance and reality pervades the play and hypocrisy is rejected by Hamlet as part of the corruption of the court at Elsinore.

The Theme of Death

In his fight against hypocrisy Hamlet comes face to face with the fact that only the harsh reality of death uncovers all appearances. Death dominates the play and an important aspect of the play is about coming to terms with death.

Hamlet's whole view of the world and of man has degenerated because of his mother's lust and his uncle's treachery. He shrinks from living in a corrupt world and is weighed down by the burden of living in a world dominated by evil. Death would end:

> *"The heart-ache and the thousand natural shocks*
> *That flesh is heir to".*   (Act 3, Scene I)

but there is *"the dread of something after death"*. Even so, he longs for death in the very first soliloquy, *Act 1, Scene II*. He wishes:

> *"that the Everlasting had not fix'd*
> *His canon 'gainst self-slaughter!"*   *(Act 1, Scene II)*

Hamlet longs to be free from the corrupt realities of life. Death is but a sleep, a release from suffering:

> *"a consummation*
> *Devoutly to be wish'd". (Act 3, Scene I)*

But he forsees the inevitable dreams to be endured in the sleep of death. Were it not for fear of the unknown, Hamlet considers that no man:

> *"would bear the whips and scorns of time".*   *(ibid)*

The question with which Hamlet struggles is whether one should choose *"To be, or not to be"*. As he debates whether the heartache is better endured or escaped from, there is a growing obsession with the physical state of death and decomposition. Hamlet uses Polonius's dead body to make some pointed remarks about death and decay:

> *"we fat all creatures else to fat us, and we fat ourselves*
> *for maggots"*   *(Act 4, Scene III)*

Everyone is equal in death:

> *"your fat king and your lean beggar is but variable service;*
> *two dishes, but to one table: that's the end".*   *(ibid)*

Hamlet observes how *"a king may go a progress through the guts of a beggar,"* Gertrude refers to the commonness and naturalness of death:

> *"Thou know'st 'tis common; all that live must die,*
> *Passing through nature to eternity".*   *(Act I, Scene II)*

but neither Gertrude nor Claudius consider deeply their own mortality, whereas Hamlet sees man as essentially *"this quintessence of dust"*. We are continually reminded of death throughout the play until the culmination of the theme of death in the graveyard.

The coarse jokes of the gravediggers contrast with Hamlet's morbid brooding throughout the play. Their familiarity with death allows no dread. It is in the graveyard scene that Hamlet confronts death head on and he questions the purpose of human life:

> *"Did these bones cost no more the breeding but to play at loggats with 'em?"*
> *(Act 5, Scene I)*

As he looks at various skulls he considers how useless were all the schemes of the politician, the courtier and the lawyer *"that would circumvent God"*. He reduces the dust of Alexander the Great and imperious Caesar to such ignoble uses as *"stopping a bung-hole"*.

In the end, Hamlet recognises that the inevitability of death is the condition of being human. As he meditates on death he comes to terms with the mystery of life. He realises the insignificance of man in the face of death. In the final act he seems to accept the impersonal face of death but he is moved by the sight of Yorick's skull and the burial of Ophelia.

In the graveyard Hamlet no longer meditates on death as something he longs for but as the common destiny of man – a destiny which he now appears to accept:

> *"Since no man has aught of what he leaves, what is't to leave betimes?"*
> *(Act 5, Scene II)*

The Nature of Man

The theme of death raises questions about the value of existence and the nature of man.

Hamlet believes that man is the highest form of creation, next to the angels. He refers to man as *"the beauty of the world"*. His deep idealism is reflected in the apostrophe to man in *Act 2, Scene II*. Man is *"noble in reason"*, *"infinite in faculty"*, *"like an angel"*, *"like a god"*. Hamlet speaks of his father in terms which suggest godlike qualities. He has *"the front of Jove"*, *"An eye like Mars"*, and *"A station like the herald Mercury"*. His qualities are such that

> *"every god did seem to set his seal,*
> *To give the world assurance of a man".*   *(Act 3, Scene IV)*

In Hamlet's eyes his father is the embodiment of human perfection. However the ghost of his father is suffering the torments of purgatory because he was:

> *"Cut off even in the blossoms of my sin,"*   *(Act I, Scene V)*

He even refers to:

> *"the foul crimes done in my days of nature."*   *(ibid)*

Hamlet's ideal of his father is therefore over-exalted, and reality fails to meet his exacting standards with the result that he becomes progressively disillusioned. He cannot accept himself or others as imperfect creatures. It is because Hamlet's ideal of man is so high that his disillusionment is so bitter. He sees something bestial in the incestuous marriage of his mother. In fact he thinks that she has brought herself down to a level even lower than the beasts for:

> *"... a beast, that wants discourse of reason,*
> *Would have mourn'd longer..."*   *(Act I, Scene II)*

As her son, he is conscious of sharing her nature. He now has a sense of belonging to a diseased stock – descendants of Adam are tainted. Hamlet sees how far below the angels humanity can fall, by descending to the level of the beasts. He is shocked to realise the bestial qualities in man, qualities which Claudius's lust seems to exemplify. The two extremes of the potentiality of man's nature are expressed in Hamlet's striking contrast of Hyperion and the satyr. The satyr is opposed to the god, but in fact a satyr is a creature which is half man and half beast. This image conveys the dual nature of man. Man is capable of good and evil, the nature of man has aspects of the god and the beast. Claudius and King Hamlet were brothers – and represent the two faces of man. Good and evil exist side by side. Man's nature can be uplifted or downgraded. Hamlet refers to *"some vicious mole of nature"*, just one inborn defect which may damn a man's whole reputation. Hamlet is just as absolute in his condemnation of his mother and his disgust of his mother extends to all women and even life itself. Hamlet does not wish to live in a world where things are *"rank and gross"*. He cannot accept a world where the satyr seems to triumph, so he denies his own nature. Hamlet's own nature is characterised by the intermingling of goodness and weakness. He is essentially noble and honourable but his character is nonetheless flawed. He misunderstands Ophelia, is pitiless towards his mother, kills Polonius and sends Rosencrantz and Guildenstern to their deaths without regret.

Hamlet must come to terms with the human condition, which is somewhere in between the god-like and the beast-like. Man is created in God's image but is descended from Adam. There is intermingling of good and evil in life. At the end of the play, Hamlet understands that there is a mysterious design which embraces good and evil and somehow he is part of the design.

The play questions the problem of being man as Hamlet struggles with the problem of accepting or rejecting the human condition:

> *"To be, or not to be: that is the question."*   (Act 3, Scene I)

Hamlet questions the meaning of creation, *"What is a man?"* Is it to simply exist, to do no more than sleep and feed? Hamlet believes that man was created for something more glorious. Hamlet is disillusioned with man and life for the very reason that he is so sensitively aware of man's potential, so amazed by the miracle of man. Hamlet's uncertainties and doubts force us to consider the great mystery of the nature of man.

Language

Imagery and Symbolism

The images which recur throughout the play are prompted by its themes and serve to highlight the important themes. An evil king is ruling Denmark and therefore corruption is growing. The world is an *"unweeded garden"* and Hamlet asks his mother:

> *"And do not spread the compost on the weeds*
> *To make them ranker".*   (Act 3, Scene IV)

From the very beginning of the play the image of the weed is present as the ghost uses the image of the weed to incite Hamlet to revenge:

> *"And duller shouldst thou be than the fat weed*
> *That roots itself in ease on Lethe wharf*
> *Wouldst thou not stir in this".*   (Act 1, Scene V)

The weed is the symbol of corruption in Denmark and it is associated with poison and disease.

The rightful king has been poisoned and now the whole country is being poisoned, contaminated by the *"mildew'd ear"*. The ghost describes how he was poisoned, emphasising the spreading of the poison:

> *"And in the porches of mine ears did pour*
> *The leperous distilment; whose effect*
> *Holds such an enmity with blood of man*
> *That swift as quicksilver it courses through*
> *The natural gates and alleys of the body,*
> *And with a sudden vigour it doth posset*
> *And curd, like eager droppings into milk,*
> *The thin and wholesome blood"*   (ibid)

This imagery of poison and disease recurs throughout the play. There is constant reference to sickness. Gertrude speaks of her *"sick soul"*. Laertes refers to *"the sickness in my heart"*. Hamlet tells Rosencrantz and Guildenstern that his *"wit's diseased"*. He uses an image of disease to warn his mother:

> *"Lay not that flattering unction to your soul,...*
> *It will but skin and film the ulcerous place,*
> *Whiles rank corruption, mining all within,*
> *Infects unseen".*   (Act 3, Scene IV)

Claudius compares himself to *"the owner of a foul disease"*. It is ironic that he constantly sees Hamlet in terms of a disease which must be got rid of when in fact it is he who has contaminated the state of Denmark. He says:

> *".... diseases, desperate grown,*
> *By desperate appliance are reliev'd,*
> *Or not at all".*　　　　　　　　　　　　　　　*(Act 4, Scene III)*

For Claudius, the *"cure"* lies in sending Hamlet to England. Unwittingly, he instigates the cure which will rid Denmark of its disease: *"the bloat king"*.

The images of sickness and rottenness are symbolic of the corruption of Denmark and the evil in man. Hamlet describes for Horatio how human nature can be corrupted from a tiny blemish such as a birthmark. A dram of evil contaminates the whole person:

> *"... that these men,*
> *Carrying, I say, the stamp of one defect,...*
> *Their virtues else, be they as pure as grace,...*
> *Shall in the general censure take corruption*
> *From that particular fault:"*　　　　　　　*(Act 1, Scene IV)*

Hamlet refers to Claudius as the *"canker of our nature"*. Laertes uses the same image when he warns Ophelia:

> *"The canker galls the infants of the spring*
> *Too oft before their buttons be disclos'd"*　　*(Act 1, Scene III)*

The contamination of love by the lustful relationship of Claudius and Gertrude is reflected in the imagery. Throughout the play images of appetite and lust emphasise Hamlet's disgust at their incestuous relationship. The bestial level of the relationship is suggested by the many animal references. Hamlet speaks to Polonius of *"maggots in a dead dog"*. He calls Claudius *"a paddock"*; *"a bat"* and *"a gib"*. Lust is seen as the degradation of love and it is the contrasting images which brings this out:

> *"So lust, though to a radiant angel link'd,*
> *Will sate itself in a celestial bed,*
> *And prey on garbage".*　　　　　　　　　　*(Act 1, Scene V)*

The images *"angel"* and *"celestial"* contrast with *"sate"* and *"prey"*. Lust is depicted as being physically disgusting by the images which Hamlet uses as he accuses his mother of living:

> *"In the rank sweat of an enseamed bed,*
> *Stew'd in corruption, honeying and making love*
> *Over the nasty sty –"*　　　　　　　　　　*(Act 3, Scene IV)*

Claudius admits:

> *"O! my offence is rank, it smells to heaven". (Act 3, Scene III)*

The predominance of this imagery of hidden disease and rankness gives an atmosphere of corruption to the play. Similarly the constant references to mortality, images of dust and physical decay envelop the play in an atmosphere of death. The mood is sombre and the wit is macabre, in keeping with the theme of death. At the beginning of the play the queen tells Hamlet:

> *"Do not for ever with thy vailed lids*
> *Seek for thy noble father in the dust".*   *(Act I, Scene II)*

Later Hamlet faces the stark reality of death in the graveyard scene as the grave-diggers talk of the *"many pocky corpses"* and Hamlet examines various skills:

> *"...now my Lady Worm's; chapless, and knocked about the*
> *mazzard with a sexton's spade."*   *(Act 5, Scene I)*

The graveyard scene is the culmination of the death motif which runs through the play.

Another important theme in the play, the theme of hypocrisy, is reinforced by words and images. Hamlet is aware of the discrepency between appearance and reality and images of clothing, painting, disguising and acting abound. Hamlet constantly tries to get behind appearance. He is aware that his black clothes are:

> *"... but the trappings and the suits of woe."*   *(Act I, Scene II)*

Polonius cannot see beneath the surface of things. Polonius uses another clothing image in his instructions to Reynaldo:

> *"... and there put on him*
> *What forgeries you please".*   *(Act 2, Scene I)*

The connection of clothing and appearance is important, so it is significant that Hamlet informs Claudius in his letter in *Act 4, Scene VII* that he has returned to Denmark *"naked"*, that is, stripped of disguise, his true self. Undisguised man is symbolised by the skull of Yorick which has such a morbid fascination for Hamlet. This is man in his essence – dust. Man's life is a futile attempt to disguise this fact. Hamlet perceives the truth. He tells Ophelia:

> *"God hath given you one face, and you make yourselves another".*
> *(Act 3, Scene I)*

In *Act 5,* Hamlet recognises the futility of life's pretences:

> *"Now get you to my lady's chamber, and tell her, let her paint*
> *an inch thick, to this favour she must come".*   *(Act 5, Scene I)*

The importance of acting as a symbol in the play is significant. The players are introduced in *Act 3* and there is much discussion on the techniques of acting. This is not just background information. We are made aware of the discrepency between the players who act so as to reveal man to himself, to *"hold a mirror up to nature"* and the other characters who assume their roles for the purpose of concealment. Claudius assumes the role of rightful king, Gertrude of virtuous queen and Hamlet of the mad prince. Words are part of their disguise and so the language of Hamlet is full of riddles, enigmas and quibbles.

Dramatic Expression

Shakespeare's use of language intensifies the impression of mystery in the play. There are many rhetorical questions, multiple riddles and numerous ambiguities. The hypocrisy and duplicity is expressed through the language of the play. Claudius talks of *"my most painted word"* and his words belie his deeds. Words disguise the truth. Claudius's words are carefully contrived to conceal a terrible truth:

> *"... and that it us befitted*
> *To bear our hearts in grief, and our whole kingdom*
> *To be contracted in one brow of woe".*   (Act I, Scene II)

The language of the court is ceremonious and stately. Many words are used to say little. Hamlet hides his real meaning under quibbles and puns:

> *"I am too much i' the sun".*   (ibid)

Hamlet unpacks his heart with words and his abrupt changes of mood are reflected in his language. The language of his more pensive moods contrasts with the sharp wit and sarcasm of his angry moods. Hamlet on the one hand utters deeply poetic sentiments and on the other hand brutally prosaic insults. Whatever the mood, Hamlet's images are concrete, his language is close to reality. Hamlet is a master of words and words are his weapon. Whereas Claudius uses words to conceal his true feelings, Hamlet uses words to reveal the truth. But he also distrusts words, *"the candied tongue"*. Polonius shows how words lose all value when they are spoken without any depth of feeling. The language of Claudius is expressive of the mask he wears. In his addresses to the council his sentences are well balanced, his speech proper. To Laertes his speech is smooth and flattering. To Hamlet his speech is stilted and contrived as he artificially turns around noun and adjective for effect:

> *"It shows a will most incorrect to heaven,*
> *A heart unfortifted, a mind impatient,*
> *An understanding simple and unschool'd".*   (Act 1, Scene II)

When alone, Claudius' speech takes on a different quality:

> *"...Pray can I not,*
> *Though inclination be as sharp as will:*
> *My stronger guilt defeats my strong intent;*
> *And, like a man to double business bound,*
> *I stand in pause where I shall first begin,*
> *And both neglect".*   (Act 3, Scene III)

His language is also more direct when he is trying to obtain information, when he is plotting with Laertes, when he is not in public.

In Hamlet there is a variety of register, ranging from the language of Hamlet's grand soliloquies to his colloquial wit. Most of the play is written in blank verse. The play within the play is clearly distinguished by the use of rhyme and the language is bombastic. Hamlet speaks in verse and prose. His use of prose disturbs the rhythm of the play and this reflects the disorder of his mind. The alternation of verse and prose is used to dramatic effect. When Hamlet wishes to pretend madness he speaks in prose which is less precise than the disciplined blank verse. It is significant that Hamlet uses verse in *Act 5*, indicating his now ordered thoughts.

Characterisation

Fortinbras

> *"Whose spirit, with divine ambition puff'd,*
> *Makes mouths at the invisible event".*   (Act 4, Scene IV)

Horatio presents a clear picture of Fortinbras in the opening scene. Horatio describes to his friends the pact between Hamlet's father and the father of Fortinbras whereby the elder Fortinbras forfeited the lands seized by the victorious King Hamlet. In Horatio's opinion, Fortinbras is a young man *"Of unimproved mettle hot and full"*. Determined to recapture the forfeited lands, he *"Shark'd up a list of lawless resolutes"* and without his uncle's blessing prepared to attack Denmark. Fortinbras has betrayed his father's word and defied a legally binding agreement. Horatio's estimate of him as a hothead is borne out by the spurious campaign against Poland. Deprived of the opportunity to invade Denmark, Fortinbras finds a new fight.

Fortinbras possesses a sense of purpose, a will to action, which Hamlet lacks, but he is unscrupulous and insensitive, risking:

> *"The imminent death of twenty thousand men,*
> *That, for a fantasy and trick of fame,*

> *Go to their graves like beds, fight for a plot*
> *Whereon the numbers cannot try the cause".*   *(ibid)*

Therefore the character of Fortinbras may be said to act as a foil to Hamlet. His moral integrity is somewhat questionable, but he is strong and very much a man of action. Hamlet names Fortinbras as heir to the throne, thus approving a man of courage and daring as ruler of Denmark.

Fortinbras is not clearly portrayed as a character in his own right. He serves a dramatic purpose in the political theme – highlighting the state of unrest in Denmark by posing a threat from without. He also offsets Hamlet's role as a dispossessed son who does not take immediate action to redress a wrong to his father. The meeting between Hamlet and Fortinbras is dramatically significant as it emphasises two opposing sets of values. But it is really only at the end of the play when it becomes clear that Fortinbras is to be successor that his importance as a character is realised.

Rosencrantz and Guildenstern

> *"in the full bent,*
> *To lay our service freely at your feet,*
> *To be commanded".*   *(Act 2, Scene II)*

Rosencrantz and Guildenstern are not really individualised. They appear together, act together and seem to echo one another. We learn that they have been childhood friends of Hamlet, yet they betray that friendship by siding with the king. They are basically self-seeking, flattering the king to gain favour. They are totally committed to the wishes of the king and express this in exaggerated courtesies:

> *"Both your Majesties*
> *Might, by the sovereign power you have of us,*
> *Put your dread pleasures more into command*
> *Than to entreaty".*   *(ibid)*

Rosencrantz and Guildenstern express their belief in the absolute authority of the king, a principle accepted by the Elizabethans. Nevertheless they are portrayed as disloyal to Hamlet, keeping him under constant surveillance and posing a threat to him by their very presence. Hamlet detests their hypocrisy and deceitfulness and describes them very well by using the image of a sponge:

> *"that soaks up the King's countenance, his rewards, his authorities".*   *(Act 4, Scene II)*

Rosencrantz and Guildenstern have little moral sense. They are also portrayed as having little intelligence. Hamlet's poetic speech about the splendour of the universe is lost on them. Rosencrantz smiles foolishly when Hamlet says *"man delights not me"*. Obviously his mind is very literal. He completely misunderstands the general sense of Hamlet's statement and explains that he is smiling:

> *"To think, my lord, if you delight not in man, what lenten*
> *entertainment the players shall receive from you". (Act 2, Scene II)*

Hamlet implies that they are much too stupid to understand his sarcasm. When Rosencrantz protests:

> *"I understand you not, my lord".*   *(Act 4, Scene II)*

Hamlet retorts:

> *"I am glad of it: a knavish speech sleeps in a foolish ear". (ibid)*

Rosencrantz and Guildenstern are of little real interest as characters. They are hardly even distinguishable separately.

Their function is to highlight that Hamlet is surrounded by enemies in the court of Denmark. They further the plot by being tools in the hands of the king. They are the immediate means by which Hamlet is to be removed from the court of Denmark. There is nothing to indicate that they know of the king's plot to murder Hamlet, but their very complicity in spying on Hamlet makes them guilty. Hamlet sends them to their death without qualms of conscience and they are dismissed by him thus:

> *"'Tis dangerous when the baser nature comes*
> *Between the pass and fell-incensed points*
> *Of mighty opposites".*   *(Act 5, Scene II)*

Horatio

> *"A man that Fortune's buffets and rewards*
> *Hast ta'en with equal thanks".*   *(Act 3, Scene II)*

Horatio contrasts with Hamlet's false friends Rosencrantz and Guildenstem. Hamlet trusts Horatio absolutely. He is the only person in the play to whom Hamlet reveals his true feelings:

> *"Since my dear soul was mistress of her choice*
> *And could of men distinguish, her election*
> *Hath seal'd thee for herself".*   *(ibid)*

With Horatio, Hamlet can be his true self, so although Horatio's role in the play is passive for the most part, he serves an important dramatic function.

We meet Horatio before we meet Hamlet. He is respected by the others. He is a *"scholar"* so they expect him to know how to address the ghost. Horatio is a key witness in identifying the ghost as the late king of Denmark. He is sceptical about the existence of ghosts. He *"will not let belief take hold of him"*. However when confronted with the appearance of the ghost he matter-of-factly accepts *"the sensible and true avouch/Of mine own eyes"*. He is exact in his account of the ghost's appearance. He shows courage in confronting the ghost:

> *"I'll cross it, though it blast me"*.   *(Act I, Scene I)*

He shows compassion for the tormented spirit, and concern for the fate of Denmark:

> *"If there by any good thing to be done,*
> *That may to thee do ease and grace to me,*
> *Speak to me:*
> *If thou art privy to thy country's fate,*
> *Which happily foreknowing may avoid,*
> *O! speak"*.   *(ibid)*

Horatio is calm and matter of fact, consistent and well balanced. Hamlet admires these qualities in Horatio. He describes him as the man whose patience and fortune are such that in suffering all he suffers nothing. Horatio is loyal and true. He tries to prevent Hamlet from taking part in the fencing match. When he sees the imminent death of his friend, he too wishes to die. However, as a good friend, he is willing to fulfill Hamlet's request to vindicate his name and he lives on to tell:

> *"the yet unknowing world*
> *How these things came about"*.   *(Act 5, Scene II)*

Polonius

> *"a foolish prating knave"*.   *(Act 3, Scene IV)*

In *Act 1, Scene II* we get a clear idea of the importance of Polonius in the court. Claudius says to Laertes:

> *"The head is not more native to the heart,*
> *The hand more instrumental to the mouth,*
> *Than is the throne of Denmark to thy father"*.

Polonius is loyal to the throne. He has obviously concurred with the succession of Claudius. He will stoop to anything to gain favour in the king's eyes. He is prepared to spy on Hamlet and even to use his own daughter as a decoy. In fact it must be noted that Polonius frequently stoops to spying in the play. He sends Reynaldo to spy on his own son. He himself spies on Hamlet and Ophelia and he meets his death spying on Hamlet and Gertrude. He is deceitful and cunning. He tells Reynaldo *"By indirections find directions out"*. He even permits Reynaldo to sully the reputation of his son provided he obtains the information he wants:

> *"...put on him*
> *What forgeries you please"*.   *(Act 2, Scene I)*

For Polonius the end justifies the means and he is unscrupulous in his methods. Polonius has low moral standards. *"Forgeries"* are permitted, *"taints of liberty"* are excusable, *"slight sullies"* are acceptable.

Polonius is a man of the world. He advises Laertes about his conduct but his maxims are shallow. His moral advice is worldy-wise, aimed at looking after oneself and distrusting others. His words have little depth of meaning. There is irony in his advice to his son:

> *"Give every man thine ear, but few thy voice;" (Act I, Scene III)*

as Polonius himself is extremely garrulous. Polonius loves to hear himself talk, to the point of irritation. The queen effectively sums up Polonius's weakness when she orders him to speak:

> *"More matter, with less art".*   *(Act 2, Scene II)*

For all his wordiness, Polonius's speeches have little substance. Moreover, for Polonius everything is black and white:

> *"Why day is day, night night, and time is time".*   *(ibid)*

Polonius is pretentious and likes to air his knowledge in the company of others. He pretends to be very knowledgeable about acting. Yet it is obvious that he does not appreciate the speech of the First Player and he complains *"This is too long"*. Polonius is dogmatic and self-opinionated. He boastfully asks the king:

> *"Hath there been such a time, – I'd fain know that, –*
> *That I have positively said, ''Tis so,'*
> *When it prov'd otherwise?"*   *(ibid)*

Here he positively asserts that Hamlet is mad for love of Ophelia. Yet he had been equally dogmatic in insisting to Ophelia that Hamlet didn't really love her. He himself realises that perhaps he should have considered Hamlet's love for Ophelia *"with better heed and judgment"*. He admits he was wrong but then jumps to a conclusion which is the other extreme altogether.

Polonius is unsympathetic towards his daughter. Although he freely dispenses advice he shows little real understanding of Ophelia's situation:

> *"Affection! pooh! you speak like a green girl". (Act I, Scene III)*

He is motivated not just by concern for his daughter but concern for himself, his position in court:

> *"Tender yourself more dearly;*
> *Or, – not to crack the wind of the poor phrase,*
> *Running it thus, – you'll tender me a fool".*   *(ibid)*

Two extreme views of Polonius emerge in the play. Claudius considers him to be faithful and honourable. Hamlet dismisses him as a:

"wretched, rash, intruding fool".   *(Act 3, Scene IV)*

Laertes

"The flash and outbreak of a fiery mind".   *(Act 2, Scene I)*

In *Act 1, Scene II* we learn that Laertes has dutifully returned to the court for the coronation but wishes to return to France. He is a pleasure-loving young man and Ophelia is quick to point out that Laertes is not particularly virtuous.

He completely misjudges the sincerity of Hamlet's love for Ophelia. His view of the world is worldly-wise. For him, marriage between a prince and an ordinary girl is an impossibility. Laertes is somewhat like his father. We learn that he has gained his father's consent to return to France *"by laboursome petition"*. Like his father he indulges in laboursome advice to Ophelia. Yet Laertes is concerned about his sister, understanding her vulnerability. His advice to Ophelia is well meant. Moreover he is obviously deeply moved by the death of his sister and he speaks of her with feeling.

Laertes is an obvious contrast to Hamlet. He is a man of action. He sweeps to his revenge without waiting for proof of who is to blame. Laertes is impulsive and thoughtless. He rushes into the court roaring for blood, ready to smash all in his way. The idea of revenge presents no dilemma for him. He proclaims that patience would proclaim him a bastard. He is prepared to defy his king, his God and his conscience. Laertes is blinded by rage and becomes a mere pawn in Claudius's plot. Laertes allows Claudius to divert his anger and use him for his own ends. Claudius plays on Laertes's qualities of pride and rivalry and succeeds in manipulating him.

Laertes succumbs to dishonour when he agrees to the king's plan and offers to poison his rapier. It is an unfair contest, but Laertes ignores any qualms of conscience and goes along with the treachery. Even his acceptance of Hamlet's apology is ungracious. In the end he redeems himself somewhat by telling Hamlet the truth and asking his forgiveness.

Ophelia

"Dear maid, kind sister, sweet Ophelia!"   *(Act 4, Scene V)*

Ophelia is a dutiful daughter who obeys her father without question. She is young and innocent, inexperienced in the ways of the world. She is docile, timid and gentle. She is not calculating like her father or worldly-wise like her brother. She loves Hamlet and believes that his love for her is honourable. Although she tries to defend him against her father's cynicism, she is not strong enough to stand up to her father. By submitting to her father's command to stop seeing Hamlet, she seems to confirm the fickleness of women. Because of her obedient resignation she fails to restore Hamlet's belief in love. Ophelia describes Hamlet's visit to her in her closet with sympathetic understanding, despite his behaviour. She deals with Hamlet's madness with dignity but she is not equal to his harshness nor is she equal to the shock of her father being killed by the man she loved. She is helpless and bewildered and the cumulative effect of the death of her father and the loss of Hamlet results in her loss of reason. Ophelia's madness is a pathetic counterpoint to Hamlet's assumed madness.

Ophelia is the very opposite of what Hamlet despises in his mother. Her naivety and simplicity contrast with the queen's character. Gertrude recognises Ophelia's qualities, her goodness and her beauty. She believes in Ophelia:

> *"so shall I hope your virtues*
> *Will bring him to his wonted way again".*   (Act 3, Scene I)

She is prepared to accept Ophelia as a bride for her son and grieves at her death:

> *"I hop'd thou shouldst have been my Hamlet's wife;*
> *I thought thy bride-bed to have deck'd, sweet maid,*
> *And not have strew'd thy grave".*   (Act 5, Scene I)

Gertrude

> *"most seeming-virtuous queen".*   (Act 1, Scene V)

Gertrude plays a very passive part in the play's action, but her presence influences the play's themes. She emerges as a weak and somewhat shallow woman. She seemed to love King Hamlet. According to Hamlet *"she would hang on him"*. Yet according to the ghost of King Hamlet she was unfaithful to him even while he was alive as he refers to his brother as *"that adulterate beast"*. She acts the part of the mourning widow:

> *"she follow'd my poor father's body,*
> *Like Niobe, all tears;"*   (Act 1, Scene II)

yet within a month she married Claudius. Since she scarcely mourns her husband, she does not like Hamlet to continue mourning. In *Scene II* of the first act she seems impatient and her words are cold and unsympathetic:

> *"Why seems it so particular with thee?"*   (ibid)

She wishes that Hamlet would make peace with Claudius. She is in fact totally submissive to the wishes of Claudius and appears to be always in his shadow. Although Claudius refers to her as *"The imperial jointress"* of the state she has little effect.

There is no hint in the play that Gertrude felt any remorse for the past. Infuriated at her lack of moral sense Hamlet sets her up:

> "a glass
> Where you may see the inmost part of you".   (Act 3, Scene IV)

She appears to be genuinely bewildered at Hamlet's storm of abuse:

> "What have I done that thou dar'st wag thy tongue
> In noise so rude against me?"   (ibid)

She is blind to the presence of the ghost which suggests her moral blindness. However her cries of anguish:

> "O! speak to me no more;
> These words like daggers enter in mine ears;
> No more..."   (ibid)

are an indication that Hamlet's words have moved her. She sees the *"black and grained spots"* tainting her soul. It is the beginning of an awareness of sin. Hamlet however has little faith in her repentance. Bitterly he tells her:

> "Assume a virtue, if you have it not".   (ibid)

Morally blind and insensitive as she may be, Gertrude is shocked to learn that her husband was murdered. She promises Hamlet not to reveal to the king what he has said and she sincerely wishes to protect her son:

> "Be thou assur'd, if words be made of breath,
> And breath of life, I have no life to breathe
> What thou hast said to me".   (ibid)

Gertrude is also kind to Ophelia and hopes that the gentle girl can help restore Hamlet's sanity. She does not blame Ophelia. In fact she says:

> "I do wish
> That your good beauties be the happy cause
> Of Hamlet's wildness".   (Act 3, Scene I)

At Ophelia's funeral it is Gertrude who strews her grave with flowers.

Gertrude's redeeming feature is her love for her son. She is delighted by Hamlet's success in the fencing match and it is in drinking to his success that she dies. Her death is pathetic. She dies a victim of Claudius's treachery, knowing that he has murdered Hamlet as well as herself.

Claudius

"smiling, damned villain".   (Act I, Scene V)

Hamlet sums up Claudius's character in the bedroom scene with his mother. He calls him:

> *"A murderer, and a villain;*
> *A slave that is not twentieth part of the tithe*
> *Of your precedent lord; a vice of kings;*
> *A cutpurse of the empire and the rule,*
> *That from a shelf the precious diadem stole,*
> *And put it in his pocket."*   (Act 3, Scene IV)

Claudius is a murderer and an adulterer, yet he acts as if he is rightfully king and makes a striking courtly figure. Claudius would appear to make a good king. He is courteous and dignified. He handles affairs of state with confidence. He is a diplomat, a man of words. However, his speech is excessive, stilted and artificial; his smiling kindness overdone. In his attempt to excuse *"mirth in funeral"* he resorts to figures of speech which show little real feeling:

> *"our whole kingdom*
> *To be contracted in one brow of woe".*   (Act I, Scene II)

Claudius is a consummate hypocrite. He puts on a show of sorrow for the brother he has murdered. He is shrewd. He has succeeded in gaining the acquiescence of his counsellors to his kingship and marriage. He is careful to maintain their approval. Before sending Hamlet to England he prudently decides:

> *"we'll call up our wisest friends;*
> *And let them know, both what we mean to do,*
> *And what's untimely done".*   (Act 4, Scene I)

He is gracious in granting favours, he is anxious to win over Hamlet. He is shrewd enough to realise that there is danger in Hamlet's melancholy:

> *"There's something in his soul*
> *O'er which his melancholy sits on brood;*
> *And, I do doubt, the hatch and the disclose*
> *Will be some danger".*   (Act 3, Scene I)

Claudius is very perceptive. He shows more insight than the others with regard to Hamlet:

> *"what he spake, though it lack'd form a little,*
> *Was not like madness".*   (ibid)

He is quick to realise the danger to himself in the fact that Hamlet killed Polonius, and he takes immediate action:

> *"The sun no sooner shall the mountains touch*
> *But we will ship him hence".*   *(Act 4, Scene I)*

Even when under threat, Claudius shows masterly control. He remains calm and dignified in the face of Laertes' threats and even manages to win over the hot-tempered Laertes, cunningly using him to kill Hamlet so that:

> *"for his death no wind of blame shall breathe". (Act 4, Scene VII)*

Like Polonius, Claudius is unscrupulous about spying. He agrees to eavesdrop with Polonius on the meeting between Ophelia and Hamlet. He permits Polonius to hide behind the arras in the queen's bedroom. He uses Hamlet's childhood friends, Rosencrantz and Guildenstern:

> *"to gather,*
> *So much as from occasion you may glean."*   *(Act 2, Scene II)*

Claudius is utterly ruthless. When Polonius is killed his immediate concern is that he should not be blamed. He is indifferent to the death of Polonius and he seems equally indifferent to the news of Ophelia's death. His ultimate act of treachery is when he allows Gertrude to drink the poison.

According to Hamlet's interpretation of Claudius, he is a beast, a *"a satyr"*. Certainly Claudius is fond of drink, carousing and merriment. He calls out for the king's *"rouse"* despite the recent death of his brother. However he is not totally devoid of conscience and a spiritual side to him is highlighted in *Scene III* of the third act as he reflects on his crime. The re-enactment of the murder in *The Mouse Trap* jolts him. His poise is shattered as he rushes away. Although he seems unmoved by the dumb show, the conversation about remarriage and remembrance disturbs him as he questions Hamlet about the suitability of the plot. Claudius's conscience moves him to express contrition for his offence which *"smells to heaven"*. He knows the full horror of his sin but acknowledges that he cannot hope for forgiveness since he cannot give up what he gained by murdering his brother. Claudius faces the truth about himself and the prayer scene is the only occasion in the play when we see behind the smiling mask.

Hamlet

> *"The expectancy and rose of the fair state..."*   *(Act 3, Scene I)*

There is an underlying awareness throughout the play that the melancholic Hamlet we see is not the real Hamlet. Basically Hamlet has a love of life, an interest in worldy activities such as fencing and the theatre. The arrival of the players delights Hamlet, but his delight is tempered by the dilemma he faces and the speech of the player is an expression of the issues uppermost in his mind. Hamlet tells Rosencrantz and Guildenstern:

> *"I have of late, – but wherefore I know not, – lost all my mirth,*
> *forgone all custom of exercises;"*   (Act 2, Scene II)

which suggests that he is not naturally of a gloomy disposition, but an active and cheerful man. Towards his friends Hamlet is friendly, and he is hospitable towards the players. He appears natural and at ease in such company, mixing well. Indeed his behaviour towards the Players and Horatio and his friends is very different from his behaviour in the presence of the king and queen and courtiers.

According to Ophelia, Hamlet had been a soldier, scholar and courtier:

> *"The glass of fashion and the mould of form".* (Act 3, Scene I)

We know from Claudius that Hamlet is loved by the people of Denmark. He is respected. Fortinbras believes:

> *"he was likely, had he been put on,*
> *To have prov'd most royally".*   (Act 5, Scene II)

Hamlet's moral being is shaken by the murder of his father and his mother's lust. The consequent loss of belief in the nobleness of man affects his whole personality.

> *"To be, or not to be..."*   (Act 3, Scene I)

Hamlet makes his appearance in the second scene of the play and is striking by his aloofness from the rest of the court, he is isolated and in black. He is gloomy and sardonic. Hamlet was obviously a dutiful and affectionate son who respected and admired his father:

> *"He was a man, take him for all in all,*
> *I shall not look upon his like again".*   (Act I, Scene II)

His grief for his father's death is heartfelt. He is obviously highly emotional and sensitive and is shocked to the core at his mother's remarriage to his uncle so soon. In the first soliloquy we get a glimpse of Hamlet's thoughts. He is disillusioned at life. The world is *"weary, stale, flat and unprofitable"*. It is *"an unweeded garden"*. His melancholy leads him to thoughts of suicide.

Yet although Hamlet expresses his disillusionment with the world, he is deeply appreciative of its beauty and the wonder of man.

Hamlet knows the earth to be a *"goodly frame"* and the firmament to be a *"majestical roof fretted with golden fire"*. He is very much the philosopher and poet. As a thinking man he is very much aware of the sufferings endured by mankind:

> *"The slings and arrows of outrageous fortune,...*
> *The heart-ache and the thousand natural shocks*
> *That flesh is heir to...*
> *   the whips and scorns of time,*
> *The oppressor's wrong...".*   (Act 3, Scene I)

So Hamlet's thoughts turn to death. It is only his religious consciousness, a fear of the after-life that prevents him from suicide. At the opening of the play the Hamlet we see is sunk in apathy, his feelings dulled by shock and revulsion. The ghost's revelation stirs his feelings to intense anger. Hamlet tries to keep alive this passionate anger as only anger will motivate him to revenge. He tries to recharge his emotion by asking the player to recite a passionate speech. As the player relates the grief of Hecuba, Hamlet makes the comparison with his mother and this renews his purpose of revenge.

Hamlet from the very outset is inwardly divided. Reason and passion are at war with one another. Passion makes him respond:

> *"Haste me to know't, that I, with wings as swift*
> *As meditation or the thoughts of love,*
> *May sweep to my revenge"*   (Act 1, Scene V)

but reason cautions:

> *".... O cursed spite,*
> *That ever I was born to set it right!"*   (ibid)

Hamlet is torn by indecision – *"To be, or not to be"*. He is beset by doubts:

> *"... The spirit that I have seen*
> *May be the devil."*   (Act 2, Scene II)

He is torn by self-reproach:

> *"O! what a rogue and peasant slave am I".*   (ibid)

He wonders:

> *"Whether 'tis nobler in the mind to suffer*
> *The slings and arrows of outrageous fortune,*
> *Or to take arms against a sea of troubles,*
> *And by opposing end them".*   (Act 3, Scene I)

He concludes:

> *"Thus conscience does make cowards of us all".*   (ibid)

He believes that:

> *"the native hue of resolution*
> *Is sicklied o'er with the pale cast of thought".*   (ibid)

The instinctive nature of man is to act, but often his reason restrains him. Man is no better than a beast if he does not use his reason, yet using it he finds no answers. Hamlet wonders if he may have been *"thinking too precisely on the event"*; yet in point of fact he seldom reasons out alternative courses of action. His first soliloquy is a passionate outpouring of disgust which ends in resigned acceptance:

> *"But break, my heart, for I must hold my tongue!" (Act I, Scene II)*

In the second soliloquy the passionate response to the player's speech is followed by a passionate denunciation of himself and an angry outburst against Claudius. There is little concrete reasoning of specific problems such as how to actually effect his revenge.

Hamlet's meditations are long and complex, usually dominated by passion. Instead of reasoning, Hamlet verbalises his emotions, he does not evoke reason. His deeply felt failure to come to terms with his situation finds an outlet in words. Hamlet knows that he has become helplessly caught up in a tempest of passion:

> *"... This is most brave*
> *That I, the son of a dear father murder'd,*
> *Prompted to my revenge by heaven and hell,*
> *Must, like a whore, unpack my heart with words,*
> *And fall a-cursing, like a very drab,*
> *A scullion!"*   *(Act 2, Scene II)*

Hamlet describes his own feelings accurately but he does not understand them. He criticises himself for being *"Like John-a-dreams"* who does nothing. He accuses himself of being:

> *"A dull and muddy-mettled rascal".*   *(ibid)*

He asks himself if he has delayed because he is insensitive or a coward. Neither cowardice nor insensitivity are qualities one could attribute to Hamlet.

> **"Yet have I in me something dangerous..."**   *(Act 5, Scene I)*

Hamlet shows himself to be a man capable of action. He is an excellent fencer. He expertly kills Laertes and Claudius, not to mention Polonius behind the arras. He bravely boards a pirate ship. He is well able to deal with Rosencrantz and Guildenstern. When Hamlet fights he is prompt and resolute. Hamlet is not afraid of physical danger. He follows the ghost bravely:

> *"My fate cries out,*
> *And makes each petty artery in this body*
> *As hardy as the Nemean lion's nerve".*   *(Act I, Scene IV)*

Hamlet admires soldiers like his father and Fortinbras and when he is dead he is seen by a soldier as a soldier.

Hamlet is courageous, capable of action. He is also capable of swift decisions. When he discovers what the king's sealed letters contain, he loses no time in taking action:

> *"Being thus benetted round with villanies, –*
> *Ere I could make a prologue to my brains*
> *They had begun the play. I sat me down,*
> *Devis'd a new commission..."*   *(Act 5, Scene II)*

There is a savage side to Hamlet which emerges in his brutal verbal attack on Ophelia and Gertrude, his speech as Claudius kneels at prayer and his ruthlessness towards Rosencrantz and Guildenstern. But Hamlet is not cruel by nature. He even has to plead with his mother so as not to weaken his resolution:

> *"Do not look upon me;*
> *Lest with this piteous action you convert*
> *My stern effects: then, what I have to do*
> *Will want true colour; tears, perchance, for blood". (Act 3, Scene IV)*

Hamlet sums up his character very well when he says:

> *"For though I am not splenetive and rash*
> *Yet have I in me something dangerous".*   *(Act 5, Scene I)*

> *"It is not madness/That I have utter'd..."*   *(Act 3, Scene IV)*

Hamlet's antic disposition is a kind of second self which disguises his instability as he alternates between weary apathy and sudden outbursts of passion, deep meditation and bitter mockery. The *"antic disposition"* is a good cover for his distraught feelings. It allows him to ask pointed questions, and make sarcastic retorts with madness as the excuse. Hamlet assumes and discards his madness at will. Conversing rationally with Horatio before the play in *Act 3, Scene II*, he suddenly switches at the arrival of the court saying, *"I must be idle"*. The success of Hamlet's assumption of an *"antic disposition"* is evident in *Act 2, Scene II*. Claudius refers to Hamlet's *"transformation"*. Gertrude refers to *"My too much changed son"* and Polonius speaks of *"the madness wherin now he raves"*. However, even Polonius recognises:

> *"Though this be madness, yet there is method in't". (Act 2, Scene II)*

Hamlet in fact never loses contact with reality. His speech is enigmatic but not incoherent. His *"madness"* takes the form of ironic mockery which his opponents cannot counter. In Hamlet's *"mad"* exchange with Polonius in *Act 3, Scene II* Hamlet makes a total fool of the bewildered Polonius;

Hamlet   *"Do you see yonder cloud that's almost in shape of a camel?*

Polonius   *By the mass, and 'tis like a camel, indeed.*

Hamlet   *Methinks it is like a weasel.*

Polonius   *It is backed like a weasel.*

Hamlet   *Or like a whale?*

Polonius   *Very like a whale."*

The very form of Hamlet's speech, the images he uses:

> *"O Jephthah, judge of Israel what a treasure hadst thou!" (Act 2, Scene II)*

is an indication of his rationality. Indeed, Hamlet is sometimes more in control in his so-called *"mad"* scenes than he is in some of his soliloquies, where he is so dominated by passion that he is dangerously irrational:

> *"now could I drink hot blood,*
> *And do such bitter business as the day*
> *Would quake to look on".*   *(Act 3, Scene II)*

> **"he was likely, had he been put on,/To have prov'd most royally..."**   *(Act 5, Scene II)*

Hamlet returns from the voyage to England a changed man, with an air of self-possession, and confidence. He has come to terms with his identity. He proclaims:

> *"This is I,*
> *Hamlet the Dane"*   *(Act 5, Scene I)*

thus claiming Denmark as his kingdom. He is also prepared now to admit his love for Ophelia and he declares in front of all at the graveside *"I lov'd Ophelia"*. The *"antic disposition"* has disappeared. His last display of anger is provoked by Laertes jumping into Ophelia's grave but Hamlet quickly regains control and apologises with dignity. His thoughts seem to have taken a new direction. There are no more bitter self-reproaches. He no longer doubts that he will act against Claudius and calmly asks Horatio:

> *"is't not perfect conscience*
> *To quit him with this arm?"*   *(Act 5, Scene II)*

Although he meditates on death in *Act 5, Scene I*, there is no morbid longing for it. His fortunate escape from death has taught him:

> *"There's a divinity that shapes our ends".*   *(ibid)*

He has found no solution to life's mystery but now he is ready for whatever is to happen. He is learning to accept reality for what it is . *"The readiness is all"*, being prepared and yet submitting to divine providence. Hamlet accepts that man cannot control fate. The accidents that saved his life were providential. He shrugs off his premonition of danger and defies *"augury"*. He accepts what's to be:

> *"If it be now, 'tis not to come; if it be not to come, it will be now; if it be not now, yet it will come: the readiness is all".*   *(ibid)*

He has no fear of dying:

> *"Since no man has aught of what he leaves, what is't to leave betimes?"*   *(ibid)*

Hamlet's death is noble. He kills Claudius, knowing now that it is clearly just to kill one who has treacherously killed so many. He forgives Laertes. Hamlet's death is not a renunciation of the world. He is concerned about the honour of his reputation and he settles the succession of the kingdom on Fortinbras. Hamlet's submission to fate may be seen as disillusioned resignation, but his references to heaven, divinity and providence suggest a belief in a great moral design beyond man's comprehension. Hamlet's words:

> *"there's a special providence in the fall of a sparrow"*   *(ibid)*

suggest faith, not despair.

Conclusion

Horatio sums up unequivocally the tragic dimension of *Hamlet*. It is a play

> *"Of carnal, bloody, and unnatural acts,*
> *Of accidental judgments, casual slaughters;*
> *Of deaths put on by cunning and forc'd cause,*
> *And, in this upshot, purposes mistook*
> *Fall'n on the inventors' heads."*   *(Act 5, Scene II)*

Yet our final impression of the play is not so much concerned with the nature of the plot as the nature of the character of Hamlet. We see the play almost entirely from the point of view of Hamlet and so we identify with him. We admire Hamlet's moral sensitivity, his abhorrence of evil, his contempt for hypocrisy. Hamlet has a sensitive awareness of the beautiful, of the good, of what man could and should be. Hamlet shows us the values of conscience and honour. Because we admire his spiritual sensitivity we tend to accept his cruelty towards Ophelia and Gertrude and his indifference to the deaths of Polonius, Rosencrantz and Guildenstern.

Hamlet's dilemma is the dilemma of civilised man who questions his existence. Hamlet does not answer questions. He poses them and forces us to consider the nature of man and the mystery of life.

Glossary of Dramatic Terms

Action: the sequence of important events on which the interest depends. The action in *Hamlet* moves more swiftly in the fourth and fifth acts.

Acts: the Elizabethan dramatists followed Horace's dictate of five acts in a play.

Aside: a speech or a remark made in a lower tone and not intended to be heard generally. It is a useful dramatic device. In *Act I Scene II*, Hamlet's aside *"A little more than kin, and less than kind"* lets the audience know that there is something wrong with Hamlet's relationship with Claudius.

Atmosphere: the spirit which pervades a play; an atmosphere of corruption and death pervades *Hamlet*.

Catastrophe: an event which overturns the order of things – the final outcome of a dramatic play. Hamlet's catastrophe is his fatal battle with Laertes who has poisoned his sword.

Catharsis: Aristotle's belief that the spectator was purified by the emotions of terror and pity and the overwhelming spectacle of sadness in tragedy.

Characterisation: it is important that the audience believes in the characters, otherwise they cannot experience pity or terror. What a character says and does must be consistent with his character. It is the characterisation of Hamlet which engrosses us most in *Hamlet*. A character undergoes profound modification in a play. Hamlet is a very different man at the end of the play from what he was in *Act 1*.

Comic Relief: a diversion which provokes laughter and releases the audience momentarily from the tension of the tragedy. The graveyard scene in *Hamlet* is an example of comic relief. Nevertheless the comedy is restrained by the pathos of preparing the grave for Ophelia.

Conflict: struggle; the essence of all drama. In classical tragedy the hero was in conflict with fate. In modern tragedy the hero is in conflict with his own nature. Hamlet's duty to avenge his father's death is in conflict with all that is noble in his nature.

Contrast:	to compare in order to state the difference between: to show the opposition of certain qualities. For example King Hamlet is contrasted with King Claudius.
Crisis:	a critical or decisive moment; a turning point. In *Hamlet* the prayer scene is the crisis point of the plot – Hamlet has the opportunity of killing Claudius. He does not do so and instigates the catastrophe by killing Polonius instead.
Denouement:	the unravelling of the plot, the outcome of the action; the denouement is synonymous with the catastrophe in tragedy.
Dialogue:	John Galsworthy defined good dramatic dialogue as *"Good dialogue, again, is character, marshalled so as continually to stimulate interest or excitement"*. Dramatic dialogue reveals the character of the speaker and unfolds the plot simultaneously. We discover the character through the dialogue.
Dramatic Irony:	occurs when the audience recognises that facts are not what the characters believe them to be. An audience can recognise that the opinions expressed by a character are the opposite to the truth. Hamlet's words regarding his father *"I shall not look upon his like again"* are an example of dramatic irony as the audience is aware that Hamlet will probably come face to face with his father's ghost. There is dramatic irony in the fact that Claudius encourages Hamlet's relationship with the players which is what contributes to his downfall. A striking example of dramatic irony is to be found at the end of the prayer scene, when just as Hamlet leaves, Claudius states that he is not able to pray.
Dramatis Personae:	persona is a Latin word for the mask worn by the actor in classical Greek drama and represented the characteristics of the person whose part he was taking. Dramatis Personae in Shakespeare's time meant the characters in the drama.
Effective:	for a scene to be dramatically effective, it must produce a definite impression. The ghost scenes in *Hamlet* are dramatically effective because they heighten our sense of unease and prepare us for the discovery of the murder.
Exposition:	the explication and development of the plot.

Hero:
: hero in the sense of the tragic hero means more than simply a man of courage, or the main protagonist. The tragic hero is always a man of high degree, a man of exceptional nature who has a divided soul.

Plot:
: the arrangement of the incidents in the play, the design of the story. The nature of the characters determines the progress of the plot. Shakespeare cared little about his plots as such, taking them from stories already well-known and altering them to suit his purpose. He focuses on character and the plot unfolds through characterisation.

Retribution:
: reward or punishment for good or bad actions. In tragedy, the hero's death is his retribution for his tragic flaw and is consequently accepted as inevitable.

Soliloquy:
: a monologue addressed to the self. In *Hamlet* the hero's soliloquies reveal his inner self and ensure the sympathy of the audience.

Stage:
: The Shakespearian stage was like an apron and partly projected into the auditorium. In the prologue to *King Henry V*, the stage is referred to as a *"...wooden O...."* The chorus asks the audience *"... can this cockpit hold/ The vastyfield of France? or may we cram/Within this wooden O the very casques/That did affright the air at Agincourt?"*

Symbolism:
: a symbol is a concrete thing which is, at the same time, itself and representative of something else. In *Hamlet* the ghost may be regarded as the symbol that something is *"rotten"* in Denmark. There is an accumulation of symbolic references to corruption and death.

Sympathy:
: sharing another's emotions; being affected by the suffering of another. The sympathy of the audience with the tragic hero is essential for catharsis. In *Hamlet* the audience identifies with Hamlet because Hamlet is the dominant consciousness through which we see the action.

Theme:
: the central idea; but there may be several themes.

Time:
: Shakespeare largely ignores time in *Hamlet*. There is a sense of time standing still. It is Ophelia who tells us in the third act of the play that it is now *"twice two months"* since the death of the king. In the original legend of Hamlet, Amleth returned to Denmark one year after he had left for England but the dramatic time of Shakespeare's *Hamlet* is much less.

Tragedy:
: the essence of tragedy is the death of a great soul which fills the audience with such pity and terror that it purifies the mind.

Questions and Sample Answers

Act 1

Scene I

1. Discuss the significance of the appearance of the ghost in the first scene of the play.

2. Outline the background information on the state of Denmark presented in this scene.

3. Horatio speaks more in this scene than in any scene in the play. What are your impressions of him as a character?

Scene II

1. What do we learn of the character of Claudius in this scene?

2. Describe the confrontation between Claudius and Hamlet. What does Gertrude contribute to the interview?

3. Study Hamlet's soliloquy. What does it reveal about his state of mind?

4. What effect on Hamlet has Horatio's report of the ghost?

Scene III

1. Discuss the relationship between Polonius, Ophelia and Laertes. Is this a typical family scene?

2. Summarise Polonius' advice to Laertes.

3. What do we learn of the relationship between Ophelia and Hamlet in this scene? Discuss the reasons given by Laertes and Polonius for discouraging the relationship.

Scene IV

1. Compare this scene with the first scene in which the ghost appeared on the battlements.

2. Would you agree with Horatio that Hamlet *"waxes desperate with imagination"*?

3. Discuss the significance of Marcellus' remark *"Something is rotten in the state of Denmark"*.

4. What is the dramatic effect of dividing *Scenes IV* and *V*?

Scene V

1. What important facts do we learn from the conversation of Hamlet and the ghost?

2. Discuss the importance of Hamlet's exclamation *"O my prophetic soul!"*

3. What is the effect on Hamlet of the ghost's revelation? How would you describe his state of mind at the end of the scene?

4. Why do you think that Hamlet decides to put on an *"antic disposition"*?

5. Discuss the dramatic effectiveness of this scene.

Act 2

Scene I

1. What are Polonius' instructions to Reynaldo? In the light of his earlier advice to his children, does it surprise you?

2. What do we learn of Hamlet's feelings for Ophelia in this scene? Would you agree with Polonius that *"This is the very ecstasy of love"*?

3. The scene between Hamlet and Ophelia is reported indirectly. Is this dramatically effective?

Scene II

1. What is the attitude of the court towards Hamlet at this stage of the play?

2. Comment on the significance of Hamlet's words to Polonius.

3. Describe Hamlet's meeting with Rosencrantz and Guildenstern.

4. Would you agree with Polonius that Hamlet is *"far gone"*? Discuss Hamlet's mental condition as it has been revealed in this scene.

5. Examine carefully the tale of Æneas to Dido. What elements in the speech are related to the situation in the play?

6. What background knowledge about the theatre in Shakespeare's time is acquired from this scene?

Act 3

Scene I

1. How successful is Hamlet in assuming his antic disposition?

2. Study Hamlet's soliloquy *"To be, or not to be"*. What insight does this give into Hamlet's attitude to life?

3. (a) Discuss the change in the relationship between Hamlet and Ophelia.

   (b) Do you think that Hamlet's treatment of Ophelia is justified?

4. Examine the role of Ophelia in the play so far.

5. Hamlet accuses himself of being *"proud, revengeful, ambitious"*. From what you have seen of him so far in the play, would you agree with this estimation of himself?

Scene II

1. Contrast Hamlet's behaviour in the presence of the players and Horatio with his behaviour towards the king and queen, Polonius and Ophelia, Rosencrantz and Guildenstern.

2. What have you learned about Shakespeare's views on acting from Hamlet's discussion with the players?

3. Describe the qualities in Horatio's character which Hamlet admires.

4. Do you consider that the device of the play-within-a-play is dramatically successful?

5. What themes are reinforced by the presentation of *The Murder of Gonzago*?

6. How does this scene advance the plot?

Scene III

1. What aspects of Claudius' character are revealed in this scene?

2. What reasons are put forward by Hamlet for not killing the king? Are you convinced these are the real reasons?

3. Consider the dramatic significance of Hamlet rejecting the opportunity of killing the king at this point in the play.

Scene IV

1. Would you agree that Polonius can be considered as *"a wretched, rash, intruding fool"*?

2. This is the only scene in the play when Hamlet is alone with his mother. Describe their interview. What effect have Hamlet's reproaches on Gertrude?

3. Discuss the dramatic effectiveness of the reappearance of the ghost. Is there any significance in the fact that he is visible only to Hamlet?

4. What light does this scene throw on the character of Queen Gertrude?

5. What is the purpose of Hamlet's *"presentment of two brothers"*? In what way are they contrasted?

6. Discuss Hamlet's attitude towards (a) his mother; (b) Polonius; (c) Rosencrantz and Guildenstern.

7. Are you surprised at Hamlet killing Polonius? Is his action in keeping with his character as you have understood it so far?

Act 4

Scene I

1. What effect does the news of the death of Polonius have on Claudius?

2. What is the dramatic function of this short scene?

Scene II

1. Would you agree with Hamlet that Rosencrantz and Guildenstern are like sponges?

2. What do you understand by Hamlet's comment *"knavish speech sleeps in a foolish ear"*? Discuss the truth of this statement in the light of Hamlet's conversation with Rosencrantz and Guildenstern. You may refer to previous scenes to illustrate your opinion.

Scene III

1. How does this scene speed up the action of the play?

2. Is Claudius in control of the situation at this point in the play?

3. Show how Hamlet uses Polonius' dead body to make some pointed remarks about death and decay.

Scene IV

1. What is the dramatic value of having Hamlet meet up with Fortinbras' army?

2. Contrast the characters of Hamlet and Fortinbras.

3. Study again Hamlet's soliloquy in *Act 2, Scene II "O! what a rogue and peasant slave am I"*. Then examine the soliloquy *"How all occasions do inform against me"*. Compare Hamlet's thoughts and state of mind. Has Hamlet made any progress?

4. Would you agree that Hamlet's problem is *"thinking too precisely on the event"*?

Scene V

1. Discuss Ophelia's madness.

   (a) Is there any significance in the songs she sings?

   (b) What is the dramatic effect of Ophelia's reappearance with the flowers?

   (c) In what way is her madness clearly differentiated from Hamlet's?

2. Contrast Laertes's behaviour with that of Hamlet.

3. How does Claudius act when faced with danger?

4. What do we learn about the present state of affairs in Denmark from this scene?

Scene VI

1. What important information is contained in Hamlet's letter to Horatio?

Scene VII

1. What further light is thrown on the character of Laertes in this scene?

2. Compare Hamlet's letter to Horatio and his letter to the king.

3. What aspects of Claudius' character are highlighted in this scene?

4. What is the effect of the description of Ophelia's death?

5. Show how the scene is set for a tragic denouement in the final act.

Act 5

Scene I

1. Discuss the effect of the comic buffoonery of the clowns.

2. Describe Ophelia's funeral.

3. Comment on the significance of the queen's words *"I hop'd thou shouldst have been my Hamlet's wife"*.

4. What do you think of the behaviour of Laertes in this scene?

5. Summarise Hamlet's meditation on life and death.

6. What new side to Hamlet's character emerges in this scene?

Scene II

1. Show how this scene ties up the various strands of the plot.

2. Why do you think Osric is introduced at this late stage of the play?

3. Give an account of the duel between Hamlet and Laertes.

4. *"For by the image of my cause, I see/The portraiture of his."* Discuss the similarity in the cause of Hamlet and Laertes and consider each character's approach to revenge.

5. What is your final impression of (a) Claudius, (b) Gertrude, (c) Laertes, (d) Horatio?

6. Are you satisfied by the succession of Fortinbras to the throne of Denmark? Has be been fully developed as a character?

7. Discuss the accomplishment of Hamlet's revenge.

Sample Questions for Ordinary Level

1. Discuss the importance of the appearance of the ghost in the first scene of the play.

2. Describe Hamlet's reaction to the ghost in scenes 4 and 5 of Act 1.

3. From your reading of the play, what do you learn of the relationship between Hamlet and his father?

4. Examine the causes for Hamlet's delay in taking revenge in the play. Are any of his reasons justified?

5. Hamlet tells Rosencrantz, *"My wit's diseased"*. To what extent do you think Hamlet was mad throughout the play?

6. Discuss the relationship between Hamlet and his mother. Do you approve of his behaviour towards his mother?

7. Discuss the relationship between Hamlet and Ophelia. Do you think Ophelia deserved to be rejected by Hamlet?

8. In Act 2 scene 2 Polonius reads out the letter written by Hamlet to Ophelia. Write out the letter you imagine Ophelia might have written in reply to Hamlet, if she had not been forbidden to communicate with Hamlet.

9. Discuss the importance of Polonius in the play. Do you think he deserved his fate?

10. Discuss the importance of Claudius in the play.

11. Claudius says of Gertrude, *"She's so conjunctive to my life and soul"*. Discuss the relationship of Claudius and Gertrude as it is portrayed in the play.

12. Discuss the importance of each of the following characters in Hamlet:

    (i) Laertes (ii) Rosencrantz and Guildenstern (iii) Fortinbras

13. Horatio appears in only nine out of the twenty scenes in the play and says little. Could he have been left out of the play altogether in your opinion?

14. Choose one of these phrases that you think best describes Hamlet and explain your choice:

    – *noble and sensitive*

    – *weak and indecisive*

    – *ruthless and cruel*

15. At the end of the play the stage is strewn with dead bodies.

    (a) How did you feel about the deaths of (i) Laertes (ii) Gertrude (iii) Claudius (iv) Rosencrantz and Guildenstern (v) Hamlet?

    (b) Is there any hope underlying the tragic ending?

Sample Answer for Ordinary Level

The play, *Hamlet*, has many exciting scenes. Briefly describe one scene that had a strong effect on you and explain why it had such an effect.

I think the most exciting and tense scene in the play is *Act 3, Scene III*. This scene is very dramatic and is exciting for a number of reasons. It is a scene where Claudius, the villain, confesses his guilt, and where Hamlet has a perfect opportunity to avenge his father's murder.

The drama in this scene is created by what has happened in the previous scene. In that scene, Hamlet used *The Mousetrap* to test his uncle's guilt. When Claudius stood up and left the play, his guilt was confirmed to Hamlet. As *Act 3, Scene III* opens, Claudius is very angry, and wants to do something about Hamlet. He says,

> *"The terms of our estate may not endure*
> *Hazard so dangerous as doth hourly grow*
> *Out of his lunacies."*

He decides to get Hamlet out of the way by sending him to England with Rosencrantz and Guildenstern.

Claudius is then left alone and one of the most dramatic moments of the play happens. He confesses his guilt. He says,

> *"O! my offence is rank, it smells to heaven;*
> *It hath the primal eldest curse upon't;*
> *A brother's murder!"*

This is shocking to the audience. Claudius then reveals that he killed King Hamlet because of *"My crown, mine own ambition, and my queen"*. This is a very tense moment. Claudius is kneeling in prayer, and the tension increases even more when Hamlet enters.

Claudius does not hear Hamlet. This is the perfect moment for the young prince to avenge his father. He says, *"Now might I do it, pat"*. The audience wonders if Hamlet will at last kill Claudius. However, Hamlet's fatal flaw is procrastination. He always finds a reason not to act. He says that he cannot kill Claudius because he is praying. A person killed while praying goes straight to heaven, no matter what his sins. Hamlet decides not to kill Claudius until he

> *"is drunk asleep, or in his rage,*
> *Or in the incestuous pleasure of his bed"*

and goes off to visit his mother's room.

There are many exciting scenes in *Hamlet*. However, I think *Act 3, Scene III* is the most dramatic of all of the scenes in the play, because it is filled with tension and anticipation.

Sample Questions for Higher Level

1. "Hamlet is a deeply reluctant agent of revenge." Discuss.

2. "Hamlet is alternately irresolute and passionate." Do you agree with this statement?

3. "Hamlet's soliloquies reveal a deeply thoughtful, troubled and passionate man." Discuss.

4. "The play ends with the deaths of all of the major characters. Ultimately, the blame for this tragedy must lie with Hamlet and his inability to act decisively." Discuss.

5. "Claudius is the great villain of the play Hamlet." Discuss.

6. "Gertrude is an extremely complex and sympathetic figure. Her great tragedy lies in the fact that she put personal happiness above moral duty." Discuss.

7. "Deception is a key theme in Shakespeare's *Hamlet*." Discuss.

8. "*Hamlet's* greatness lies in the extraordinary power of Shakespeare's language and imagery." Discuss.

9. "*Hamlet* is a play about power and kingship. Claudius' desire for power corrupts the kingdom of Denmark and creates the tragedy of the play." Discuss.

10. "Loyalty and betrayal are key themes in Shakespeare's *Hamlet*." Discuss.

11. Discuss the character of Ophelia. Would you agree that she is pathetic rather than tragic?

12. Show how the imagery of corruption contributes to the atmosphere and meaning of the play.

13. The Hamlet we see in Act 5 is transformed from the Hamlet of the previous four acts. Discuss this view of the dramatic change in Hamlet's character.

14. Discuss Ophelia's three-fold view of Hamlet as a courtier, soldier and scholar.

15. Would you agree with G. Wilson Knight that *"the theme of Hamlet is death"*?

Sample Answer for Higher Level

"Claudius is the consummate villain."

Discuss this statement in view of your study of Shakespeare's *Hamlet*. Support your answer with appropriate reference and quotation.

> *"Thus was I, sleeping, by a brother's hand,*
> *Of life of crown of queen, at once dispatched;"*   Ghost, Act 1, Scene V

Claudius is a regicide. A combination of jealousy and naked ambition led him to plan and carry out the murder of King Hamlet. This crime, regicide, is not only a crime against the person of the king, but also a crime against God and the nation of Denmark itself. Claudius' act and his subsequent attempts to protect his fraudulent position lead directly to the death of many members of the Danish court. He is an intelligent, clever man and a skilful politician, and he suffers the pangs of conscience that make him a very human and recognisable villain. However, the fact is his actions devastate Prince Hamlet, corrupting his view of the world until he becomes cynical and violent. Those close to the king suffer due to his duplicitous, selfish behaviour. Polonius, Claudius' minister and confidante, is killed and his children, Ophelia and Laertes, suffer tragic fates. Rosencrantz and Guildenstern, loyal subjects of the king, meet a bloody end in England as a direct result of one of Claudius' Machiavellian schemes. And Gertrude, the queen for whom Claudius continually expresses his passionate love, is also sacrificed in a desperate and rather pathetic attempt by the murderer to cover his crimes. There can be no doubt that Claudius is, indeed, a consummate villain.

Claudius first appears on stage in *Act 1, Scene II* and he presents a noble and dignified figure. His is eloquent as he comments on recent events in the kingdom of Denmark.

> *"Though yet of Hamlet our dear brother's death*
> *The memory be green, and that it us befitted*
> *To bear our hearts in grief, and our whole kingdom*
> *To be contracted in one brow of woe"*

He appears genuinely distinguished and stately, and goes on to display the political wisdom and gravitas expected of a worthy king. He sends envoys to Norway, in a clever attempt to circumvent the threat posed to his new kingdom by the Norwegian Prince Fortinbras, who Claudius notes holds *"a weak supposal of our worth"*. He refers to his *"dear brother's death"* and comments on the love he feels for Gertrude, *"our sometime sister, now our queen"*. The performance is immaculate. Claudius appears to be a moral, benign, worthy king. *Act 1,*

Scene II is the last time Claudius appears this way in the play, for, as it soon becomes clear, Claudius' appearance belies a very different reality.

Hamlet meets the Ghost of his father in *Act 1, Scene V*, and Claudius' villainy is revealed. The Ghost bluntly states that

> *"The serpent that did sting thy father's life*
> *Now wears his crown."*

These words devastate Hamlet. King Hamlet was murdered by his brother who

> *"stole*
> *With juice of cursed hebona in a vial,*
> *And in the porches of mine ears did pour*
> *The leperous distilment".*

Hamlet swears to avenge his father's death and his epic struggle to punish his uncle, the *"smiling, damned villain"*, begins. Claudius' method, his choice of weapon, is important. He does not choose the sword or the knife, but instead selects poison. This is the tool of the duplicitous, dishonest, treacherous coward.

Hamlet's behaviour following the meeting with his father's spectre causes Claudius to feel anxious. The regicide has given him the power denied to him by primogeniture, and the wife he genuinely appears to love. He does not want anyone, especially his nephew, to interfere with or threaten his position. He therefore turns to Polonius, his chief minister and close confidante, for advice. In *Act 2, Scene II*, Polonius announces to the king that he has found the *"very cause of Hamlet's lunacy"*. Claudius is delighted with this news, and, turning to the queen, says,

> *"He tells me, my sweet queen, that he hath found*
> *The head and source of all your son's distemper."*

His apparent innocence is confounded by his wife's no-nonsense reply,

> *"I doubt it is no other but the main;*
> *His father's death, and our o'erhasty marriage."*

Unlike his wife, Claudius is unable or unwilling to admit that his actions have had significant consequences. He cares only about himself, and the depth of his corruption becomes evident as the play progresses.

His dishonesty is a feature of all of his relationships. He readily agrees when Polonius suggests he will *"loose my daughter to him"*, and this strategy leads directly to Ophelia's breakdown and subsequent suicide. She is an innocent young lady, and yet Claudius has no hesitation in using her to protect his position. The king is supposed to be the moral centre of the nation. This usurper king shows little moral fibre. Later in the play, when Gertrude announces Ophelia's death in *Act 4, Scene VII*, Claudius' immediate thoughts are not for the *"poor wretch"* and his role in her tragic death. Instead, he expresses frustration that his attempts to placate Laertes have been undermined:

> *"How much I had to do to calm his rage!*
> *Now fear I this will give it start again."*

Even the news of Polonius' death, in *Act 4, Scene I*, elicits a selfish reaction,

> *"O heavy deed!*
> *It had been so with us, had we been there.*
> *His liberty is full of threats to all."*

This man, who claims to care about others, is concerned only with his own position and his own survival. The deaths of the members of his court are a direct result of this passionate self-interest. He really is a complete villain.

The Mousetrap, in *Act 3, Scene II*, truly startles and frightens Claudius. He is presented with the reality of his sins and is disturbed. The very fact that he is troubled by his conscience makes it clear that he is no psychopathic monster. That would almost excuse his actions, or at least serve to explain them. But Claudius has no such avenue of escape. He tries to pray in *Act 3, Scene III*, and admits his

> *"offence is rank, it smells to heaven;*
> *It hath the primal eldest curse upon't;*
> *A brother's murder!"*

He is aware of the enormity of his crime, and wonders *"Is there not rain enough in the sweet heavens"* to wash his bloody hands *"white as snow"*. He knows his crime, regicide, prevents him from entry to heaven, unless he confesses and begs forgiveness. It is at this point that the essential self-interest at the centre of his character becomes apparent. He wonders *"may one be pardoned and retain the offence"* because he is still

> *"possess'd*
> *Of those effects for which I did the murder,*
> *My crown, mine own ambition and my queen."*

He is faced with the choice between redemption and the retention of the fruits of his crime, and opts to retain his ill-gotten gains. He truly is a consummate villain.

The final scene of the play witnesses the restoration of order that is so vital in a Shakespearean tragedy. The villain, Claudius, is finally unmasked and punished. The hero, Hamlet, at last avenges his father's death. However, it is in this final scene, *Act 5, Scene II*, that any lingering doubts about the nature of Claudius' character are removed. His underhand and duplicitous scheming leads him to poison Hamlet's cup. When Gertrude lifts the cup to drink in tribute to her son's fencing prowess, Claudius is presented with his last chance to redeem himself. He asks her not to drink, but will not risk exposure by warning her of the poison. Instead he sits back and mutters, *"It is the poison'd cup! it is too late."* Gertrude, the woman he has professed to love throughout the play, is also sacrificed in an attempt to protect his position. When Hamlet kills him with the words *"Here, thou incestuous, murderous, damned Dane"*, the audience can feel no sympathy for this selfish man whose unrestrained ambition, duplicitous character and egocentric nature has led to the destruction of so many lives.

Claudius, the villain of the Shakespeare's *Hamlet*, truly is a consummate villain. He takes on the position of king and totally fails to provide the moral leadership intrinsic in that role. Fittingly, it is Hamlet's words to Gertrude in *Act 3, Scene IV* that encapsulate the character of the wretched Claudius. He is

> *"A murderer, and a villain;*
> *A slave that is not twentieth part the tithe*
> *Of your precedent lord; a vice of kings;*
> *A cutpurse of the empire and the rule,*
> *That from a shelf the precious diadem stole,*
> *And put it in his pocket!"*

Past Higher Level Exam Questions

2001

1. "The struggle between Hamlet and Claudius is a fascinating one."

   Discuss this statement, supporting your answer by reference to the play, *Hamlet*.

2. Choose the scene from Shakespeare's *Hamlet* that in your view was the most dramatic. Discuss your choice, supporting your answer by reference to the play.

   [Textual support may include reference to a particular performance of the play that you have seen.]

2002

1. "The appeal of Shakespeare's *Hamlet* lies primarily in the complex nature of the play's central character, Hamlet."

   To what extent would you agree with the above statement? Support your view by reference to the play.

2. What is your view of the importance of **either** Gertrude **or** Ophelia in Shakespeare's play, *Hamlet*?

   Support the points you make by reference to the play.

2005

1. In your opinion, what is the appeal of the play, *Hamlet*, for a twenty-first century audience?

   Support the points you make by reference to the text.

2. "We admire Hamlet as much for his weaknesses as for his strengths."

   Write a response to this view of the character of Hamlet, supporting your points by reference to the text.

Suggested Reading List

A.C. Bradley *Shakespearean Tragedy*

C. Brooks *The Well Wrought Urn*

H. Granville-Barker *Prefaces to Shakespeare*

W. Hazlitt *"Hamlet"*

S. Johnson *The Plays of William Shakespeare*

G. Wilson Knight *The Wheel of Fire*

L.C. Knights *Some Shakespearean Themes*

E.M.W. Tillyard *The Elizabethan World Picture*

J. Dover Wilson *What Happens in Hamlet*